The Essential

JOSEPH

SMITH

The Essential
JOSEPH
SMITH

FOREWORD BY

MARVIN S. HILL

SIGNATURE BOOKS
SALT LAKE CITY
1995

Jacket Design: Randall Smith Associates

Signature Books is a registered trademark of Signature Books, Inc.
Printed in the United States of America.
∞ Printed on acid free paper.
99   98   97   96   95   6   5   4   3   2   1

LIBRARY OF CONGRESS CATALOGING-IN-PUBLICATION DATA
Smith, Joseph, 1805-1844.
    [Selections.   1995]
    The essential Joseph Smith / foreword by Marvin S. Hill.
        p.   cm.
    Includes bibliographical references and index.
    ISBN 0-941214-71-0
    1. Smith, Joseph, 1805-1844.   2. Church of Jesus Christ of Latter
-Day Saints—Doctrines.   3. Mormon Church—Doctrines.   I. Title.
BX8621.S522   1995
289.3'2—dc20   94-37258
                                                        CIP

Contents

Publisher's Preface

Devout Mormons place Joseph Smith (1805-44) second only to Jesus Christ in redeeming the world from darkness. As God's prophet, he is said to have accessed absolute truth, brought forth "the world's most perfect book," and restored necessary knowledge and ritual for people to fulfill their ultimate divine destinies.

Smith's sense of mission, his radical activism, inspired adoration. *The Essential Joseph Smith*—alive with the disparities and ambiguities that characterized the life, temerity, and creative energy of its author—presents a microcosm of issues still swirling around his enigmatic teachings and personality.

Those who have never been exposed to the prophet's scripture or sermons may appreciate the magnetism of his style. Readers already steeped in the official record may find the breadth and eccentricity of Smith's unedited intellectual explorations surprising.

Joseph Smith's life began in near-abject poverty on 23 December 1805 in Sharon, Vermont. He was named after his father, a barrel-maker and occasional speculator. Lucy Mack, Smith's mother, was an independent, intelligent, stabilizing influence in her son's life. The Smith family was among the poor whose self-image surpassed their financial status. They were proud, ambitious, and strongly-bonded.

In pursuing their dreams, the Smiths moved ten times during Joseph's youth through Vermont, New Hampshire, and New York, where they finally came to settle on a Manchester farm near Palmyra village. There they were exposed to the sometimes spectacular displays of religious enthusiasm that swept among the under-developed and precarious frontier communities of western New York.

Joseph's own religious loyalties were divided between his father's iconoclastic Unitarian sympathies and his mother's more conventional Methodism. Under the various influences of sectarian orthodoxy, Christian primitivism, charismatic revivalism, deism, and ritualistic mysticism, Smith reported a variety of personal religious experiences. Heavenly messengers appeared to him to reveal his life's mission of preparing the way of Jesus' second advent. As evidence of his divine calling, Smith published the Book of Mormon in 1830 as the writings of some of the lost tribes of Israel in the New World, which addressed religious issues disputed among Smith's American frontier neighbors.

The spiritual audacity exhibited by Smith transcended his initial bashfulness. With revelatory byproducts in hand and charged with adolescent ambition and magnetism, he was soon in a class above other neighborhood visionaries. The prophet's following grew beyond his extended family circle, and adherents were drawn by his bold claim to new revelation and his utopian vision of a society free of structure and dogma. Less quickly but just as surely, stewards of traditional institutions bristled at his revolutionary and disruptive vision.

Within a decade Smith's following coalesced from an ill-defined movement into a church. The early Church of Christ comprised a string of Mormonite branches organized throughout New York, Pennsylvania, and Ohio, where members met in neighbors' homes and enjoyed gatherings characterized by congregational autonomy, gifts of the Spirit, and miracle-works. Smith's concerns, depicted in his writings of the early 1830s and often expressed in prophetic voice, centered on the impending Millennium, gathering the elect to Jesus, and balancing individual spirituality with organizational uniformity.

Gradually Smith expanded and rigidified church offices into a hierarchy answerable to him. Latter-day Saints, as they were now called, were instructed to gather to specially designated sites in Missouri and Ohio and to deed their possessions to church authorities for more equitable distribution. In vision, Smith saw that Independence, Missouri, was to be the New Jerusalem, called Zion, where Jesus would soon appear.

A remarkable degree of cohesion existed at this time. But when Smith's prophecies about Missouri did not immediately materialize, when outsiders heard of Mormon political ambitions, when Smith's Ohio bank failed due to bad timing and mismanagement, and when rumors of polygamy spread, antagonism grew without and within. Mormons organized vigilante bands to defend against agitators, but Ohioans and Missourians mustered their own militias to drive Smith and his followers from their states. Eventually church leaders were jailed for treason. During this period the prophet's writings were marked by rationalization and regret, especially for the loss of Zion.

Smith escaped from prison, and during the early 1840s he established a new gathering place in western Illinois. As crops were planted and cities built, a renewed unanimity of purpose surfaced. Also, the Illinois populace welcomed the Saints as refugees. But soon Smith faced new problems. More than before he was challenged by his own followers' increasing disillusionment over rumors of "spiritual wifery" and establishment of an authoritarian political theocracy. To counteract dissent, Smith excommunicated many, while rewarding a tight-knit inner circle with secret knowledge guarded by oaths and ritual. The prophet's rhetoric in Illinois illustrates this move toward stratification, esoteric wisdom, and secret ordinances.

A SYSTEM OF GOVERNMENT RULED BY PRIESTS

THE ART OF EFFECTIVELY USING LANGUAGE

TO BECOME ARRANGED IN LAYERS

During the last years of his brief life, Smith produced his most radical theological revisions. Inhabited worlds without number, gods and goddesses as human-like beings, humans as gods in embryo, and the pre-mortal existence and innate goodness of human spirits permeated his sermons. He also organized the political Kingdom of Heaven on Earth in the covert Council of Fifty. As mayor of Nauvoo he imposed martial law, including around-the-clock patrols. Before his death, the Mormon kingdom had become a police state.

Neighbors and disaffected Mormons oppressed Smith's political and spiritual empire. Dissidents published the *Nauvoo Expositor* to expose the secret rituals, polygamy, and the Council of Fifty's political plans, and state judicial officers arrested Smith when he ordered the *Expositor* and its printing press destroyed. Before he could be brought to answer the charge, a vigilante group stormed the jail where he was held and assassinated him and his older brother Hyrum.

Disloyal

The evolution of Smith's writings and their polarizing effect on audiences present two roadblocks to the production of an "essential Joseph Smith." A third difficulty is the process by which Smith's discourse was recorded and distributed. Not only were few public sermons and private letters preserved—especially for the early period—but, as Mormon historian Dean Jessee has observed, Smith was more concerned with ideas than syntax. Later church editors wielded a sometimes heavy hand in preparing Smith-related documents for publication. Forced to interpret incomplete transcripts, they periodically refined ideas as well as spelling. Also, Smith's reliance on scribes blurred the distinction between first- and third-person voice, resulting in the addition of material from other sources and its attribution to Smith.

Ultimately, readers today can rely on few texts credited to the prophet as completely authentic. In this compilation care has been taken to present writings and speeches that are unquestionably Smith's, and, though often recorded by fallible scribes, to offer them in their original manuscript or early published forms. Archaic grammatical constructions and spellings are usually unaltered, while obvious typographical errors, such as letter transpositions, have been frequently corrected. Puncutation has been supplied occasionally to facilitate comprehension. Editorial insertions appearing in sources that have been previously published are usually retained.

Some of these texts may be familiar to those who have read official versions without the contradictions, digressions, or occasional earthiness, which are preserved in this volume. Other documents have been published in scholarly journals, multi-volume works, or various anthologies. For more definitive editions of many of these documents, readers are directed to Andrew F. Ehat and Lyndon W. Cook, comp., *The Words of Joseph Smith: The Contemporary Accounts of the Nauvoo Discourses of the Prophet Joseph* (Provo, Utah: Religious Studies Center at Brigham Young University, 1980); Dean C. Jessee, ed., *The Papers of Joseph Smith* (Salt Lake City: Deseret Book Co., 1989-), 2+ vols.; Dean C. Jessee, ed., *The Personal Writings of Joseph Smith* (Salt Lake City: Deseret Book Co., 1984); Scott H. Faulring, ed., *An American Prophet's Record: The Diaries and Journals of Joseph Smith* (Salt Lake City: Signature Books in association with Smith Research Associates, 1987); and Dan Vogel, ed., *Early Mormon Documents* (Salt Lake City: Signature Books, 1995-), 1+ vols.

Rather than an exhaustive, fully annotated edition, this volume provides a readable, representative selection which spans Smith's entire lifetime, including letters, diary entries, reminiscences, revelations, visions, and speeches. As an introduction to the Mormon prophet, *The Essential Joseph Smith* should acquaint readers with the nucleus of his work and hopefully inspire further investigation.

Foreword

Marvin S. Hill

One of the things historians learn when they begin to delve into historical sources is that the great men and women of the past have always been the subject of bitter controversy. While these people have had their defenders, they have had their critics too. In the 1790s, for example, one famous hero of the Revolutionary Era wrote to another, "As to you, sir, the world will be puzzled to decide whether you are an apostate or an imposter, whether you have abandoned good principles or whether you ever had any."[1] The author of this vituperation was Thomas Paine, whose pamphlet *Common Sense* was the catalyst of the American demand for independence from Great Britain in 1776. The recipient of this vitriolic letter was George Washington.

According to another political partisan of the 1790s, a prominent leader of the opposition party was guilty of the "most ambitious spirit, the most overweening pride and hauteur, so that the externals of pure democracy afford but a flimsy veil to the internal evidences of aristocratic splendor, sensuality, and Epicureanism."[2] The critic here was a friend of Alexander Hamilton; the object of his denunciation was Thomas Jefferson, champion of American democracy. Still another American who was extremely controversial during his years in public office was excoriated as "illiterate, course [sic] and vulgar," as a "mobocrat, a Southern hater, a lunatic and a chimpanzee." This belittled man was Abraham Lincoln.[3]

Like other great Americans Joseph Smith (1805-44) was not exempt from such disparagement. He had friends who spoke well of him, and he had critics who were often embittered. The result was broad disagreement as to his character and personality. If we consider such traits as his personal appearance the first impressions he made on others, his treatment of people, his linguistic and oratory skills, and his financial integrity, we find much controversy among his acquaintances.

During his lifetime Smith developed from a poor farm boy in Palmyra, New York, to the leader of a large, influential church. In considering his early appearance we must keep in mind his poverty.

One of those who knew him as a young man was Daniel Hendrix, who worked in a store in Palmyra and who said that Smith came in almost daily. Hendrix described him as "the most ragged . . . fellow in the place, and that is saying a good deal." Hendrix remembered him as "about twenty-five years old, I can see him now, in my mind's eye, with his torn and patched trousers, held to his form by a pair of suspenders made out of sheeting, with his calico shirt as dirty and black as earth, and his uncombed hair sticking through the holes in his old, battered hat. In winter I used to pity him, for his shoes were so worn out that he must have suffered in the snow and slush."[4]

Pomeroy Tucker, editor of a local newspaper, the *Wayne Sentinel*, said Smith was remembered in Palmyra from the ages of twelve to twenty as a "dull-eyed, flaxen-haired youth."[5] Isaac Hale, Smith's future father-in-law, described him in 1825 as "a careless young man."[6]

It is hard to find a description of Smith in this early period by his friends. Those that exist do not provide all the details we would like. Parley P. Pratt's description is a good example. He said that in 1830 "President Joseph Smith was in person tall and well built, strong and active, of light complexion, light hair, blue eyes, very little beard, and of an expression peculiar to himself, on which the eye naturally rested with interest."[7] Pratt does not mention Smith's apparel, details which would have been helpful in assessing what David Hendrix said.

If we consider Smith's appearance in later life, we find continued variance. Charles Francis Adams, later American minister to Great Britain during the Civil War, said that when he met Smith in 1844 Smith was "clad in the costume of a journeyman carpenter when about his work. He was a hearty, athletic looking fellow, with blue eyes standing prominently out upon his light complexion, a long nose, and a retreating forehead. He wore striped pantaloons, and a linen jacket, which had not lately seen the washtub, and a beard of some three days growth."[8] But Bathsheba Smith, a Mormon, remembered Smith more favorably: "The Prophet was a handsome man—splendid looking, a large man, tall and fair and his hair was light. He had a very nice complexion, his eyes were blue, and his hair a golden brown and very pretty."[9]

If we examine the sort of first impression Joseph Smith made, again we find a polarity. Orlando Saunders, who lived in Palmyra as a boy and worked with Smith on the Smith farm, said Joseph was a good worker but a "greeny, both large and strong."[10] By "greeny" Saunders meant an awkward, somewhat unsophisticated rustic. One investigator agreed, saying he lost interest in the church after discovering that Smith was "not such a [good] looking man as I expected to see. He looked green and not very intelligent. I felt disappointed and returned home."[11] On the other hand Jonathan Crosby, who joined the church, found Smith's unpretentiousness refreshing. He said, "I thought he was a quear [sic] man for a Prophet, at first, he didn't appear exactly as I expected to see a Prophet of God. . . . I found him to be a friendly, cheerful pleasant agreeable man. I could not help liking him."[12]

Nancy Towles, who met Smith just after he moved to Kirtland, Ohio, in early 1831, said that he was an "ignorant plough-boy," a "good natured,—low bred sort of chap."[13] But Newel Knight, who was Smith's friend and convert in Chenango County, New York, said that from the first Smith made a favorable impression on the Knights. He was a hard worker and, Newel said, "I never knew anyone to gain the advantage over him, yet he was always kind and kept the good will of his playmates."[14] Some non-Mormons, however, remembered Smith as bad tempered. Michael Morse, later a brother-in-law, said he recalled that when Smith was courting Emma Hale, some of her brothers were ill disposed toward him "and took occasion to annoy and vex him." Finally Smith had had enough and "threw off his coat and proposed to defend himself."[15]

Luke Johnson, a Mormon, said that when a certain man who had grown up with Smith came to Kirtland as a minister of another denomination, the man displayed bad manners. After staying overnight at Smith's house, he called Smith a "hypocrite and imposter." Luke Johnson reported that Smith "covered the minister's ears with both hands and kicked him out with his foot."[16] Peter H. Burnett, who was Smith's lawyer in Missouri and later governor of California, said he attended a meeting in which a certain John McDaniel said publicly that he did not believe in Smith's ability to prophesy. The next day, a Sunday, when Smith rose to speak he was enraged and said, "Nobody could slander him in that way, and that if the brethren present would not do something about it he would."[17]

Again, however, there were those who saw Smith quite differently. Daniel Tyler, a Mormon, told of a time in Kirtland when William Smith—Joseph's younger brother—and some others openly challenged Smith's leadership of the church, and tempers were hot. Smith called a special meeting and then opened with prayer, the tears running down his cheeks. Turning his back so that his sorrow would be less visible, Smith prayed. Tyler recorded: "I had heard men and women pray—especially the former—from the most ignorant, both as to letters and intellect, to the most learned and eloquent, but never until then had I heard a man address his maker as though he was present, listening as a kind father would listen to the sorrows of a dutiful child. [The prayer] was in behalf of those who accused him of having gone astray and fallen into sin, that the Lord would forgive them and open their eyes that they might see aright. . . . There was no ostentation, no raising of the voice as by enthusiasm, but a plain conversational tone, as a man would address a present friend. . . . It was crown of all the prayers I had ever heard."[18]

In his treatment of others, some non-members thought Smith abrupt, even rude. William A. West, a visitor to Kirtland, said he went toward the temple one day and saw Smith talking with several of the brethren. They were "talking bank, money, steam mills and so on, and the Prophet was very busy." West said that Smith finally broke away, but then another man caught up with him and asked to speak with him for a moment longer. In frustration Smith exclaimed, "O God, I wish I were translated," and walked away grumbling that "everyone want[s] to speak with him for just a minute."[19] Later, at an outdoor meeting in Nauvoo, Illinois, Smith was upset when the congregation was distracted by a flock of geese that flew over while he was speaking. He stopped his sermon and walked off the stand, saying, "If you are more interested in the quak [sic] of a flock of geese than in what I am saying it's all right."[20]

There are several stories that render an entirely different view of Smith. Emma recalled to her son Joseph III how often the elders sought out her husband and how much he enjoyed their company. She said to her son: "Well Joseph . . . I do not expect you can do much more in the garden than your father would, and I never wanted him to go into the garden to work for if he did it would not be fifteen minutes before there would be three or four, or sometimes a dozen men round him and they would tramp the ground faster than he would hoe it up."[21]

Jane S. Richards said emphatically that Smith took "a personal interest in all his people."[22] A story which seems to support this is told about his last days in Nauvoo. During a heavy rain some members of the Nauvoo Legion, a quasi-military organization, had been out all night on patrol looking for mobbers that threatened the city. When his men rode in at dawn foot-sore and tired, Smith was waiting for them and began inquiries about their work. After a time he noticed that one of the men had bled on a log where they were sitting, and Smith found that the man's shoes were worn to ribbons and his feet badly cut. Looking further he found others in the same condition. He immediately invited the men to his store for a new pair of shoes. When the storekeeper told him there were no shoes but only expensive boots, Smith said, "Let them have boots then."[23]

Another story provides further support. While Smith was conversing with some of the brethren near his home in Nauvoo, a man came up who said that his home had just been burned down by a mob. Smith took out five dollars, looked at the other men, and said, "I feel sorry for this brother to the amount of five dollars; how much do you feel sorry?"[24]

Not only have some of Smith's critics said he was rude to strangers, they have even affirmed that he was contemptuous toward his father. Isaac Hale said that Smith was "very sassy and insolent toward his father."[25] Yet a story related by Joseph Knight suggests a bond of love between Smith and his father. When Smith saw Martin Harris and his father, Joseph Sr., baptized, he was almost overcome with emotion. Knight related: "Joseph was filled with the spirit to a great degree to see his father and Mr. Harris that had been with him so much [baptized]. He burst out with . . . joy and appeared to want to get out of sight of everybody and would sob and cry and after a while he came in, but he was the most wrought that I have ever seen any man."[26]

The author of the *History of Wayne County, New York*, said he heard reports indicating Smith tended to be taciturn* unless spoken to.[27] Daniel Hendrix, however, remembered that Smith had a "jovial, easy, I-don't-care way about him that made him a lot of friends." Hendrix said, "He was a good talker, and would have made a fine stump speaker, if he had the training."[28] Peter H. Burnett said that in "conversation he was slow, and used too many words to express ideas, and would not generally go directly to the point." Burnett affirmed that Smith was an "awkward but vehement speaker."[29] Yet Christopher Crary, a non-Mormon, said, "His language, so far as I was qualified to judge, was correct, forcible, and right to the point and convincing."[30] Wandle Mace said Smith was "very interesting and

*[handwritten margin note:] * INCLINED TO SILENCE

eloquent in speech,"[31] while Job Smith said he was "powerful in invective and occasionally sarcastic."[32]

A Universalist minister who met Smith complained that he disliked Smith's "swagger and brag."[33] But David Whitmer, a close friend of Smith, said that when he first met Smith, "he was a very humble and meek man."[34] There is another discrepancy between the Wayne County historian, who said that Smith was "never known to laugh,"[35] and U.S. congressman Elisha Potter, who said that Smith had "a keen wit."[36] And still another between Benjamin F. Johnson, who said that no one made greater mistakes in his choice of associates than did Smith,[37] and Peter H. Burnett, who said that Smith was a good judge of men.[38]

A resident of Kirtland, Sam Brown, claimed that near the end of the Mormon stay in Kirtland, he was unwilling to lend more money to Smith for fear he would not get it back.[39] Christopher Crary, on the other hand, said that Smith was always scrupulously honest in paying debts.[40] While temporarily estranged from the prophet following the failure of the Kirtland Safety Society Bank, Apostle Parley P. Pratt accused Smith of charging "extortionary prices" for three lots of land.[41] David Osborne, however, said that on another occasion Smith was upset with some of the rich brethren who bought government land cheaply and resold it in small lots to the poor for a high price.[42] Whatever the issue at hand concerning Joseph Smith, one can find contradictory testimony.

With so much that is controversial about Smith, how does one go about finding the truth? How does one separate fact from fiction? To start with let us consider the matter of Joseph Smith's appearance and the initial impressions he made upon people. In trying to assess Daniel Hendrix's remarks about how destitute Smith looked, we must keep several things in mind. Daniel Hendrix was eighty-seven years old when he was interviewed as to his recollections of Smith, and it is difficult to determine how accurate his memory might have been. He indicates that Smith was habitually dressed in old, tattered clothes. This seems possible in these years, for we know that the Smith family was having a hard time financially.[43] Yet, on the other hand, some of the things Hendrix says are not born out by other facts that are firmly established. He says Smith was lazy, but this is contradicted by other testimony from the period when Smith was in Palmyra. It is also contradicted by much direct evidence that comes from a later period.[44] Consequently, one must be careful with an account like Hendrix's, written at a time when it was popular to say disparaging things about Smith.

It is significant, I think, that when Parley P. Pratt described Smith in 1830, he said nothing of what Smith wore but indicated his general size, complexion, and personality. When Pratt told us Smith was a person upon whom his eye rested with interest, he was saying that he responded affirmatively to Smith and that he was more interested in his character and personality than in his outward appearance. This would appear to be characteristic of a follower. Bathsheba Smith, a Mormon, remembered that Smith's hair was "pretty" but said nothing about his clothing. One might surmise from this oversight that Smith's apparel was not unusual so far as Bathsheba was concerned. When Charles Francis Adams saw Smith as rather careless in his personal appearance, he was probably judging him by the standards of the Boston elite not by western standards.

When it comes to Smith's treatment of others, the negative evidence often seems biased. Isaac Hale remembered that Smith was unkind to his father. But one must ask how many times did Isaac Hale see Smith with his father? It could not have been many. Lucy Mack Smith reports only two occasions Smith and his father were together in Harmony, Pennsylvania.[45] Thus Hale may have made a broad generalization based on a few brief encounters. Other evidence suggests strongly that throughout most of his life Smith went out of his way to care for his father, that he loved him deeply. If there was some temporary estrangement between them in 1825 when Hale knew them, there is no evidence it continued. Hale's purpose when he wrote his affidavit for Philastus Hurlbut in 1833 was to discredit Smith. He was angry about Mormonism in general and about Smith's moving away with his daughter. His assertion therefore cannot be taken at face value.

There is enough evidence from what Smith's friends have said and from admissions by Smith himself, however, to make it evident that he did have a temper. One of his most intimate friends, Benjamin F. Johnson, said Smith "would allow no arrogance or undue liberties; and criticisms, even by associates, were rarely acceptable; and contradictions would arouse in him the lion, at once."[46] We know from newspaper accounts and court records that Smith was involved in more than one fight. Yet the evidence is plentiful that he had to be provoked by direct insult before he would resort to violence. We must remember it was customary in this period of American history for direct confrontations and even duels to be fought over personal differences. Andrew Jackson, Henry Clay, and Senator Thomas Hart Benton, to name but three, were involved in duels to protect their honor or public image.[47] Many a frontier preacher took to brawling when heckled from the crowd. This was a rough age by our standards. As for Joseph Smith we know that he did not relish fighting, that he felt deep remorse over it. He told Allen Stout in Nauvoo on one occasion that he had been too quarrelsome at times, that "in his youth he had learned to fight much against his will," and "whenever he laid his hand in anger on a fellow creature, it gave him sorrow and a feeling of shame."[48] Apparently Smith sought repentance in this area.

Nonetheless, evidence of his temper does not offset the many examples we have of his general tendency to treat people with courtesy and consideration. Peter H. Burnett said in this regard: "There was a kind, familiar look about him, that pleased you. He was very courteous in discussion, admitting what he did not intend to controvert, and would not oppose you abruptly but had due deference to your feelings."[49] If on the occasion in Kirtland he dismissed the request for another minute of his time, this is not sufficient evidence by itself of general impatience or lack of consideration. Negative or positive impressions about Smith's language and manners are again dependent upon who is doing the observing. Smith was not nor did he pretend to be educated. Still his skills seem suitable for his time and place. This was an age when Andrew Jackson reached the White House, and Jackson was neither polished nor educated.

So far as his sense of humor goes, the Wayne County historian says Smith was "good natured," thus contradicting himself on this point. We have an example of Smith's humor preserved by Willard Richards, who said that one day Smith told him he was going to study law to become "a very great lawyer." Perhaps Emma had been encouraging his studying law, for she told her son Joseph III after his father's death that Smith would have avoided many legal entanglements had he known more about the law. In any case on the occasion described by Richards, Smith's way of studying was to lie "down on the writing table with \back of the head\ on Law Books," upon which he "fell asleep and went to snoring."[50] Smith did not think much of lawyers, which was a widely held attitude in the early nineteenth century.

On the questions raised by Pratt and Sam Brown on the matter of Smith's financial integrity, this issue was the subject of much controversy at the time and still is among historians.[51] Many accused Smith of reckless speculation, even fraud. They maintained that Smith imprudently invested in land and charged exorbitant prices for it, that he established an illegal bank with intent to print worthless currency and exchange it for valuable goods, that he ran up an enormous debt and fled from Kirtland to avoid paying it. Whereas it is true that Smith bought land in Kirtland and resold it, the prices were not out of line with the general demand for land nor with land prices in nearby communities. Smith had large debts as a result of his business transactions, but he also had large assets with which he could have paid his debts had the economy not collapsed. Smith started his bank to transfer landed wealth into ready capital and, had he been able to secure a charter from the state legislature, he may have been able to establish a modest but successful bank. But in 1836-37, for political and economic reasons, the state legislature granted no new charters for banks, and Smith had to improvise. He set up an anti-banking society that was in fact a simple corporation with note-issuing powers. He may have acted on bad legal advice here, but similar banks were being established elsewhere in the state at this time.[52] When Smith learned that the notes would not circulate at face value, he withdrew his support from the bank, sustaining larger personal losses than any other person. He did not risk other people's money where he would not risk his own. Smith was a naive capitalist, but he did not envision that his gain would be anyone else's loss. When he reached Nauvoo, he ultimately declared bankruptcy, though he first tried to settle many of his Kirtland debts.

Careful research can help offset the negative interpretations some try to impose on Joseph Smith. The existence of contradictory evidence should make scholars hesitate to jump to hasty or unwarranted conclusions or to claim definitiveness for historical studies that are more in the nature of interim reports. If my characterization of Joseph Smith has seemed at times unflattering, it has come from no desire to diminish him. It comes rather from the belief that at times in the Mormon church we tend to expect too much of him, to ask him to be more than human. This may lead to some disillusionment when we inevitably find that he did not measure up to our expectations. The early Saints usually avoided that kind of mistake. Brigham Young said of Smith: "Though I admitted in my feelings and knew all the time that Joseph was a human being and subject to err, still it was none of my business to look after his faults."[53] Young chose to stress the positive side. Parley P. Pratt said that Smith was "like other men, as the prophets and apostles of old, liable to errors and mistakes which were not inspired from heaven, but managed by . . . [his] own judgment."[54]

These men knew Smith as a man with human weaknesses, yet they believed in his divine calling and in his greatness. It seemed to them that what he had achieved as a prophet far outweighed his imperfections. In the long run their love of him and their faith in his calling were decisive in shaping their lives. Seeing Smith in his various moods, they still called him a prophet of God. That seems to me to be the right attitude for faithful Latter-day Saints, who see the Lord's will at work, even though he must effect that will by the means of earthen vessels. Aware of some things earthen in Joseph Smith, Benjamin F. Johnson still had this to say of him: "From my early youth to the day of his martyrdom, I was closely associated with the Prophet Joseph Smith, was his trusted friend and business partner, his relative, and bosom friend. And I knew him as the purest, the truest and noblest of manly men."[55]

Smith said of himself, "I do not, nor never have pretended to be any other than a man, subject to passion and liable without the assisting grace of the Saviour, to deviate from that perfect path in which all are commanded to walk."[56] He also said, "God is my friend, in him I shall find comfort. I have given my life unto his hands. I am prepared to go at his call and desire to be with Christ. I count not my life dear to me only to do his will."[57] And he said, "The Lord does reveal himself to me. I know it."[58] Those who would understand Joseph Smith must give equal consideration to both his spiritual and human sides. It was his strong commitment to things spiritual which made him so aware of his human failings, so desirous to overcome weaknesses and to give his all to the work of the Lord.

NOTES

1. James Thomas Flexner, *Washington: The Indispensable Man* (Boston: Little, Brown and Co., 1974), 354.

2. Dumas Malone, *Jefferson and the Rights of Man* (Boston: Little, Brown and Co., 1951), 474.

3. Stephen B. Oates, *With Malice Toward None* (New York: Mentor Books, 1979), 203.

4. *Saint Louis Globe Democrat*, 21 Feb. 1897, 34.

5. Pomeroy Tucker, *Origin, Rise, and Progress of Mormonism* (New York: D. Appleton and Co., 1867), 16.

6. Eber D. Howe, *Mormonism Unvailed, or a Faithful Account of That Singular Imposition and Delusion, from Its Rise to the Present Time* (Painesville, OH: the Author, 1834), 263.

7. *Autobiography of Parley P. Pratt* (Salt Lake City: Deseret Book Co., 1961), 45.

8. In William A. Mulder and A. Russell Mortensen, eds., *Among the Mormons* (New York: Alfred A. Knopf, 1958), 133.

9. *Young Woman's Journal* 16 (1905): 549.

10. Frederic G. Mather, "The Early Days of Mormonism," *Lippincott's Magazine* 26 (1880): 198.

11. "Journal of Luman Andrus Shurtliff," 19, typescript, Special Collections, Harold B. Lee Library, Brigham Young University, Provo, Utah; hereafter BYU Special Collections.

12. "Journal of Jonathan Crosby," 13-14, archives, Historical Department, Church of Jesus Christ of Latter-day Saints, Salt Lake City, Utah; hereafter LDS archives.

13. Nancy Towles, *Vicissitudes Illustrated* (Portsmouth, NH: John Caldwell, 1833), 157.

14. "Newel Knight's Journal," *Scraps of Biography, Tenth Book of the Faith-Promoting Series* (Salt Lake City: Juvenile Instructor Office, 1883), 46.

15. *True Latter Day Saints Herald* 26 (15 June 1879): 190-91.

16. "History of Luke Johnson," LDS archives.

17. Peter H. Burnett, *An Old California Pioneer* (Oakland, CA: Biobooks, 1946), 34.

18. "Recollections of the Prophet Joseph Smith," *Juvenile Instructor* 27 (15 Feb. 1892): 127-28.

19. William A. West, *A Few Interesting Facts Respecting the Rise, Progress and Pretensions of the Mormons* (n.p., 1837), 14.

20. Edwin F. Parry, *Stories about Joseph Smith, the Prophet* (Salt Lake City: Deseret News Press, 1934), 22-23.

21. Emma Smith to Joseph Smith III, 1 Aug., no year, but after 1847, in the Emma Bidamon Papers, Library-Archives, Reorganized Church of Jesus Christ of Latter Day Saints, Independence, Missouri.

22. "Reminiscences of Mrs. F. D. Richards," 11, Hubert Howe Bancroft Library, University of California at Berkeley, Berkeley, California.

23. Parry, 126-28.

24. Ibid., 22.

25. Howe, 263.

26. "Autobiography of Joseph Knight," 10, LDS archives.

27. *History of Wayne County, New York* (Philadelphia: Everts & Ensign, 1877), 150.

28. *Saint Louis Globe Democrat*, 21 Feb. 1897, 34.

29. Burnett, 40.

30. Christopher Crary, *Pioneer & Personal Reminiscences* (Marshalltown, IA: Marshall Printing Co., 1893), 21.

31. "Autobiography of Wandle Mace," 37, BYU Special Collections.

32. "Diary of Job Smith," 6, Henry E. Huntington Library, San Marino, California.

33. W. S. B. was a Universalist who visited Nauvoo in 1844. See the *Universalist Union*, 27 Apr. 1844, 393.

34. *Deseret News*, 16 Aug. 1878.

35. *History of Wayne County*, 150.

36. Mulder and Mortensen, 134.

37. "An Interesting Letter from Benjamin F. Johnson to George F. Gibbs," 17, BYU Special Collections.

38. Burnett, 40.

39. James H. Kennedy, *Early Days of Mormonism* (New York: Charles Scribner's Sons, 1888), 158.

40. Crary, 21.

41. In Richard Livesey, *An Exposure of Mormonism* (Preston, Eng.: J. Livesey, 1838), 9.

42. *Juvenile Instructor* 27 (15 Mar. 1892): 173.

43. Lucy Mack Smith recounts some of the financial difficulties of the family in her *History of Joseph Smith* (Salt Lake City: Bookcraft, 1954), 65, 85, 93-99. Orlando Saunders of Palmyra told William H. Kelly that they were poor. See his testimony in "The Hill Cumorah, and the Book of Mormon," *Saints Herald* 28 (1 June 1881): 165.

44. "Journal of Newel Knight," 46; and Orlando Saunders to William H. Kelly. Joseph's history cites several occasions where he worked in the fields with the elders or on the temple, while William Walker says on many a day Joseph cut hay in Nauvoo for ten-hour stretches (*Life Incidents and Travels of Elder William Holmes Walker* [1943], 8).

45. Smith, *History of Joseph Smith*, 93, 133.

46. "Benjamin F. Johnson to George F. Gibbs," 4.

47. See Daniel J. Boorstin, *The Americans: The National Experience* (New York: Vintage Books, 1965), 208.

48. Cragun Cox, "Reminiscences of Joseph Smith," Utah State Historical Society, Salt Lake City.

49. Burnett, 40.

50. See Scott H. Faulring, ed., *An American Prophet's Record: The Diaries and Journals of Joseph Smith* (Salt Lake City: Signature Books in association with Smith Research Associates, 1987), 335.

51. Marvin S. Hill, Keith Rooker, and Larry T. Wimmer, *Kirtland Economy Revisited: A Market Critique of Sectarian Economics* (Provo, UT: Brigham Young University Press, 1977).

52. Crary, 37.

53. *Journal of Discourses*, 26 vols. (Liverpool: Latter-day Saints' Book Depot, 1855-86), 4:297.

54. *Elders Journal* 1 (July 1838): 50.

55. Benjamin F. Johnson, "Mormonism as an Issue: An Open Letter to the Editor of the *Arizona Republican*," n.d.

56. *Latter-day Saints Messenger and Advocate* 1 (Dec. 1834): 40.

57. Joseph Smith to Emma Smith, 6 June 1832, Chicago Historical Society.

58. In *New York Spectator*, 23 Sept. 1843.

{1}

"Respected Sir I Would Inform You that I Arrived at Home," Joseph Smith to Oliver Cowdery, 22 October 1829

(from copy in archives, Historical Department, Church of Jesus Christ of Latter-day Saints, Salt Lake City, Utah)

Respected Sir I would inform you that I arrived at home [Harmony, Pennsylvania] on sunday morning the 4th after having a prosperous Journey, and found all well[.] [T]he people are all friendly to us except a few who are in opposition to ev[e]ry thing unless it is some thing that is exactly like themselves and two of our most formadable persacutors are now under censure and are cited to a tryal in the church for crimes which if true are worse than all the Gold Book [Book of Mormon] business. [W]e do not rejoice in the affliction of our enimies but we shall be glad to have truth prevail[.] [T]here begins to be a great call for our books in this country[;] the minds of the people are very much excited when they find that there is a copyright obtained and that there is really [a] book [the Book of Mormon], about to be printed[.] I have bought a horse of Mr. [Josiah] Stowell and want some one to come after it as soon as convenient[.] Mr. Stowell has a prospect of getting five or six hundred dollars[.] he does not know certain that he can get it but he is a going to try and if he can get the money he wants to pay it in immediately for books[.] [W]e want to hear from you and know how you prosper in the good work, give our best respects to Father & Mother and all our brothers and Sisters, to Mr. [Martin] Harris and all the company concerned[.] [T]ell them that our prayers are put up daily for them that they may be prospered in ev[e]ry, good word and work and that they may be preserved from sin here and from the consequence of sin hereafter[.] [A]nd now dear brother be faithful in the discharge of ev[e]ry duty looking for the reward of the righteous and now may God of his infinite mercy keep and preserve us spotless untill his coming and receive us all to rest with him in eternal repose through the attonement of Christ our Lord Amen.

{2}

"The Rise of the Church of Christ
in These Last Days,"
A Revelation to the Church of Christ, circa June 1830

(from *The Evening and the Morning Star*
[Independence, Missouri] 1 [June 1832], 1:[1-2])

The rise of the Church of Christ in these last days, being one thousand eight hundred and thirty years since the coming of our Lord and Savior Jesus Christ, in the flesh; it being regularly organized and established agreeable to the laws of our country, by the will and commandments of God in the fourth month and on the sixth day of the month, which is called April: Which commandments were given to Joseph [Smith], who was called of God and ordained an Apostle of Jesus Christ, an Elder of this Church; and also to Oliver [Cowdery], who was also called of God an Apostle of Jesus Christ, an Elder of this Church, and ordained under his hand; and this according to the grace of our Lord and Savior Jesus Christ to whom be all glory both now and for ever. Amen.

For, after it was truly manifested unto this first Elder, that he had received a remission of his sins, he was entangled again in the vanities of the world, but after truly repenting God ministered unto him by an holy angel, whose countenance was as lightning, and whose garments were pure and white above all other whiteness, and gave unto him commandments which inspired him from on high, and gave unto him power, by the means which were prepared, that he should translate a Book, which Book contained a record of a fallen people, and also the fulness of the Gospel of Jesus Christ to the Gentiles; and to the Jews also, proving unto them, that the holy Scriptures are true; and also, that God does inspire men and call them to his holy work, in these last days as well as in generations of old, that he might be the same God forever. Amen.

Which Book was given by inspiration, and is called The Book of Mormon, and is confirmed to others by the ministering of angels, and declared unto the world by them: Wherefore, having so great witnesses, by them shall the world be judged, even as many as shall

2

hereafter receive this work, either to faith and righteousness, or to the hardness of heart in unbelief, to their own condemnation, for the Lord God hath spoken it, for we, the Elders of the Church, have heard and bear witness to the words of the glorious Majesty on high; to whom be glory for ever and ever. Amen.

Wherefore, by these things we know, that there is a God in Heaven, who is infinite and eternal, from everlasting to everlasting, the same unchangeable God, the maker of Heaven and earth and all things that in them is, and that he created man male and female, and after his own image, and in his own likeness created he them; and that he gave unto the children of men commandments, that they should love and serve him the only being whom they should worship, but by the transgression of these holy laws, man became sensual and devilish, and became fallen man: Wherefore the Almighty God gave his only begotton Son, as it is written in those Scriptures, which have been given of him, that he suffered temptations, but gave no heed unto them, that he was crucified, died, and rose again the third day, and that he ascended into Heaven to sit down on the right hand of the Father, to reign with Almighty power, according to the will of the Father. Therefore, as many as would believe and were baptized in his holy name, and endured in faith to the end, should be saved; yea, even as many as were before he came in the flesh, from the beginning, who believed in the words of the holy Prophets, who were inspired by the gift of the Holy Ghost, which truly testifies of him in all things, as well as those who should come after, who should believe in the gifts and callings of God, by the Holy Ghost, which beareth record of the Father and of the Son, which Father and Son and Holy Ghost, is one God, infinite and eternal, without end. Amen.

And we know, that all men must repent and believe on the name of Jesus Christ, and worship the Father in his name, and endure in faith on his name to the end, or they cannot be saved in the Kingdom of God: And we know, that Justification through the grace of our Lord and Savior Jesus Christ, is just and true; and we know, also, that Sanctification through the grace of our Lord and Savior Jesus Christ, is just and true, to all those who love and serve God with all their mights, minds, and strength, but there is a possibility that men may fall from grace and depart from the living God. Therefore let the church take heed and pray always, lest they fall into temptation; yea, and even he that is sanctified also; and we know, that these things are true and agreeable to the Revelation of John, neither adding to, nor diminishing from the prophecy of his Book; neither to the holy Scriptures; neither to the Revelations of God which shall come hereafter, by the gift and power of the Holy Ghost; neither by the voice of God; neither by the ministering of angels, and the Lord God hath spoken it; and honor, power, and glory be rendered to his holy name both now and ever. Amen.

And again, by way of commandment to the Church, concerning the manner of baptism: Behold whosoever humbleth himself before God and desireth to be baptized, and comes forth with a broken heart and a contrite spirit, and witnesseth unto the Church that they have truly repented of all their sins and are willing to take upon them the name of Christ, having a determination to serve him unto the end, and truly manifest by their works that they have received the spirit of Christ unto the remission of their sins, then shall they be received unto baptism into the Church of Christ.

The duty of the Elders, Priests, Teachers, Deacons and members of the Church of Christ. An Apostle is an Elder, and it is his calling to baptize and to ordain other Elders, Priests, Teachers and Deacons, and to administer the flesh and blood of Christ, according to the Scriptures, and to teach, expound, exhort, baptize, and watch over the Church, and to confirm the Church by the laying on of the hands, and the giving of the Holy Ghost, and to take the lead of all meetings. The Elders are to conduct the meetings as they are led by the Holy Ghost. The Priests' duty is to preach, teach, expound, exhort and baptize, and administer the Sacrament, and visit the house of each member, and exhort them to pray vocally and in secret, and attend to all family duties; and ordain other Priests, Teachers, and Deacons, and take the lead in meetings; but none of these offices is he to do when there is an Elder present, but in all cases is to assist the Elder. The Teachers' duty is to watch over the Church always, and be with and strengthen them, and see that there is no iniquity in the Church, neither hardness with each other, neither lying nor back-biting nor evil speaking; and see that the Church meet together often, and also see that all the members do their duty; and he is to take the lead of meetings in the absence of the Elder or Priest, and is to be assisted always, and in all his duties in the Church by the Deacons; but neither the Teachers nor Deacons, have authority to baptize nor administer the Sacrament, are to warn, expound, exhort and teach, and invite all to come unto Christ.

4

Every Elder, Priest, Teacher, or Deacon, is to be ordained according to the gifts and callings of God unto him, by the power of the Holy Ghost which is in the one who ordains him.

The several Elders composing this Church of Christ, are to meet in Conference once in three months, to do church business whatsoever is necessary. And each Priest or Teacher, who is ordained by a Priest, is to take a certificate from him at the time, which when presented to an Elder, he is to give him a License, which shall authorize him to perform the duty of his calling.

The duty of the members after they are received by baptism. The Elders or Priests are to have a sufficient time to expound all things concerning this Church of Christ to their understanding, previous to their partaking of the Sacrament, and being confirmed by the laying on of the hands of the Elders; so that all things may be done in order. And the members shall manifest before the Church, and also before the Elders, by a godly walk and conversation, that they are worthy of it, that there may be works and faith agreeable to the holy Scriptures, walking in holiness before the Lord. Every member of the Church of Christ having children, is to bring them unto the Elders before the Church, who are to lay their hands upon them in the Lord, and bless them in the name of Christ. There cannot any one be received into the Church of Christ, who has not arrived to the years of accountability before God, and is not capable of repentance.

And baptism is to be administered in the following manner unto all those who repent: Whosoever being called of God and having authority given them of Jesus Christ, shall go down into the water with them, and shall say, calling them by name: Having authority given me of Jesus Christ, I baptize you in the name of the Father, and of the Son, and of the Holy Ghost. Amen. Then shall he immerse them in the water, and come forth again out of the water. And it is expedient that the Church meet together oft to partake of Bread and Wine, in the remembrance of the Lord Jesus; and the Elder or Priest shall administer it, and after this manner shall he do, he shall kneel with the Church, and call upon the Father in mighty prayer saying: O God the Eternal Father, we ask thee in the name of thy Son Jesus Christ, to bless and sanctify this bread to the souls of all those who partake of it, that they may eat in remembrance of the body of thy Son, and witness unto thee, O, God, the Eternal Father, that they are willing to take upon them the name of thy Son, and always remember

5

him, and keep his commandments which he hath given them, that they may always have his Spirit to be with them. Amen. The manner of administering the Wine: Behold they shall take the Cup and say, O God, the Eternal Father, we ask thee in the name of thy Son Jesus Christ, to bless and sanctify this Wine to the souls of all those who drink of it, that they may do it, in remembrance of the blood of thy Son, which was shed for them, that they may witness unto thee, O God the Eternal Father, that they do always remember him, that they may have his spirit to be with them. Amen.

Any member of this Church of Christ, transgressing or being overtaken in a fault, shall be dealt with as the Scriptures direct. It shall be the duty of the several churches, composing this Church of Christ, to send one or more of their Teachers to attend the several Conferences, held by the Elders of this Church, with a list of the names of the several members, uniting themselves with the Church since the last Conference, or send by the hand of some Priest, so that there can be a regular list of the names of the whole Church, in a Book kept by one of the Elders; whomsoever the other elders shall appoint from time to time: and also, if any have been expelled from the Church, so that their names may be blotted out of the general Church Record of names. Any member not removing from the Church where he resides, if going to a Church where he is not known, may take a letter certifying that he is a regular member and in good standing; which certificate may be signed by any Elder or Priest, if the member receiving the letter is personally acquainted with the Elder or Priest, or it may be signed by the Teachers or Deacons of the Church.

Behold, I say unto you, that all old Covenants have I caused to be done away in this thing, and this is a new and everlasting Covenant: even that which was from the beginning. Wherefore, although a man should be baptized an hundred times, it availeth him nothing, for ye cannot enter in at the straight gate by the law of Moses; neither by your dead works; for it is because of your dead works, that I have caused this last Covenant, and this Church to be built up unto me; even as in days of old. Wherefore, enter ye at the gate as I have commanded, and seek not to counsel your God. Amen.

"Dearly Beloved in the Lord
We Are under the Necessity to Disappoint You,"
Joseph Smith to Colesville [New York] Saints,
28 August and 2 December 1830

(from copies in Newel Knight Journal, typescript,
pp. 128-36 and 196-207, in private possession)

Dearly beloved in the Lord

We are under the necessity to disappoint you this time for reasons which I shall mention hereafter, but trusting that your meeting may not be an unprofitable one, may you all realize the necessity of getting together often to pray and supplicate at the Throne of Grace that the Spirit of the Lord may always rest upon you. Remember that without asking we can receive nothing, therefore ask in faith, and ye shall receive such blessings as God sees fit to bestow upon you. Pray not with covetous hearts that ye may consume it upon your lusts, but pray earnestly for the best gifts; fight the good fight of faith that ye may gain the crown which is laid up for those that endure faithful unto the end of their probation. Therefore hold fast that which ye have received so liberally from the hands of God so that when the time of refreshing shall come ye may not have labored in vain, but that ye may rest from all your labors and have fulness of joy in the Kingdom of God.

Dearly beloved brethren we are not ignorant of your tribulations, owing that ye are placed among ravening wolves, therefore we have the more earnest desire to come to see you, but our friends from the West have not yet come, and we can get no horse and wagon, and we are not able to come afoot so far, therefore we cannot come this saturday, but we look for our friends from the West every day and with safety we can promise to come next saturday, if the Lord will; therefore our desire is that ye should assemble yourselves together next saturday so that all things will be in order when we come. Be careful that the enemy of all righteousness will not get the advantage over you in getting the news abroad. Were it not for the prayers of you few, the Almighty would have thundered down his

7

wrath upon the inhabitants of that place, but be not faint, the day of your deliverance is not far distant for the judgements of the Lord are already abroad in the earth and the cold hand of death will soon pass through your neighborhood, and sweep away some of your most bitter enemies, for you need not suppose that God will be mocked at, and his commandments be trampled under their feet in such a manner as your enemies do, without visiting them in his wrath when they are fully ripe, and behold, the angel cries, thrust in your sickle for the harvest is fully ripe, and the earth will soon be reaped, that is, the wicked must soon be destroyed from off the face of the earth, for the Lord hath spoken it, and who can stay the hand of the Lord, or who is there that can measure arms with the Almighty, for at his commands the heavens and the earth must pass away, for the day is fast hastening on when the restoration of all things shall be fulfilled which all the Holy Prophets have prophesied of even into the gathering in of the House of Israel. Then shall come to pass that the lion shall lie down with the lamb, &c. But brethren be not discouraged when we tell you of perilous times, for they must shortly come, for the sword, famine, and pestilence are approaching, for there shall be great destructions upon the face of this land, for ye need not suppose that one jot or tittle of the prophecies of all the Holy Prophets shall fail, and there are many that remain to be fulfilled yet, and the Lord hath said that a short work will he make of it, and the righteous shall be saved if it be as by fire.

May the Grace of God the Father, Son and Holy Ghost be and abide with you from henceforth and forever, Amen.

&a.

Dearly beloved in the Lord

According to our prayers, the Lord hath called, chosen, ordained, sanctified and sent unto you another Servant and apostle separated unto this gospel through Jesus Christ our Redeemer, to whom be all honor praise henceforth and forever, even our beloved brother Orson Pratt, the bearer of these lines, whom I recommend unto you as a faithful Servant in the Lord, through Jesus Christ our Redeemer, Amen.

To the Church in Colesville

Having many things to write to you, but being assured that ye are not ignorant of all that I can write to you, finally I would inform you that Zion is prospering here [Fayette, New York], there are many serious inquirers in this place, who are seeking the Lord. It gave us much joy to hear from you, to hear that God is softening the hearts of the children of men in that place, it being the seat of Satan. But blessed be the name of God, it also hath become the abode of our savior and may you all be faithful and wait for the time of our Lord, for his appearing is nigh at hand. But the time, and the season, Brethren, ye have no need that I write unto you, for ye yourselves perfectly know that the day of the Lord so cometh as a thief in the night, for when they shall say peace and safety, then sudden destruction cometh upon them, as travail upon a woman, but they shall not escape. But ye, brethren, are not in darkness, therefore let us not sleep as do others, but let us watch and be sober, for they that sleep, sleep in the night, and they that be drunken are drunken in the night, but let us who be of the day, be sober, putting on the breastplate of faith and law, and for a helmet, the hope of salvation, for God hath not appointed us to wrath, but to obtain salvation through our Lord Jesus Christ. Wherefore comfort one another, even as ye also do, for perilous times are at hand, for behold the dethronement and deposition of the kings in the eastern continent, the whirlwinds in the West India, Islands, it has destroyed a number of vessels, uprooted buildings and strewed them in the air, the fields of spices have been destroyed and the inhabitants have barely escaped with their lives and many have been buried under the ruins. In Columbia, South America, they are at war and peace is taken from the earth in part and it will soon be in whole, yea destructions are at our doors and they soon will be in the houses of the wicked, and they that know not God. Yea lift up your heads and rejoice for your redemption draweth nigh. We are the most favored people that ever have been from the foundation of the world, if we remain faithful in keeping the commandments of our God. Yea, even Enoch, the seventh from Adam, beheld our day [and] rejoiced, and the prophets from that day forth have prophesied of the second coming of our Lord and Savior Jesus Christ and rejoiced at the day of rest of the Saints; yea, and the Apostles of our Savior also did rejoice in his appearance in a cloud with the host of Heaven to dwell with man on the earth a thousand years. Therefore we have reason to rejoice. Behold the prophecies of the Book of

Mormon are fulfilling as fast as time can bring it about. The Spirit of the Living God is upon me therefore who will say that I shall not prophecy. The time is soon at hand that we shall have to flee whithersoever the Lord will for safety. Fear not those who are making you an offender for a word but be faithful in witnessing unto a crooked and a perverse generation that the day of the coming of our Lord and Savior is at hand. Yea, prepare ye the way of the Lord, make strait his path. Who will shrink because of offenses for offenses must come, but woe to them by whom they come, for the rock must fall on them and grind them to pow[d]er, for the fulness of the Gentiles is come in, and woe will be unto them if they do not repent and be baptized in the name of our Lord and Savior Jesus Christ for the remission of their sins, and come in at the strait gate and be numbered with the House of Israel, for God will not always be mocked, and not pour out his wrath upon those that blaspheme his holy name, for the sword[,] famine and destruction will soon overtake them in their wild career, for God will avenge and pour out his phials [vials] of wrath and save his elect. And all those who will obey his commandments are his elect, and he will soon gather them from the four winds of heaven, from one quarter of the earth to the other, to a place whithersoever he will, therefore in your patience possess ye your souls, Amen.

Brother Hyrum [Smith], beware of the freemasons, [Alexander] McIntyre heard that you were in Manchester and he got out a warrant and went to your father's to distress the family but [Samuel] Harrison overheard their talk and they said that they cared not for the debt, if they only could obtain your body. They were there with carriages. Therefore beware of the Freemasons, this from yours & etc.

{4}

"Brother Martin I Send You This to Inform You that It Is Necessary for You to Come Here," Joseph Smith to Martin Harris, 22 February 1831

(from copy in archives, Historical Department, Church of Jesus Christ of Latter-day Saints, Salt Lake City, Utah)

Brother Martin

I send you this to inform you that it is necessary for you to come here [Kirtland, Ohio] as soon as you can in order to choose a place which may be best adopted to the circumstances of yourself and breatheren in the east to settle on as you may choose any place which may best suit yourselves any where in this part of the country so as to be as compact as possable[.] [A]nd as you will be better able to make [the] choice than we it is better for you to come before the rest of the breathren that when they come they may have places to go to[.] [Y]ou will also bring or cause to be brought all the books [copies of the Book of Mormon], as the work is here breaking forth on the east west north and south[.] [Y]ou will also inform the Elders which are there that all of them who can be spared will come here without delay if possable[.] [T]his by commandment of the Lord as he has a great work for them all in this our inheritance.

We have received the laws of the Kingdom since we came here and the Disciples in these parts have received them gladly. If You will[,] see that Father Smiths family are taken care of and sent on[.] You will send to Colesville and have either Hiram [Smith] or Newel [K. Whitney] to come immediately or both if they can be spared.

You will not sell the books for less than 10 Shillings[.]

{5}

"Again I Say unto You,"
Extract from the Laws for the Government
of the Church of Christ, 9 February 1831

(from *The Evening and the Morning Star*
[Independence, Missouri] 1 [July 1832], 2:[1])

Again I say unto you, that it shall not be given to any one to go forth to preach my gospel, or to build up my church, except he be ordained by some one who has authority, and it is known to the church that he has authority, and has been regularly ordained by the hands of the church. And again, the elders, priests, and teachers of this church, shall teach the Scriptures which are in the Bible, and the Book of Mormon, in the which is the fulness of the Gospel; and they shall observe the Covenants and church Articles to do them; and this shall be their teachings. And they shall be directed by the Spirit, which shall be given them by the prayer of faith; and if they receive not the Spirit, they shall not teach. And all this they shall observe to do, as I have commanded concerning their teaching, until the fulness of my Scriptures are given. And as they shall lift up their voices by the Comforter, they shall speak and prophesy as seemeth me good; for behold, the Comforter knoweth all things, and beareth record of the Father, and of the Son.

And now behold, I speak unto the church: Thou shalt not kill; and he that killeth, shall not have forgiveness, neither in this world, nor in the world to come. And again, thou shalt not kill; he that killeth shall die. Thou shalt not steal; and he that stealeth and will not repent, shall be cast out. Thou shalt not lie; he that lieth and will not repent, shall be cast out. Thou shalt love thy wife with all thy heart, and shall cleave unto her and none else; and he that looketh upon a woman to lust after her, shall deny the faith, and shall not have the Spirit; and if he repent not, he shall be cast out. Thou shalt not commit adultery; and he that commiteth adultery and repenteth not, shall be cast out; and he that has commiteth adultery and repenteth with all his heart, and forsaketh it, and doeth it no more, thou shalt forgive him; but if he doeth it again, he shall not be forgiven, but shall be cast out. Thou shalt not speak evil of thy neighbor, nor do him any harm. Thou knowest my laws, they are given in my Scriptures, he that sinneth and repenteth not, shall be cast out.

If thou lovest me, thou shalt serve me and keep all my commandments; and behold, thou shalt consecrate of thy properties, that which thou hast unto me, with a covenant and a deed which cannot be broken; and they shall be laid before the bishop of my church, and two of the elders, such as he shall apoint and set apart for the purpose. And it shall come to pass, that the bishop of my church, after that he has received the properties of my church, that it cannot be taken from the church, he shall appoint every man a steward over his own property, or that which he has received, inasmuch as shall be sufficient for himself and family; and the residue shall be kept to administer to him who has not, that every man who may receive according as he stands in need; and the residue shall be kept in my storehouse, to adminster to the poor and the needy, as shall be appointed by the elder of the church and the bishop; for the purpose of purchasing lands, and the building up of the New Jerusalem, which is hereafter to be revealed; that my covenant people may be gathered in one, in the day that I shall come to my temple: And this I do for the salvation of my people. And it shall come to pass, that he that sinneth and repenteth not shall be cast out, and shall not receive again that which he has consecrated unto me: For it shall come to pass, that which I spake by the mouths of my prophets shall be fulfilled; for I will consecrate of the riches of the Gentiles, unto my people which are of the house of Israel. And again, thou shalt not be proud in thy heart; let all thy garments be plain, and their beauty the beauty of the work of thine own hands, and let all things be done in cleanliness before me.

Thou shalt not be idle; for he that is idle shall not eat the bread, nor wear the garments of the laborer. And whosoever among you that are sick, and have not faith to be healed, but believeth, shall be nourished in all tenderness with herbs and mild food, and that not of the world; and the elders of the church, two or more shall be called, and shall pray for and lay their hands upon them in my name, and if they die, they shall die unto me; and if they live, they shall live unto me.— Thou shalt live together in love, insomuch that thou shalt weep for the loss of them that die, and more especially for those that have not hope of a glorious resurrection. And it shall come to pass, that those that die in me shall not taste of death, for it shall be sweet unto them; and they that die not in me, wo unto them; for their death is bitter. And again, it shall come to pass, that he that has faith in me to be healed, and is not appointed unto death, shall be healed. He who has faith to see, shall see; he who has faith to hear, shall hear; the lame who have faith to leap, shall leap; and they who have not faith to do these things, but believe in me, have power to become my sons, and inasmuch as they break not my laws, thou shalt bear their infirmities. Thou shalt stand in the place of thy stewardship: Thou shalt not take thy brother's garment; thou shalt pay for that which thou shalt receive of thy brother. And if thou obtainest more than that which would be for thy support, thou shalt give it into my storehouse, that all things may be done according to that which I have spoken. Thou shalt ask and my Scriptures shall be given as I have appointed; and for thy safety it is expedient that thou shalt hold thy peace concerning them, until ye have received them; then I give unto you a commandment that ye shall teach them unto all men; and they also shall be taught unto all nations, kindreds, tongues and people.

Thou shalt take the things which thou hast received, which thou knowest to have been my law, to be my law, to govern my church; and he that doeth according to these things shall be saved, and he that doeth them not shall be damned, if he continue. If thou shalt ask, thou shalt receive revelation upon revelation, knowledge upon knowledge, that thou mayest know the mysteries, and the peaceable things of the kingdom; that which bringeth joy, that which bringeth life eternal. Thou shalt ask and it shall be revealed unto you in mine own due time where the New Jerusalem shall be built. And behold, it shall come to pass, that my servants shall be sent forth to the, east and to the west, to the north, and to the south; and even now let him that goeth to the east, teach them that shall be converted to flee to the west; and this in consequence of that which is to come on the earth, and of secret combinations. Behold, thou shalt observe all these things, and great shall be thy reward. Thou shalt observe to keep the mysteries of the kingdom unto thyself, for it is not given to the world to know the mysteries. The laws which ye have received, and shall hereafter receive, shall be sufficient for you both here, and in the New Jerusalem. Therefore, he that lacketh knowledge, let him ask of me and I will give him liberally, and upbraid him not. Lift up your hearts and rejoice, for unto you the kingdom has been given; even so. Amen.

The priests and teachers, shall have their stewardship given them even as the members; and the elders are to assist the bishop in all things, and he is to see that their families are supported out of the property which is consecrated to the Lord, either a stewardship, or otherwise, as may be thought best by the elders & bishop.

Behold, verily I say unto you, that whatever persons among you having put away their companions for the cause of fornication, or in other words, if they shall testify before you in all lowliness of heart that this is the case, ye shall not cast them out from among you; but if ye shall find that any persons have left their companions for the sake of adultery, and they themselves are the offenders, and their companions are living, they shall be cast out from among you. And again I say unto you, that ye shall be watchful and careful, with all inquiry, that ye receive none such among you if they are married, and if they are not married, they shall repent of all their sins, or ye shall not receive them.

{6}

"Hear, O Ye Heavens, and Give Ear, O Earth," A Vision Received on 16 February 1832

(from *The Evening and the Morning Star* [Independence, Missouri] 1 [July 1832], 2:[2]; with Sidney Rigdon)

Hear, O ye Heavens, and give ear, O earth, and rejoice ye inhabitants thereof, for the Lord he is God, and beside him there is none else; and great is his wisdom; marvelous are his ways; and the extent of his doings, none can find out; his purposes fail not, neither are there any who can stay his hand: from eternity to eternity, he is the same, and his years never fail.

I the Lord am merciful and gracious unto them who fear me, and delight to honor them who serve me in righteousness, and in truth; great shall be their reward, and eternal shall be their glory; and to them will I reveal all mysteries; yea, all the hidden mysteries of my Kingdom from days of old; and for ages to come will I make known unto them the good pleasure of my will concerning all things; yea, even the wonders of eternity shall they know, and things to come will I show them, even the things of many generations; their wisdom shall be great, and their understanding reach to Heaven; before them the wisdom of the wise shall perish, and the understanding of the prudent shall come to nought; for by my Spirit will I enlighten them, and by my power will I make known unto them the secrets of my will; yea, even those things which eye has not seen, nor ear heard, nor yet entered into the heart of man.

We, Joseph [Smith] and Sidney [Rigdon], being in the Spirit on the sixteenth of February, in the year of our Lord, one thousand eight hundred and thirty two, and through the power of the Spirit, our eyes were opened, and our understandings were enlightened, so as to see and understand the things of God; even things which were from the b[e]ginning before the world was, which was ordained of the Father, through his only begotten Son, who was in the bosom of the Father, even from the beginning, of whom we bear record, and the record which we bear is the fulness of the Gospel of Jesus Christ, which is in

16

the Son, whom we saw and with whom we conversed in the Heavenly Vision; for as we sat doing the work of translation, which the Lord had appointed unto us, we came to the twenty ninth verse of the fifth chapter of John, which was given unto us thus: speaking of the resurrection of the dead who should hear the voice of the Son of man, and shall come forth; they who have done good in the resurrection of the just, and they who have done evil in the resurrection of the unjust. Now this caused us to marvel, for it was given us of the Spirit; and while we meditated upon these things, the Lord touched the eyes of our understandings, and they were opened, and the glory of the Lord shone round about; and we beheld the glory of the Son, on the right hand of the Father, and received of his fulness; and saw the holy angels, and they who are sanctified before his throne, worshiping God and the Lamb forever and ever. And now after the many testimonies which have been given of him, this is the testimony, last of all, which we give of him, that he lives; for we saw him, even on the right hand of God; and we heard the voice bearing record that he is the only begotten of the Father; that by him, and through him, and of him, the worlds are made, and were created; and the inhabitants thereof are begotten sons and daughters unto God. This we saw also and bear record, that an angel of God, who was in authority in the presence of God, who rebelled against the only begotten Son, (whom the Father loved, and who was in the bosom of the Father,) was thrust down from the presence of God and the Son, and was called Perdition; for the Heavens wept over him; for he was Lucifer, even the son of the morning; and we beheld and lo, he is fallen! is fallen! even a son of the morning. And while we were yet in the Spirit, the Lord commanded us that we should write the Vision; for behold satan, that old serpent, even the devil, who rebelled against God, and sought to take the kingdoms of our God, and of his Christ; wherefore he maketh war with the saints of God, and encompasses them about: And we saw a vision of the eternal sufferings of those w[i]th whom he maketh war and overcometh, for thus came the voice of the Lord unto us.

Thus saith the Lord, concerning all those who know my power, and who have been made partakers thereof, and suffered themselves, through the power of the devil, to be overcome unto the denying of the truth, and the defying of my power: they are they who are the sons of perdition, of whom I say it had been better for them never to have been born; for they are vessels of wrath doomed to suffer the wrath of

God, with the devil and his angels, throughout eternity: concerning whom I have said there is no forgiveness for them in this world nor in the world to come; having denied the Holy Ghost after having received it, and having denied the only begotten Son of the Father, crucifying him unto themselves, and putting him to an open shame: these are they who shall go away into the lake of fire and brimstone, with the devil and his angels, and the only ones on whom the second death shall have any power; yea, verily the only ones who shall not be redeemed in the due time of the Lord, after the sufferings of his wrath, who shall be brought forth by the resurrection of the dead, through the triumph & the glory of the Lamb; who was slain, who was in the bosom of the Father before the worlds were made. And this is the Gospel, the glad tidings which the voice out of the heavens bore record unto us, that he came into the world, even Jesus to be crucified for the world, and to bear the sins of the world, and to sanctify the world, and to cleanse it from all unrighteousness; that through him all might be saved, whom the Father had put into his power; and made by him who glorifieth the Father; and saveth all the work of his hands, except those sons of perdition, who denieth the Son after the Father hath revealed him: wherefore he saveth all save them, and these shall go away into everlasting punishment, which is endless punishment, which is eternal punishment, to reign with the devil and his angels throughout eternity, where their worm dieth not and the fire is not quenched, which is their torment, but the end thereof, neither the place thereof, and their torment, no man knoweth, neither was revealed, neither is, neither will be revealed unto man, save to them who are made partakers thereof: nevertheless I the Lord showeth it by vision unto many, but strai[gh]tway shutteth it up again: wherefore the end, the width, the height, the depth, and the misery thereof, he understandeth not, neither any man save them who are ordained unto this condemnation. And we heard the voice saying, Write the Vision for lo, this is the end of the vision of the eternal sufferings of the ungodly!

And again, we bear record for we saw and heard, and this is the testimony of the Gospel of Christ, concerning them who come forth in the resurrection of the just: they are they who received the testimony of Jesus, and believed on his name, and were baptized after the manner of his burial, being buried in the water in his name, and this according to the commandment which he hath given, that, by keeping the commandment, they might be washed and cleansed from all their sins, and receive the Holy Ghost by the laying on of the hands of him who is ordained and sealed unto this power; and who overcome by faith, and are sealed by that Holy Spirit of promise, which the Father shedeth forth upon all those who are just and true; they are they who are the church of the first-born: they are they into whose hands the Father hath given all things: they are they who are priests and kings, who having received of his fullness, and of his glory, and are priests of the most High, after the order of Melchisedek, which was after the order of Enoch, which was after the order of the only begotten Son: wherefore, as it is written, they are gods, even the sons of God: wherefore all things are theirs, whether life or death, or things present, or things to come, all are theirs and they are Christ's, and Christ is God's; and they shall overcome all things: wherefore let no man glory in man, but rather let him glory in God, who shall subdue all enemies under his feet: these shall dwell in the presence of God and his Christ forever and ever: these are they whom he shall bring with him, when he shall come in the clouds of heaven, to reign on the earth over his people: these are they who shall have part in the first resurrection: these are they who shall come forth in the resurrection of the just: these are they who are come unto mount Zion, and unto the city of the living God, the heavenly place, the holiest of all: these are they who have come to an innumerable company of angels; to the general assembly and church of Enoch, and of the first born: these are they whose names are written in Heaven, where God and Christ is the judge of all: these are they who are just men made perfect through Jesus the Mediator of the new covenant, who wrought out this perfect atonement through the shedding of his own blood: these are they whose bodies are celestial, whose glory is that of the Son, even the glory of God the highest of all; which glory the Sun of the firmament is written of as being typical.

And again, we saw the Terrestrial world, and behold and lo! these are they who are of the terrestrial, whose glory differeth from that of the church of the first born, who have received the fulness of the Father, even as that of the Moon differeth from the Sun of the firmament. Behold, these are they who died without law; and also they who are the spirits of men kept in prison, whom the Son visited and preached the Gospel unto them, that they might be judged according to men in the flesh, who received not the testimony of Jesus in the flesh, but afterwards received it: these are they who are honorable men of the earth, who were blinded by the craftiness of men:

these are they who receive of his glory, but not of his fulness: these are they who receive of the presence of the Son, but not of the fulness of the Father: wherefore they are bodies terrestrial, and not bodies celestial, and differeth in glory as the Moon differeth from the Sun: these are they who are not valiant in the testimony of Jesus: wherefore they obtained not the crown over the kingdoms of our God. And now this is the end of the vision which we saw of the terrestrial, that the Lord commanded us to write while we were yet in the Spirit.

And again, we saw the glory of the Telestial, which glory is that of the lesser, even as the glory of the stars differeth from that of the glory of the Moon in the firmament: these are they who receive not the Gospel of Christ, neither the testimony of Jesus: these are they who deny not the Holy Ghost: these are they who are thrust down to hell: these are they who shall not be redeemed from the devil, until the last resurrection, until the Lord, even Christ the Lamb, shall have finished his work: these are they who receive not of his fulness in the eternal world, but of the Holy Ghost through the administration of the terrestrial; and the terrestrial through the administration of the celestial; and also the telestial receive it of the administering of angels, who are appointed to minister for them, or who are appointed to be ministering spirits for them, for they shall be heirs of salvation.— And thus we saw in the Heavenly vision, the glory of the telestial, which surpasseth all understanding; and no man knoweth it except him to whom God hath revealed it. And thus we saw the glory of the terrestrial, which excelleth in all things the glory of the telestial, even in glory, and in power, and in might, and in dominion. And thus we saw the glory of the celestial, which excelleth in all things where God, even the Father, reigneth upon his throne forever and ever; before whose throne all things bow in humble reverence and giveth him glory forever and ever. They who dwell in his presence are the church of the first born; and they see as they are seen, and know as they are known, having received of his fullness and of his grace; and he maketh them equal in power, and in might, and in dominion. And the glory of the celestial is one, even as the glory of the Sun is one. And the glory of the Terrestrial is one, even as the glory of the Moon is one. And the glory of the Telestial is one, even as the glory of the stars is one: for as one star differeth from another star in glory, even so differeth one from another in glory in the telestial world: for these are they who are of Paul, and of Apollos, and of Cephas: they are they who say, they are some of one and some of another; some of Christ; and some of John; and some of Moses; and some of Elias;

20

and some of Esaias; and some of Isaiah; and some of Enoch, but received not the Gospel; neither the testimony of Jesus; neither the prophets; neither the everlasting covenant; last of all: these all are they who will not be gathered with the saints, to be caught up into the church of the first born, and received into the cloud; these are they who are liars, and sorcerers, and adulterers, and whorem[o]ngers, and whosoever loveth and maketh a lie: these are they who suffer the wrath of God on the earth: these are they who suffer the vengeance of eternal fire: these are they who are cast down to hell and suffer the wrath of Almighty God until the fulness of times, when Christ shall have subdued all enemies under his feet, and shall have perfected his work, when he shall deliver up the kingdom, and present it unto his Father spotless, saying: I have overcome and have trodden the wine-press alone, even the wine-press of the fierceness of the wrath of Almighty God: then shall he be crowned with the crown of his glory, to sit on the throne of his power to reign forever and ever. But behold and lo, we saw the glory and the inhabitants of the telestial world, that they were in number as innumerable as the stars in the firmament of Heaven, or as the sand upon the sea shore, and heard the voice of the Lord saying: These all shall bow the knee, and every tongue shall confess to him who sitteth upon the throne forever and ever: for they shall be judged according to their works; and every man shall receive according to his own works, his own dominion, in the mansions which are prepared; and they shall be servants of the most High, but where God and Christ dwells they cannot come, worlds without end. This is the end of the vision which we saw, which we were commanded to write while we were yet in the Spirit.

But great and marvelous are the works of the Lord and the mysteries of his kingdom which he showed unto us, which surpasseth all understanding in glory, and in might, and in dominion, which he commanded us we should not write, while we were yet in the Spirit, and are not lawful for man to utter; neither is man capable to make them known, for they are only to be seen and understood by the power of the Holy Ghost; which God bestows on those who love him and purify themselves before him; to whom he grants this privilege of seeing and knowing for themselves; that through the power and manifestation of the Spirit, while in the flesh, they may be able to bear his presence in the world of glory. And to God and the Lamb be glory, and honor, and dominion, forever and ever. Amen.

{7}

"Dear Wife I Would Inform You,"
Joseph Smith to Emma Smith,
6 June and 13 October 1832

(from Chicago Historical Society, Chicago, Illinois;
and Library-Archives, Reorganized Church of Jesus Christ
of Latter Day Saints, Independence, Missouri)

Dear Wife

I would inform you that Brother Martin [Harris] has arrived here [Greenville, Indiana] and braught the pleasing news that our Familys were well when he left there which Greately Cheared our hearts and revived our Spirits[.] we thank our hevenly Father for his Goodness unto us and all of you[.] Martin arrived on Satterday the Same week he left Chagrin haveing a prosperous time[.] we are all in good health[.] Brother [Newel K.] Whitneys [broken] leg is gaining and he thinks he Shall be able to to perform his Journy so as to get home about the 20th[.] my Situation is a very unpleasent one although I will endeaver to be Contented the Lord asisting me[.] I have visited a grove which is Just back of the town almost every day where I can be Secluded from the eyes of any mortal and there give vent to all the feelings of my heart in meaditation and prayr[.] I have Called to mind all the past moments of my life and am left to morn and Shed tears of sorrow for my folly in Sufering the adversary of my Soul to have so much power over me as he has had in times past[.] but God is merciful and has forgiven my Sins and I rejoice that he Sendeth forth the Comforter unto as many as believe and humbleeth themselves before him[.] I was grieved to hear that Hiram [Smith] had lost his little Child [Mary.] I think we Can in Some degree Simpathise with him but we all must be reconciled to our lots and say the will of the Lord be done[.] Sister [Elizabeth Ann] Whitney wrote a letter to her husband [Newel K.] which was very chearing but and being unwell at that time and filled with much anxiety it would have been very Consoling to me to have received a few lines from you but as you did not take the trouble I will try to be contented with my lot knowing that God is my friend[.] in him I shall find comfort[.] I have given my life into his hands[.] I am prepared to go at his Call[.] I desire to be with Christ[.] I Count not my life dear to me only to do his will[.] I am not pleased to hear that William Mclelin has come back and disobayed the voice of him who is altogether Lovely for a woman[.] I am astonished at Sister Emaline [Emeline Miller] yet I cannot belive she is not a worthy sister[.] I hope She will find him true and kind to her but have no reason to expect it[.] his Conduct merits the disapprobation of every true follower of Christ[.] but this is a painful subject [and] I hope you will excuse my warmth of feeling in mentioning this subject and also my inability in convaying my ideas in writing[.] I am happy to find that you are still in the faith of Christ and at Father Smiths[.] I hope you will Comfort Father and Mother in their trials and Hiram and Jerusha and the rest of the Family[.] tell Sophronia I remember her and Kalvin in my prayrs[.] my respects to the rest[.] I Should Like [to] See little Julia and once more take her on my knee and converse with you on all the subjects which concerns us[,] things I cannot[,] is not prudent for me to write[.] I omit all the important things which could I See you I could make you acquainted with[.] tell Brother [Frederick G.] Williams that I and Brother Whitney will arrange the business of that farm when we Come[.] give my respects to all the Brotheren[.] Br- Whitney['s] Family tell them he is Chearfull and patient and a true Brother to me[.] I subscribe myself your Husband[.] the Lord bless you[.] peace be with [you] so Farewell untill I return[.]

ૐ

My Dear Wife

This day I have been walking through the most splended part of the City of New Y[ork.] the buildings are truly great and wonderful to the astonishing of eve[r]y beholder and the language of my heart is like this[:] can the great God of all the Earth maker of all thing[s] magnificent and splendid be displeased with man for all these great inventions saught out by them[?] my answer is no[.] it can not be[,] seeing these works are calculated to mak[e] men comfortable[,] wise[,] and happy[.] therefore not for the works can the Lord be displeased only aga[i]nst man is the anger of the Lord Kindled because they Give him not the Glory[.] therefore their iniquities shall be visited upon their heads and their works shall be burned up with unquenchable fire[.] the inequity of the people is printed in every countinance and

nothing but the dress of the people makes them look fair and b[ea]uti-
ful[.] all is deformity[.] their is something in every countinance that is
disagreable with few exceptions[.] Oh how long Oh Lord Shall this
order of things exist and darkness cover the Earth and gross darkness
cover the people[?] after beholding all that I had any desire to behold
I returned to my room to meditate and calm my mind and behold the
thaughts of home[,] of Emma and Julia[,] rushes upon my mind like a
flood[,] and I could wish for [a] moment to be with them[.] my breast
is fill[e]d with all the feelings and tenderness of a parent and a
Husband[,] and could I be with you I would tell you many things[.]
yet when I reflect upon this great city like Ninevah not desearning
their right hand from their left[,] yea more then two hundred thousand souls[,] my bowels is filled with compasion towards them and I
am determined to lift up my voice in this City and leave the Event
with God who holdeth all things in his hands and will not suffer an
hair of our heads unnoticed to fall to the ground[.] there is but few
Cases of the chol[e]ra in this City now and if you should see the
people you would not know that they had ever heard of the
chol[e]ra[.] I hope you will excuse me for writting this letter so soon
after w[r]iting for I feel as if I wanted to say something to you to
comfort you in your beculier [peculiar] triel and presant affliction[.] I
hope God will give you strength that you may not faint[.] I pray God
to soften the hearts of those arou[n]d you to be kind to you and take
the burdon of[f] your shoulders as much as posable and not afflict
you[.] I feel for you for I know you[r] state and that others do not[.]
but you must comfort yourself knowing that God is your friend in
heaven and that you hav[e] one true and living friend on Earth your
Husband[.]

PS while Brother [Newel K.] Whitney [is] Selecting goods I have
nothing to [do] but to sit in my room and pray for him that he may
have strength to indure his labours[.] for truly it is [a] tedious Job to
stand on the feet all day to select goods[.] it wants good Judgement
and a long acquantence with goods to git good ones and a man must
be his own Judge for no one will Judge for him[,] and it is much
pepleccity [perplexity] of mind[.] I prefer reading and praying and
holding comuneion with the holy spirit and writing to you[,] then
walking the streets and beholding the distraction of man[.] I have had
some conversation with few which gave satisfaction[,] and one very
b[ea]utiful young gentleman from Jersy whose countinance was very

sollam[.] he came and set by my side and began to converce with me about the Chol[e]ra[,] and I learned he had been seased with it and came very near die[i]ing with it[.] he said the Lord had spared him for some wise pu[r]pose[.] I took advantage of this and opened a long discours with him[.] he received my teaching appearan[t]ly with much pleasure and becam[e] very strongly attacth to me[.] we talkd till late at night and concluded to omit conversation till the next day[,] but having some business to do he was detained untill the boat was ready to go out and must leave[.] he came to me and bid me Farewell and we parted with much reluctance[.] Brother Whitney is received with great kindness by all his old acquaintance[s.] he is faithful in prayr and fervant in spirit and we take great comfort together[.] there is about one hundred boarders and sometimes more in this house every day from one to two from all parts of the world[.] I think you would hav[e] laughed right harty if you could [havel been whe[r]e you could see the waiters to day noon [as they] waited on the table both Black and white and molato runing[,] bowing[,] and maneuvering[,] but I must conclude[.] I remain your affectionate Husband until Death[.]

{8}

"A History of the Life of Joseph Smith, Jr.,"
1832

(from Scott H. Faulring, ed., *An American Prophet's Record:*
The Diaries and Journals of Joseph Smith
[Salt Lake City: Signature Books in association
with Smith Research Associates, 1987], pp. 3-8)

An account of his [Joseph Smith Jr.'s] marvilous experience and of all the mighty acts which he doeth in the name of Jesus Ch[r]ist the Son of the Living God of whom he beareth record. Also an account of the rise of the Church of Christ in the eve of time according as the Lord brought forth and established by his hand. Firstly, he receiving the testamony from on high. Seccondly, the ministering of Angels. Thirdly, the reception of the Holy Priesthood by the ministring of Angels to admin[i]ster the letter of the Gospel the Law and commandments as they were given unto him and the ordinenc[e]s. Fo[u]rthly, a confirmation and reception of the High Priesthood after the Holy Order of the Son of the Living God [with] power and ordinence[s] from on high to preach the Gospel in the administration and demonstration of the spirit, the Kees of the Kingdom of God confered upon him and the continuation of the blessings of God to him &c.

I was born in the town of Charon [Sharon] in the State of Vermont, North America on the twenty third day of December AD 1805 of goodly parents who spared no pains to instructing me in the Christian religion.

At the age of about ten years my Father Joseph Smith, Siegnior [Senior,] moved to Palmyra, Ontario County in the State of New York. And being in indigent circumstances [we] were obliged to labour hard for the support of a large Family having nine chilldren. As it required the exertions of all that were able to render any assistance for the support of the Family, therefore we were deprived of the bennifit of an education. Suffice it to say I was mearly instructid in reading, writing, and the ground rules of Arithmatic which const[it]uted my whole literary acquirements.

At about the age of twelve years my mind become seriously imprest with regard to the all important concerns for the wellfare of my immortal Soul which led me to searching the scriptures believe-ing, as I was taught, that they contained the word of God. Thus applying myself to them and my intimate acquaintance with those of differant denominations led me to marvel excedingly. For I discovered that they did not adorn their profession by a holy walk and Godly coversation agreeable to what I found contained in that sacred deposi-tory. This was a grief to my Soul.

Thus from the age of twelve years to fifteen I pondered many things in my heart concerning the sittuation of the world of mankind, the contentions and divisions, the wickedness and abominations, and the darkness which pervaded the minds of mankind. My mind be-come excedingly distressed for I become convicted of my sins and by searching the scriptures I found that mankind did not come unto the Lord but that they had apostatised from the true and living faith. There was no society or denomination that built upon the gospel of Jesus Christ as recorded in the New Testament and I felt to mourn for my own sins and for the sins of the world.

For I learned in the scriptures that God was the same yesterday, to day, and forever. That he was no respecter to [of] persons, for he was God. For I looked upon the sun, the glorious luminary of the earth. And also the moon rolling in their magesty through the heavens. Also the stars, shining in their courses. And the earth also upon which I stood. And the beast of the field and the fowls of heaven and the fish of the waters. And also man walking forth upon the face of the earth in magesty and in the strength of beauty whose power and intiligence in governing the things which are so exceding great and marvilous even in the likeness of him who created them.

When I considered upon these things my heart exclaimed, "Well hath the wise man said it is a fool that saith in his heart, 'there is no God.'" My heart exclaimed, "All these bear testimony and bespeak an omnipotent and omnipreasant power. A being who makith Laws and decreeeth and bindeth all things in their bounds. Who filleth Eternity. Who was, is, and will be from all Eternity to Eternity." When I considered all these things and that that being seeketh such to worship him as worship him in spirit and in truth. Therefore I cried unto the Lord for mercy for there was none else to whom I could go and obtain mercy. The Lord heard my cry in the wilderness and while in the attitude of calling upon the Lord in the 16th year of my age a pillar of light above the brightness of the sun at noon day come down from above and rested upon me. I was filled with the spirit of God and the Lord opened the heavens upon me and I saw the Lord.

He spake unto me saying, "Joseph my son thy sins are forgiven thee. Go thy way, walk in my statutes and keep my commandments. Behold I am the Lord of Glory. I was crucifyed for the world that all those who believe on my name may have Eternal life. Behold the world lieth in sin at this time and none doeth good, no not one. They have turned asside from the gospel and keep not my commandments. They draw near to me with their lips while their hearts are far from me and mine anger is kindling against the inhabitants of the earth to visit them acording to their ungodliness and to bring to pass that which hath been spoken by the mouth of the prophets and Apostles. Behold and lo, I come quickly as it [is] written of me, in the cloud clothed in the glory of my Father."

My soul was filled with love and for many days I could rejoice with great Joy and the Lord was with me. But [I] could find none that would believe the he[a]venly vision. Nevertheless, I pondered these things in my heart. But after many days I fell into transgression and sinned in many things which brought a wound upon my soul. There were many things which transpired that cannot be writ[t]en and my Father's family have suffered many persicutions and afflictions.

And it came to pass when I was seventeen years of age, I called again upon the Lord and he shewed unto me a heavenly vision. For behold an angel of the Lord came and stood before me. It was by night and he called me by name and he said the Lord had forgiven me my sins. He revealed unto me that in the Town of Manchester, Ontario County, N[ew] Y[ork] there was plates of gold upon which there was engravings which was engraven by Maroni [Moroni] and his fathers, the servants of the living God in ancient days, deposited by the commandments of God and kept by the power thereof and that I should go and get them. He revealed unto me many things concerning the inhabitants of the earth which since have been revealed in commandments and revelations.

It was on the 22d day of Sept[ember] AD 1822. Thus he appeared unto me three times in one night and once on the next day. Then I immediately went to the place and found where the plates was deposited as the angel of the Lord had commanded me and straightway made three attempts to get them. Then being excedingly fright-ened I supposed it had been a dreem of Vision, but when I con-sid[e]red I knew that it was not. Therefore I cried unto the Lord in the agony of my soul, "Why can I not obtain them?"

Behold the angel appeared unto me again and said unto me, "You have not kept the commandments of the Lord which I gave unto you. Therefore you cannot now obtain them, for the time is not yet fulfilled. Therefore thou wast left unto temptation that thou mightest be made acquainted with the power of the advisary. Therefore repent and call on the Lord [and] thou shalt be forgiven. And in his own due time thou shalt obtain them."

For now I had been tempted of the advisary and saught the Plates to obtain riches and kept not the commandment that I should have a eye single to the glory of God. Therefore I was chastened and saught dilegently to obtain the plates and obtained them not untill I was twenty one years of age.

In this year, I was married to Emma Hale, Daughter of Isaach Hale, who lived in Harmony, Susquehana County, Pen[n]sylvania on the 18th [of] January AD 1827. On the 22d day of Sept[ember] of this same year I obtained the plates.

In December following, we mooved to Susquehana [Harmony] by the assistence of a man by the name of Martin Harris who became convinced of the visions and gave me fifty Dollars to bare my ex-pences. Because of his faith and this righteous deed the Lord ap-peared unto him in a vision and shewed unto him his marvilous work which he was about to do.

He imediately came to Susquehannah and said the Lord had shown him that he must go to New York City with some of the characters, so we proceeded to coppy some of them. He took his Journy to the Eastern Cittys and to the Learned saying, "Read this I pray thee" and the learned said, "I cannot," but if he would bring the plates they would read it but the Lord had forbid it. He returned to me and gave them to me to translate and I said, "I cannot for I am not learned," but the Lord had prepared spectacles for to read the Book. Therefore I commenced translating the characters. Thus the Propicy [prophecy] of Isiaah was fulfilled which is writ[t]en in the 29[th] chapter concerning the book.

And it came to pass that after we had translated 116 pages that he desired to carry them to read to his friends that p[er]adventure he might convince them of the truth. Therefore, I inquired of the Lord and the Lord said unto me that he must not take them. I spoke unto him (Martin) the word of the Lord and he said inquire again. I inquired again and also a third time and the Lord said unto me, "Let him go with them, only he shall covenant with me that he will not shew them to only but four persons." He covenented with the Lord that he would do according to the word of the Lord.

Therefore he took them and took his journey unto his friends to [in] Palmira, Wayne County, State of N[ew] York. He brake the covenent which he made before the Lord and the Lord suffered the writings to fall into the hands of wicked men. Martin was chastened for his transgression and I also was chastened also for my transgression for asking the Lord the third time. Wherefore the Plates was taken from me by the power of God and I was not able to obtain them for a season.

And it came to pass after much humility and affliction of soul, I obtained them again when [the] Lord appeared unto a young man by the name of Oliver Cowdery and shewed unto him the plates in a vision, also the truth of the work, and what the Lord was about to do through me his unworthy servant. Therefore, he was desirous to come and write for me and translate. Now my wife had writ[t]en some for me to translate and also my Brother Samuel H. Smith but we had become reduced in property and my wive's father was about to turn me out of doors. I had not where [nowhere] to go and I cried unto the Lord that he would provide for me to accomplish the work whereunto he had commanded me.

{9}

"Joseph Smith, Jr. Record Book," Excerpts from Joseph Smith's First Diary, 27 November to 6 December 1832

(from Scott H. Faulring, ed., *An American Prophet's Record: The Diaries and Journals of Joseph Smith* [Salt Lake City: Signature Books in association with Smith Research Associates, 1987], pp. 9-11)

Joseph Smith, Jr. Record Book Baught [bought] for to note all the minute circumstances that comes under my observation

Joseph Smith, Jr.'s Book for Record Baught on the 27th of November 1832 for the purpose to keep a minute ac[c]ount of all things that come under my obse[r]vation &c.

Oh may God grant that I may be directed in all my thaughts. Oh bless thy servent. Amen.

November 28th [1832] This day I have [spent] in reading and writing. This Evening my mind is calm and serene for which I thank the Lord.

November 29th This day [I] road from Kirtland to Chardon to see my Sister Sop[h]ronia and also ca[lled] to see my Sister Catherine [and found] them [well].

This Evening Brother Frederic[k G. Williams] Prophecyed that next spring I should go to the city of Pittsburg to establish a Bishop-wrick and within one year I should go to the City of New York. The Lord spare the life of thy servent. Amen.

November 30th 1830 [1832] This day retu[r]ned home to Kirtland [and] found all well to the joy and satisfaction of my soul. On my return home stopped at Mr. King's [and] bore testimony to him and Family &c.

December 1th [1st, 1832] /[I] bore testimony to Mr. Gilmore/ [I] wrote and corrected revelations &c.

December 2th [2nd] The Sabath, [I] went to meeting &c.

December 3d Ordained Brother Packherd with my own hand[s].

Also Brother Umfiry [Humphery who] came to see me from the East and braught news from Brother Lyman Johnson and Orson Pratt &c.

Also held a conference in the Evening. Br[others] Jes[s]e [Gause] and Mo[r]gan and William McLel[l]en was excommunicated from the Church &c.

December 4th This day I [have] been unwell [and] done but lit[t]le, been at home all day. Regulated some things this Evening. [I] feel better in my mind then I have for a few days back. Oh Lord deliver thy servent out of tem[p]tations and fill his heart with wisdom and understanding.

December 5th This day wrote let[t]ers, copying letters, and translating. In [the] evening held a council to advise with Brother Solomon Humphry. It was ordered by the council that he should be a companion with Brother Noah Packard in the work of the ministry.

December 6th Translating and received a revelation explaining the Parable [of] the wheat and the tears [tares] &c.

{10}

"Sir, Considering the Liberal Principles,"
Joseph Smith to N. C. Saxton, editor,
American Revivalist, and Rochester Observer,
4 January 1833

(from *Times and Seasons* [Nauvoo, Illinois]
5 [15 November 1844], 21:705-707)

Sir, Considering the liberal principles, upon which your interesting and valuable paper is published, myself being a subscriber, and feeling a deep interest in the cause of Zion and in the happiness of my brethren of mankind, I cheerfully take up my pen to contribute my mite, at this very interesting and important period.

For some length of time I have been carefully viewing the state of things, as they now appear, throughout our christian land; and have looked at it with feelings of the most painful anxiety, while upon one hand, beholding the manifest withdrawal of God's Holy Spirit, and the vail of stupidity which seems to be drawn over the hearts of the people; and upon the other hand beholding the judgments of God that have swept, and are still sweeping hundreds and thousands of our race, (and I fear unprepared) down to the shades of death.— With this solemn and alarming fact before me I am led to exclaim, "O that my head were waters, and mine eyes a fountain of tears, that I might weep day and night," &c.

I think that it is high time for a christian world to awake out of sleep, and cry mightily to that God, day and night, whose anger we have justly incurred. Are not these things a sufficient stimulant to arouse the faculties, and call forth the energies of every man, woman, and child, that possesses feelings of sympathy for their fellows, or that is in any degree endeared to the budding cause of our glorious Lord? I leave an intelligent community to answer this important question, with a confession, that this is what has caused me to overlook my own inability, and expose my weakness to a learned world: but, trusting in that God, who has said these things are hid from the wise and prudent and revealed unto babes, I step forth into the field to tell you what the

Lord is doing, and what you must do, to enjoy the smiles of your Saviour in these last days.

The time has at last arived when the God of Abraham, of Isaac, and of Jacob has set his hand again, the second time, to recover the remnants of his people, which have been left from Assyria, and from Egypt, and from Pathros, &.c., and from the islands of the sea, and with them to bring in the fulness of the Gentiles, and establish that covenant with them, which was promised when their sins should be taken away. See Romans 11:25, 26, and 27, and also, Jeremiah 31:31, 32 and 33. This covenant has never been established with the house of Israel, nor with the house of Judah, for it requires two parties to make a covenant, and those two parties must be agreed, or, no covenant can be made.

Christ, in the days of his flesh, proposed to make a covenant with them, but they rejected him and his proposals, and in consequence thereof, they were broken off, and no covenant was made with them at that time. But their unbelief has not rendered the promise of God of none effect: no, for there was another day limited in David, which was the day of his power; and then his people, *Israel*, should be a willing people;—and he would write his laws in their hearts, and print them in their thoughts; their sins and their iniquities he would remember no more.

Thus after this chosen family had rejected Christ and his proposals, the heralds of salvation said to them "lo we turn unto the Gentiles," and the Gentiles received the covenant, and were grafted in from whence the chosen family were broken off: but the Gentiles have not continued in the goodness of God, but have departed from the faith that was once delivered to the saints, and have broken the covenant in which their fathers were established: (see Isaiah 24:5,) and have become high minded, and have not feared; therefore, but few of them will be gathered with the chosen family. Has not the pride, high-mindedness, and unbelief of the Gentiles provoked the Holy One of Israel to withdraw his Holy Spirit from them, and send forth his judgments to scourge them for their wickedness? This is certainly the case.

Christ said to his deciples, (Mark 16:17 and 18,) that these signs should follow them that believe: in my name shall they cast out devils; they shall speak with new tongues; they shall take up servants [serpents], and if they drink any deadly thing it shall not hurt them; they shall lay hands on the sick and they shall recover; and also, in connexion with this, read 1st Corinthians 12th chapter. By the foregoing testimonies, we may look at the christian world and see the apostacy there has been from the apostolic platform; and who can look at this and not exclaim, in the language of Isaiah, "the earth is defiled under the inhabitants thereof, because they have transgressed the laws, changed the ordinances, and broken the everlasting covenant."

The plain fact is this, the power of God begins to fall upon the nations, and the light of the latter day glory begins to break forth through the dark atmosphere of sectarian wickedness, and their iniquity rolls up into view, and the nations of the Gentiles are like the waves of the sea, casting up mire and dirt, or, all in commotion, and they hastily are preparing to act the part allotted them, when the Lord rebukes the nations; when he shall rule them with a rod of iron, and break them in peaces like a potters vessel. The Lord declared to his servants, some eighteen months since, that he was withdrawing his spirit from the earth; and we can see that such is the fact, for not only the churches are dwindling away, but there are no conversions, or, but very few; and this is not all, the governments of the earth are thrown into confusion and division; and DESTRUCTION, to the eye of the spiritual beholder, seems to be written by the finger of an invisible hand, in large capitals upon almost every thing we behold.

And now what remains to be done, under circumstances like these? I will proceed to tell you what the Lord requires of all people, high and low, rich and poor, male and female, ministers and people, professors of religion, and non-professors, in order that they may enjoy the Holy Spirit of God to a fulness, and escape the judgments of God, which are almost ready to burst upon the nations of the earth.— Repent of all your sins, and be baptised in water for the remission of them, in the name of the Father, and of the Son, and of the Holy Ghost, and receive the ordinance of the laying on of the hands of him who is ordained and sealed unto this power, that ye may receive the Holy Spirit of God; and this is according to the Holy scriptures, and of the Book of Mormon; and the only way that man can enter into the Celestial kingdom. These are the requisitions of the new covenant, or first principles of the gospel of Christ; then "add to your faith, virtue; and to virtue, knowledge; and to knowledge, temperance; and to temperance, patience; and to patience, brotherly kindness; and to brotherly kindness, charity; (or love,) and if these things be in you, and abound, they make you to be neither barren, nor unfruitful, in the knowledge of our Lord Jesus Christ."

The Book of Mormon is a record of the forefathers of our western

35

tribes of Indians; having been found through the ministration of an holy angel, and translated into our own language by the gift and power [of] God, after having been hid up in the earth for the last fourteen hundred years, containing the word of God which was delivered unto them. By it we learn that our western tribes of Indians are descendants from that of Joseph that was sold into Egypt, and that the land [of] America is a promised land unto them, and unto it, all the tribes of Israel will come, with as many of the Gentiles as shall comply with the requisitions of the new covenant. But the tribe of Judah will return to old Jerusalem. The City of Zion, spoken of by David, in the one hundred and first Psalm, will be built upon the land of America, "and the ransomed of the Lord shall return and come to it with songs and everlasting joy upon their heads," and then they will be delivered from the overflowing scourge that shall pass through the land. But Judah shall obtain deliverance at Jerusalem. See Joel 2:32. Isaiah 26:20, and 21st. Jeremiah 31:12. Psalms 50:5. Ezekiel 34:11, 12, and 13. These are testimonies, that the good Shepherd will put forth his own sheep, and lead them out from all nations where they have been scattered in a cloudy and dark day, to Zion, and to Jerusalem: besides many more testimonies which might be brought.

And now I am prepared to say by the authority of Jesus Christ, that not many years shall pass away, before the United States shall present such a scene of *bloodshed* as has not a parallel in the history of our nation; pestilence, hail, famine, and earthquakes will sweep the wicked of this generation from off the face of the land, to open and prepare the way for the return of the lost tribes of Israel from the north country. The people of the Lord, those who have complied with the requisitions of the new covenant, have already commenced gathering together to Zion, which is in the State of Missouri; therefore I declare unto you the warning which the Lord has commanded me to declare unto this generation, remembering that the eyes of my Maker are upon me, and that to him I am accountable for every word I say, wishing nothing worse to my fellow men than their eternal salvation; therefore, "fear God and give glory to him for the hour of his judgment is come"—Repent ye, repent ye, and embrace the everlasting covenant, and flee to Zion before the overflowing scourge overtake you, for there are those now living upon the earth whose eyes shall not be closed in death until they see all these things, which I have spoken, fulfilled. *Remember* these things; call upon the Lord while he is near, and seek him while he may be found, is the exhortation of your unworthy servant.

11

"Respected Uncle Silas
It Is with Feelings of Deep Interest,"
Joseph Smith to Silas Smith,
26 September 1833

(from copy in Lucy Mack Smith, "Preliminary History,"
archives, Historical Department, Church of Jesus Christ
of Latter-day Saints, Salt Lake City, Utah)

Respected Uncle Silas

It is with feelings of deep interest for the wellfare of mankind which fills my mind on the reflection that all were formed by the hand of him who will call the same to give an impartial account of all their works on that great day to which you and myself in common with them are bound, that I take up my pen and seat myself in an attitude to address a few though imperfect lines to you for your perusal.

I have no doubt but that you will agree with me that men will be held accountable for the things which they have and not for the things they have not or that all the light and intelligence communicated to them from their benifficen[t] creator whether it is much or little by the same they in justice will be judged, and that they are required to yield obedience and improve upon that and that only which is given for man is not to live by bread alone but by every word that proceeds out of the mouth of God.

Seeing that the Lord has never given the world to understand by anything heretofore revealed that he had ceased forever to speak to his creatures when saught unto in a proper manner why should it be thought a thing incredible that he should be pleased to speak again in these last days for their salvation. Perhaps you may be surprized at this assertion that I should say for the salvation of his creatures in these last days since we have already in our possesion a vast volume of his word which he has previously given—But you will admit that the word spoken to Noah was not sufficent for Abraham or it was not required of Abraham to leave the land of his nativity and seek an Inheritance in a strange Country upon the word spoken to Noah but for himself he obtained promises at the hand of the Lord and walked in that perfection that he was called the friend of God Isaac the promised seed was not required to rest his hope upon the promises made to his father Abraham but was priviledged with the assurance of his approbation in the sight of Heaven by the direct voice of the Lord to him. If one man can live upon the revelations given to another might not I with propriety ask why the necessity then of the Lord speaking to Isaac as he did as is recorded in the 26 chapter of Genesis for the Lord there repeats or rather promises again to perform the oath which he had previously sworn unto Abraham and why this repet[it]ion to Isaac. Why was not the first promise as sure for Isaac as it was for Abraham. Was not Isaac Abraham's son And could he not place implicit confidence in the word of his father as being a man of God.

Perhaps you may say that he was a very peculiar man and different from men in these last days consequently the Lord favored him with blessings peculiar and different as he was different from men in this age[.] I admit that he was a peculiar man and was not only peculiarly blessed but greatly blessed. But all the peculiarity that I can discover in the man or all the difference between him and men in this age is that he was more holy and more perfect before God and came to him with a purer heart and more faith than men in this day.

The same might be said on the subject of jacobs history. Why was it that the Lord spake to him concerning the same promise after he had made it once to Abraham and renewed it to Isaac why could not Jacob rest contented upon the word spoken to his fathers. When the time of the promise drew nigh for the deliverance of the children of Israel from the land of Egypt why was it necessary that the Lord should begin to speak to them. The promise or word to Abraham was that his seed should serve in bondage and be afflicted four hundred years and after that they should come out with great substance. Why did they not rely upon this promise and when they had remained in Egypt in bondage four hundred [years] come out without waiting for further revelation but act entirely upon the promise given to Abraham that they should come out.

Paul said to his Hebrew brethren that God b[e]ing more abundantly willing to show unto the heirs of his promises the immutability of his council ["]confirmed it by an oath." He also exhorts them who throug[h] faith and patience inherit the promises.

"Notwithstanding we (said Paul) have fled for refuge to lay hold of the hope set before us which hope we have as an anchor of the soul both sure and steadfast and which entereth into that within the vail." Yet he was careful to press upon them the necessity of continuing on untill they as well as those who inherited the promises might have the assurance of their salvation confirmed to them by an oath from the mouth of him who could not lie[.] for that seemed to be the example anciently and Paul holds it out to his brethren as an object attainable in his day[,] and why not I admit that by reading the scriptures of truth saints in the days of Paul could learn beyond the power of contradiction that Abraham Isaac and jacob had the promise of eternal life confirmed to them by an oath of the Lord[;] but that promise or oath was no assurance to them of their salvation[,] but they could by walking in the footsteps and continuing in the faith of their fathers obtain for themselves an oath for confirmation that they were meet to be partake[r]s of the inheritance with the saints in light.

If the saints in the days of the Apostles were priviledged to take the saints for example and lay hold of the same promises and attain to the same exhalted priviledges of knowing that their names were writen in the Lambs book of life[,] and that they were sealed there as a perpetual memorial before the face of the most high[,] will not the same faithfulness[,] the same purity of heart[,] and the same faith bring the same assurance of eternal life and that in the same manner to the children of men now in this age of the world.

I have no doubt but that the holy prophets and apostles and saints in ancient days were saved in the Kingdom of God. Neither do I doubt but that they held converse and communion with them while in the flesh as Paul said to the corinthian brethren that the Lord jesus showed himself to above 500 saints at one time after his resure[c]tion. job said that he knew that his Redeemer lived and that he should see him in the flesh in the latter days. I may believe that Enoch walked with God[.] I may believe that Abraham communed with God and conversed with angels. I may believe that Isaac obtained a renewal of the covenant made to Abraham by the direct voice of the Lord. I may believe that jacob conversed with holy angels and heard the word of his Maker[,] that he wrestled with the angel until he prevailed and obtained a blessing[.] I may believe that Elijah was taken to Heaven in a chariot of fire with fiery horses[.] I may believe that the saints saw the Lord and conversed with him face to face after his resurection[.] I may believe that the Hebrew Church came to Mount Zion and unto the

39

city of the living God the Heave[n]ly Jerusalem and to an inumerable company of angels. I may believe that they looked into Eternity and saw the Judge of all, and Jesus the Mediator of the new covenant; but will all this purchase an assurance for me, or waft me to the regions of Eternal day with my garments spotless, pure, and white? Or, must I not rather obtain for myself, by my own faith and dilligence, in keeping the commandments of the Lord, an assurance of salvation for myself[.] And have I not an equal priviledge with the ancient saints? and will not the Lord hear my prayers, and listen to my cries, as soon [as] he ever did to their's if I come to him in the manner they did or is he a respecter of persons?

I must now close this subject for the want of time; and I may say with propriety at the begining: we would be pleased to see you in Kirtland and more pleased to have you embrace the New Covenant. I remain.

Yours affectionately

12

"Beloved Brother Edward,
I Commence Answering Your Letter,"
Joseph Smith to Edward Partridge,
2 May 1833

(from copy in archives, Historical Department,
Church of Jesus Christ of Latter-day Saints,
Salt Lake City, Utah)

Beloved Brother Edward,

I commence answering your letter & sincere request to me, by begging your pardon for not having addressed you, more particularly in letters which I have written to Zion [Independence, Missouri], for I have always felt as though a letter written to any one in authority in Zion, would be the property of all, & it matters but little to whom it was directed. But I am satisfied that this is an error, for instruction that is given pointedly, and expressly to us, designating our names as individuals, seems to have double power and influence over our minds[.] I am thankful to the Lord for the testimony of his spirit, which he has given me, concerning your honesty, and sincerity before him, and the Lord loveth you, and also Zion, for he chasteneth whom he loveth, and scourgeth every son & daughter whom he receiveth, and he will not suffer you to be confounded, and of this thing you may rest assured, notwithstanding, all the threatning of the enemy, and your perils among false brethren[.] For verily I say unto you, that this is my prayer, and I verily believe the prayer of all the saints in Kirtland, recorded in heaven, in these words, Heavenly Father in the name of Jesus Christ thy son, preserve brother Edward, the bishop of thy church, and give him wisdom, knowledge & power, & the holy ghost, that he may impart to thy saints in Zion, their inheritance, & to every man his portion of meat in due season[.] [A]nd now, this is our confidence & record on high, therefore fear not little flock, for it has been your fathers good will to give you the kingdom, and now I will proceed to tell you my views, concerning consecration, property, and giving inheritances &c[.] The law of the Lord, binds you to receive,

41

whatsoever property is consecrated, by deed[.] The consecrated property, is considered the residue kept for the Lords store house, and it is given for this consideration, for to purchase inheritances for the poor[.] [T]his, any man has a right to do, agreeable to all laws of our country, to donate, give or consecrate all that he feels disposed to give, and it is your duty, to see that whatsoever is given, is given legally[.] [T]herefore, it must be given for the consideration of the poor saints, and in this way no man can take any advantage of you in law[.] [A]gain, concerning inheritances, you are bound by the law of the Lord, to give a deed, securing to him who receives inheritances, his inheritance, for an everlasting inheritance, or in other words, to be his individual property, his private stewardship, and if he is found a transgressor [he] should be cut off, out of the church, his inheritance is his still and he is delivered over to the buffetings of satan, till the day of redemption[.] But the property which he consecrated to the poor, for their benefit, & inheritance, [and] stewardship, he cannot obtain again by the law of the Lord[.] Thus you see the propriety of this law, that rich men cannot have power to disinherit the poor by obtaining again that which they have consecrated, which is the residue, signified in the law, that you will find in the second paragraph of the extract from the law, in the second number[.] [A]nd now brother Edward, be assured that we all feel thankful, that the brethren in Zion are beginning to humble themselves, & trying to keep the commandments of the Lord, which is our prayer to God, [that] you may all be able to do[.] [A]nd now, may the grace of God be with all, amen.

{13}

"Blessed of the Lord,"
Blessings, dated 18 December 1833

(from Scott H. Faulring, ed., *An American Prophet's Record:
The Diaries and Journals of Joseph Smith*
[Salt Lake City: Signature Books in association
with Smith Research Associates, 1987], pp. 17-19)

Blessed of the Lord is Bro[ther] Oliver [Cowdery]. Nevertheless there are two evils in him that he must needs forsake or he cannot altogeth[er] escape the buffettings of the adver[sar]y. If he shall forsak[e] these evils he shall be forgiven and shall be made like unto the bow which the Lord hath set in the heavens. He shall be a sign and an ensign unto the nations. Behold he is blessed of the Lord for his constancy and steadfastness in the work of the Lord. Wherefore he shall be blessed in his generation and they shall never be cut off. He shall be helped out of many troubles and if he keep[s] the commandments and harken unto the council of the Lord his rest shall be glorious.

Again blessed of the Lord is my father and also my mother and my brothers and my sisters. For they shall yet find redemption in the House of the Lord and their of[f]springs shall be a blessing, a Joy, and a comfort unto them.

Blessed is my mother for her soul is ever fill[ed] with benevolence and phylanthropy and notwithstanding her age yet she shall receive strength and shall be comforted in the midst of her house. She shall have eternal life.

Blessed is my father. For the hand of the Lord shall be over him. For he shall see the affliction of his children pass away when his head is fully ripe. He shall behold himself as an olive tree whose branches are bowed down with much fruit. He shall also possess a mansion on high.

Blessed of the Lord is my brother Hyrum for the integrity of his heart. He shall be girt about with truth and faithfulness shall be the strength of his loins from generation to generation. He shall be a shaft in the hand of his God to exicute Judgement upon his enemies. He shall be hid by the hand of the Lord that none of his secret parts shall

43

be discovered unto his hu[r]t. His name shall be accounted a blessing among men. When he is in trouble and great tribulation hath come upon him he shall remember the God of Jacob and he will shield him from the power of Satan. He shall receive[counsel] in the House of the Most High that he may be streng[t]hened in hope that the going of his feet may be established for eve[r].

Blessed of the Lord is [my] bro[ther] Samuel because the Lord shall say unto him, "Sam[ue]l, Sam[ue]l." Therefore he shall be made a teacher in the House of the Lord and the Lord shall mature his mind in Judgement. Thereby he shall obtain the esteem and fellowship of his brethren. His soul shall be established and he shall benefit [from] the House of the Lord because he shall obtain answer[s] to [his] prayer[s] in his faithfulness.

[My] Bro[ther] William is as the fi[e]rce Lion who divideth not the spoil because of his strength. In the pride of his heart he will neglect the more weighty matters until his soul is bowed down in sorrow. Then he shall return and call on the name of his God and shall find forgiveness and shall wax valient. Therefor[e] he shall be saved unto the utter most. As the roaring Lion of the forest in the midst of his prey so shall the hand of his generation be lifted up against those who are set on high that fight against the God of Israel. Fearless and unda[u]nted shall they be in battle in avenging the [w]rongs of the innocent and relieving the oppressed. Ther[e]for[e] the blessings of the God of Jacob shall be in the midst of his house notwithstanding his rebelious heart.

And now O God let the residue of my father's house ever come up in remembrance before thee. That thou mayest save them from the hand of the oppressor and establish their feet upon the rock of ages. That they may have place in thy house and be saved in thy Kingdom. Let all these things be even as I have said for Christ's sake. Amen.

{14}

"I Shall Now Endeavor to Set Forth,"
Two Sermons Delivered on 12 February
and 21 April 1834

(from "Kirtland [Ohio] Council Minute Book,"
original in archives, Historical Department,
Church of Jesus Christ of Latter-day Saints,
Salt Lake City, Utah)

This evening the high Priests and Elders of the Church in Kirtland [met] at the house of bro. Joseph Smith Jun. in Council for Church business. The council was organized, and opened by bro. Joseph Smith Jun in prayer. Bro. Joseph then rose and said: I shall now endeavor to set forth before this council, the dignity of the office which has been conferred upon me by the ministring of the Angel of God, by his own will and by the voice of this Church. I have never set before any council in all the order in which a Council ought to be conducted, which, perhaps, has deprived the Council of some, or many blessings.

He said, that no man was capable of judging a matter in council without his own heart was pure, and that we frequently are so filled with prejudice, or have a beam in our own eye, that we are not capable of passing right decissions, &c. But to return to the subject of the order. In ancient days Councils were conducted with such strict propriety, that no one was allowed to whisper, be weary, leave the room, or get uneasy in the least, until the voice of the Lord, by revelation, or by the voice of the council by the Spirit was obtained: which has not been observed in the church to the present. It was understood in ancient days, that if one man could stay in Council another could, and if the president could spend his time, the members could also. But in our councils, generally, one would be uneasy, another asleep, one praying another not; one's mind on the business of the council and another thinking on something else &c. Our acts are recorded, and at a future day they will be laid before us, and if we should fail to judge right and injure our fellow beings, they may there perhaps condemn us; then they are of great consequence, and to me

45

the consequence appears to be of force beyond any thing which I am able to express &c. Ask yourselves, brethren, how much you have exercised yourselves in prayer since you heard of this council; and if you are now prepared to sit in judgment upon the soul of your brother. Br Joseph then went on to give us a relation of his situation at the time he obtained the record, the persecution he met with &c. He also told us of his transgression at the time he was translating the Book of Mormon. He also prophecied that he should stand and shine like the sun in the firmament when his enemies and the gainsayers of his testimony should be put down and cut off and their names blotted out from among men.

॰॰

This day a conference of the Elders of the Church of Christ assembled at the dwelling house of bro. [Benjamin] Carpenters at 10 O'clock A.M. . . . Bro. Joseph Smith Jun. read the 2nd Chapter of the prophecy of Joel & took the lead in prayer, after which, he commenced addressing the congregation, as follows. It is very difficult for us to communicate to the Churches all that God has revealed to us, in consequence of tradition; for we are differently situated from any other people that ever existed upon this Earth. [C]onsequently those former revelations cannot be suited to our condition, because they were given to other people who were before us; but in the last days, God was to call a remnant, in which was to be deliverance, as well as in Jerusalem, and Zion. Now, if God should give no more revelations, where will we find Zion and this remnant. He said that the time was near when desolation was to cover the earth and then God would have a place of deliverance in his remnant, and in Zion, &c. He then gave a relation of obtaining and translating the Book of Mormon, the revelation of the priesthood of Aaron, the organization of the Church in the year 1830, the revelation of the high priesthood, and the gift of the Holy Spirit poured out upon the Church, &c. Take away the book of Mormon, and the revelations, and where is our religion? We have none; for without a Zion and a place of deliverance, we must fall, because the time is near when the sun will be darkened, the moon turn to blood, the stars fall from heaven and the earth reel to and fro; then if this is the case, if we are not sanctified and gathered to the places where God has appointed, [despite] our former professions and our great love for the bible, we must fall, we cannot stand, we cannot be saved; for God will gather out his saints from the gentiles and then comes desolation or destruction and none can escape except the pure in heart who are gathered, &c.

{15}

"We Shall, in this Lecture, Speak of the Godhead," from Lecture Fifth and Lecture Sixth, Lectures on Faith, 1834-35

(from *Latter Day Saints' Messenger and Advocate*
[Kirtland, Ohio] 1 [May 1835], 8:122-26;
with Sidney Rigdon)

Lecture Fifth.

1 In our former lectures we treated of the being, character, perfections and attributes of God. What we mean by perfections, is, the perfections which belong to all the attributes of his nature. We shall, in this lecture, speak of the Godhead: we mean the Father, Son and Holy Spirit.

2 There are two personages who constitute the great, matchless, governing, and supreme power over all things—by whom all things were created and made, that are created and made, whether visible or invisible, whether in heaven, on earth, or in the earth, under the earth, or through-out the immensity of space— They are the Father and the Son: The Father being a personage of spirit, glory and power: possessing all perfection and fullness: The Son, who was in the bosom of the Father, a personage of tabernacle, made, or fashioned like unto man, or being in the form and likeness of man, or, rather man was formed after his likeness, and in his image;—he is also the express image and likeness of the personage of the Father: possessing all the fullness of the Father, or; the same fullness with the Father; being begotten of him, and ordained from before the foundation of the world to be a propitiation for the sins of all those who should believe on his name, and is called the Son because of the flesh— and descended in suffering below that which man can suffer, or, in other words, suffered greater sufferings, and was exposed to more powerful contradictions than any man can be. But notwithstanding all this, he kept the law of God, and remained without sin: Showing thereby that it is in the power of man to keep the law and remain also without sin. And also, that by him a righteous judgment might come upon all flesh, & that all who walk not in the law of God, may justly be condemned by the law,

48

and have no excuse for their sins. And he being the only begotten of the Father, full of grace and truth, and having overcome, received a fullness of the glory of the Father—possessing the same mind with the Father, which mind is the Holy Spirit, that bears record of the Father and the Son, and these three are one, or in other words, these three constitute the great, matchless, governing and supreme power over all things: by whom all things were created and made, that were created and made: and these three constitute the Godhead, and are one: The Father and the Son possessing the same mind, the same wisdom, glory, power and fulness: Filling all in all—the Son being filled with the fulness of the Mind, glory and power, or, in other words, the Spirit, glory and power of the Father—possessing all knowledge and glory, and the same kingdom: sitting at the right hand of power, in the express image and likeness of the Father—a Mediator for man—being filled with the fulness of the mind of the Father, or, in other words, the Spirit of the Father: which Spirit is shed forth upon all who believe on his name and keep his commandments: and all those who keep his commandments shall grow up from grace to grace, and become heirs of the heavenly kingdom, and joint heirs with Jesus Christ; possessing the same mind, being transformed into the same image or likeness, even the express image of him who fills all in all: being filled with the fullness of his glory, and become one in him, even as the Father, Son and Holy Spirit are one.

3 From the foregoing account of the Godhead, which is given in his revelations, the Saints have a sure foundation laid for the exercise of faith unto life and salvation, through the atonement and mediation of Jesus Christ, by whose blood they have a forgiveness of sins, and also, a sure reward laid up for them in heaven, even that of partaking of the fulness of the Father and the Son, through the Spirit. As the Son partakes of the fulness of the Father through the Spirit, so the saints are, by the same Spirit, to be partakers of the same fulness, to enjoy the same glory; for as the Father and the Son are one, so in like manner the saints are to be one in them, through the love of the Father, the mediation of Jesus Christ, and the gift of the Holy Spirit, they are to be heirs of God, and joint heirs with Jesus Christ. . . .

Lecture Sixth.

1 Having treated, in the preceding lectures, of the ideas of the character, perfections and attributes of God, we next proceed to treat of the knowledge which persons must have, that the course of life

which they pursue is according to the will of God, in order that they may be enabled to exercise faith in him unto life and salvation.

2 This knowledge supplies an important place in revealed religion; for it was by reason of it that the ancients were enabled to endure as seeing him who is invisible. An actual knowledge to any person that the course of life which he pursues is according to the will of God, is essentially necessary to enable him to have that confidence in God, without which no person can obtain eternal life. It was this that enabled the ancient saints to endure all their afflictions and persecutions, and to take joyfully the spoiling of their goods, knowing, (not believing merely,) that they had a more enduring substance. Heb. 10: 34.

3 Having the assurance that they were pursuing a course which was agreeable to the will of God, they were enabled to take, not only the spoiling of their goods, and the wasting of their substance, joyfully, but also to suffer death in its most horrid forms; knowing, (not merely believing,) that when this earthly house of their tabernacle was dissolved, they had a building of God, a house not made with hands, eternal in the heavens. Second Cor. 5: 1.

4 Such was and always will be the situation of the saints of God, that unless they have an actual knowledge that the course they are pursuing is according to the will of God, they will grow weary in their minds and faint; for such has been and always will be the opposition in the hearts of unbelievers and those that know not God, against the pure and unadulterated religion of heaven, (the only thing which ensures eternal life,) that they will persecute to the utermost, all that worship God according to his revelations, receive the truth in the love of it, and submit themselves to be guided and directed by his will, and drive them to such extremities that nothing short of an actual knowledge of their being the favorites of heaven, and of their having embraced the order of things which God has established for the redemption of man, will enable them to exercise that confidence in him necessary for them to overcome the world, and obtain that crown of glory which is laid up for them that fear God.

5 For a man to lay down his all, his character and reputation, his honor and applause, his good name among men, his houses, his lands, his brothers and sisters, his wife and children, and even his own life also, counting all things but filth and dross for the excellency of the knowledge of Jesus Christ, requires more than mere belief, or supposition that he is doing the will of God, but actual knowledge: realizing,

that when these sufferings are ended he will enter into eternal rest, and be a partaker of the glory of God.

6 For unless a person does know that he is walking according to the will of God, it would be offering an insult to the dignity of the Creator, were he to say that he would be a partaker of his glory when he should be done with the things of this life. But when he has this knowledge, and most assuredly knows that he is doing the will of God, his confidence can be equally strong that he will be a partaker of the glory of God.

7 Let us here observe, that a religion that does not require the sacrifice of all things, never has power sufficient to produce the faith necessary unto life and salvation; for from the first existence of man, the faith necessary unto the enjoyment of life and salvation never could be obtained without the sacrifice of all earthly things: it was through this sacrifice, and this only, that God has ordained that men should enjoy eternal life; and it is through the medium of the sacrifice of all earthly things, that men do actually know that they are doing the things that are well pleasing in the sight of God. When a man has offered in sacrifice all that he has, for the truth's sake, not even withholding his life, and believing before God that he has been called to make this sacrifice, because he seeks to do his will, he does know most assuredly, that God does and will accept his sacrifice and offering, and that he has not nor will not seek his face in vain.— Under these circumstances, then, he can obtain the faith necessary for him to lay hold on eternal life.

8 It is in vain for persons to fancy to themselves that they are heirs with those, or can be heirs with them, who have offered their all in sacrifice, and by this means obtain faith in God and favor with him so as to obtain eternal life, unless they in like manner offer unto him the same sacrifice, and through that offering obtain the knowledge that they are accepted of him.

9 It was in offering sacrifices that Abel, the first martyr, obtained knowledge that he was accepted of God.— And from the days of righteous Abel to the present time, the knowledge that men have that they are accepted in the sight of God, is obtained by offering sacrifice: and in the last days, before the Lord comes, he is to gather together his saints who have made a covenant with him by sacrifice. Ps. 50: 3, 4, 5. Our God shall come, and shall not keep silence: a fire shall devour before him, and it shall be very tempestuous round about him. He

shall call to the heavens from above, and to the earth, that he may judge his people. Gather my saints together unto me; those that have made a covenant with me by sacrifice.

10 Those, then, who make the sacrifice will have the testimony that their course is pleasing in the sight of God, and those who have this testimony will have faith to lay hold on eternal life, and will be enabled, through faith, to endure unto the end, and receive the crown that is laid up for them that love the appearing of our Lord Jesus Christ. But those who do not make the sacrifice cannot enjoy this faith, because men are dependent upon this sacrifice in order to obtain this faith; therefore they cannot lay hold upon eternal life, because the revelations of God do not guarantee unto them the authority so to do; and without this guarantee faith could not exist.

11 All the saints of whom we have account in all the revelations of God which are extant, obtained the knowledge which they had of their acceptance in his sight, through the sacrifice which they offered unto him; and thro' the knowledge thus obtained, their faith became sufficiently strong to lay hold upon the promise of eternal life, and to endure as seeing him who is invisible; and were enabled, through faith, to combat the powers of darkness, contend against the wiles of the adversary, overcome the world, and obtain the end of their faith, even the salvation of their souls.

12 But those who have not made this sacrifice to God, do not know that the course which they pursue is well pleasing in his sight; for whatever may be their belief or their opinion, it is a matter of doubt and uncertainty in their mind; and where doubt and uncertainty are, there faith is not, nor can it be. For doubt and faith do not exist in the same person at the same time. So that persons whose minds are under doubts and fears cannot have unshaken confidence, and where unshaken confidence is not, there faith is weak, and where faith is weak, the persons will not be able to contend against all the opposition, tribulations and afflictions which they will have to encounter in order to be heirs of God, and joint heirs with Christ Jesus; and they will grow weary in their minds, and the adversary will have power over them and destroy them.

"I Have Something to Lay before the Council," A Sermon Delivered on 27 February 1835

(from "A record of the transactions of the Twelve apostles
of the Church of the Latter-Day Saints
from the time of their call to the apostleship
which was on the 14th Day of Feby. A. 1835,"
original in archives, Historical Department,
Church of Jesus Christ of Latter-day Saints,
Salt Lake City, Utah)

I have something to lay before the council [of Twelve Apostles], an item which they will find to be of great importance to them. I have for myself learned a fact by experience which on recollection gives me deep sorrow. It is a fact that if I now had in my possession every decision which has been given upon important items of doctrine and duties since the rise of this church, they would be of incalcuable worth to the saints, but we have neglected to keep record of such things, thinking that perhaps that they would never benefit us afterwards, which had we now, would decide almost any point that might be agitated; and now we cannot bear record to the church nor unto the world of the great and glorious manifestations that have been made to us with that degree of power and authority which we otherwise could if we now had these things to publish abroad.

Since the twelve are now chosen, I wish to tell them a course which they may pursue and be benefitted hereafter in a point of light of which they, perhaps, are not now aware. At all times when you assemble in the capacity of a council to transact business let the oldest of your number preside and let one or more be appointed to keep a record of your proceedings and on the decision of every important time, be it what it may, let such decision be noted down, and they will ever after remain upon record as law, covenant and doctrine. Questions thus decided might at the time appear unimportant, but should they be recorded and one of you lay hands upon them afterward, you might find them of infinite worth not only to your brethren but a feast also to your own souls.

Should you assemble from time to time and proceed to discuss important questions and pass decisions upon them and omit to record such decisions, by and by you will be driven to straits from which you will not be able to extricate yourselves—not being in a situation to bring your faith to [bear] with sufficient perfection or power to obtain the desired information. Now in consequence of a neglect to write these things when God reveal them not esteeming them of sufficient worth the spirit may withdraw and God may be angry and here is a fountain of knowledge[, the] importance [of] which is now lost. What was the cause of this. The answer is slothfulness, or a neglect to appoint a man to occupy a few moments in writing. Here let me prophecy the time will come when if you neglect to do this, you will fall by the hands of unrighteous men. Were you to be brought before the authorities and accused of any crime or misdemeanor and be as innocent as the angels of God unless you can prove that you were somewhere else, your enemies will prevail against you: but if you can bring twelve men to testify that you were in some other place at that time you will escape their hands. Now if you will be careful to keep minutes of these things as I have said, it will be one of the most important and interesting records ever seen. I have now laid these things before you for your consideration and you are left to act according to your own judgments.

{17}

"I Am Happy in the Enjoyment of this Oppertunity," A Sermon Delivered on 12 November 1835

(from Scott H. Faulring, ed., *An American Prophet's Record: The Diaries and Journals of Joseph Smith* [Salt Lake City: Signature Books in association with Smith Research Associates, 1987], pp. 56-58)

I am happy in the enjoyment of this oppertunity of meeting with this Council [of Twelve Apostles] on this occasion. I am satisfyed that the spirit of the Lord is here. I am satisfied with all the breth[r]en present. I need not say that you have my utmost confidence and that I intend to uphold you to the uttermost. For I am well aware that you have to sustain my character against the vile calumnies and reproaches of this ungodly generation and that you delight in so doing. Darkness prevails at this time as it was at the time Jesus Christ was about to be crucified. The powers of darkness strove to obscure the glorious sun of righteousness that began to dawn upon the world and was soon to burst in great blessings upon the heads of the faithful.

Let me tell you brethren that great blessings awate us at this time and will soon be poured out upon us if we are faithful in all things. For we are even entitled to greater blessings than they were because the[y] had the person of Christ with them to instruct them in the great plan of salvation. His personal presence we have not, therefore we need great faith on account of our peculiar circumstances. I am determined to do all that I can to uphold you. Although I may do many things invertanbly [inadvertently] that are not right in the sight of God.

You want to know many things that are before you that you may know how to prepare your selves for the great things that God is about to bring to pass. But there is on[e] great deficiency or obstruction in the way that deprives us of the greater blessings. And in order to make the foundation of this Church complete and permanent, we must remove this obstruction which is to attend to certain duties that we have not as yet attended to.

I supposed I had established this Church on a permanent foundation when I went to the Missouri. Indeed I did so, for if I had been taken away it would have been enough, but I yet live. Therefore God requires more at my hands.

The item to which I wish the more particularly to call your attention to night is the ordinance of washing of feet. This we have not done as yet, but it is necessary now as much as it was in the days of the Saviour. We must have a place prepared that we may attend to this ordinance aside from the world. We have not desired much from the hand of the Lord with that faith and obediance that we ought. Yet we have enjoyed great blessings and we are not so sensible of this as we should be.

When or wher[e] has God suffered one of the witnesses or first Elders of this Church to fall? Never nor nowhere amidst all the calamities and judgments that have befallen the inhabitants of the earth. His almighty arm had sustained us. Men and Devils have raged and spent the[ir] malice in vain.

We must have all things prepared and call our Solem[n] Assembly as the Lord has commanded us that we may be able to accomplish his great work. It must be done in God's own way. The House of the Lord must be prepared and the Solem[n] Assembly called and organized in it according to the order of the House of God. In it we must attend to the ordinance of washing of feet. It was never intended for any but official members. It is calculated to unite our hearts that we may be one in feeling and sentiment and that our faith may be strong so that Satan cannot over throw us, nor have any power over us.

The Endowment you are so anxious about you cannot comprehend now. Nor could Gabriel explain it to the understanding of your dark minds, but strive to be prepared in your hearts. Be faithful in all things that when we meet in the Solem[n] Assembly that is such as God shall name out of all the official members will meet and we must be clean ev[e]ry whit. Let us be faithful and silent brethren and if God gives you a manifestation keep it to yourselves. Be watchful and prayerful and you shall have a prelude of those joys that God will pour out on that day. Do not watch for iniquity in each other. If you do you will not get an endowment, for God will not bestow it on such. But if we are faithful and live by every word that proce[e]des forth from the mouth of God I will venture to prophesy that we shall get a blessing that will be worth remembering if we should live as long as John the Revelator. Our blessings will be such as we have not realized before, nor in this generation.

The order of the House of God has and ever will be the same. Even after Christ comes and after the termination of the thousand years it will be the same and we shall finally roll into the Celestial Kingdom of God and enjoy it forever. You need an Endowment brethren in order that you may be prepared and able to over come all things. Those that reject your testimony will be damned. The sick will be healed, the lame made to walk, the deaf to hear and the blind to see through your instrumentality. But let me tell you that you will not have power after the Endowment to heal those who have not faith, nor to benifit them. For you might as well expect to benefit a devil in hell as such an one who is possessed of his spirit and are willing to keep it. For they are habitations for the devils and only fit for his society.

But when you are endowed and prepared to preach the gospel to all nations, kindred and toungs [tongues] in there own languages you must faithfully warn all and bind up the testimony and seal up the law. The destroying angel will follow close at your heels and execute his tremendeous mission upon the children of disobediance and destroy the workers of iniquity, while the Saints will be gathered out from among them and stand in holy places ready to meet the bride groom when he comes.

I feel disposed to speak a few words more to you my brethren concerning the Endowment. All who are prepared and are sufficiently pure to abide the presence of the Saviour will see him in the Solem[n] Assembly.

{18}

"After So Long a Time, and after So Many Things Having Been Said, I Feel It My Duty to Drop a Few Hints," Joseph Smith to the Elders of the Church of the Latter Day Saints, 1 September, 1 November, and 1 December 1835

(from *Latter Day Saints' Messenger and Advocate* [Kirtland, Ohio] 1 [September 1835], 1:179-82; 2 [November 1835], 2:209-12; and 2 [December 1835], 3:225-30)

After so long a time, and after so many things having been said, I feel it my duty to drop a few hints, that, perhaps the elders, traveling through the world to warn the inhabitants of the earth to flee the wrath to come, and save themselves from this untoward generation, may be aided in a measure, in doctrine, and in the way of their duty. I have been laboring in this cause for eight years, during which time I have traveled much, and have had much experience. I removed from Seneca county, N.Y. to Geauga county, Ohio, in February, 1831.

Having received, by an heavenly vision, a commandment, in June following, to take my journey to the western boundaries of the State of Missouri, and there designate the very spot, which was to be the central spot for the commencement of the gathering together of those who embrace the fulness of the everlasting gospel—I accordingly undertook the journey with certain ones of my brethren, and, after a long and tedious journey, suffering many privations and hardships, I arrived in Jackson county Missouri; and, after viewing the country, seeking diligently at the hand of God, he manifested himself unto me, and designated to me and others, the very spot upon which he designed to commence the work of the gathering, and the upbuilding of an holy city, which should be called Zion: —Zion because it is to be a place of righteousness, and all who build thereon, are to worship the true and living God—and all believe in one doctrine even the doctrine of our Lord and Savior Jesus Christ.

"Thy watchmen shall lift up the voice; with the voice together shall they sing: for they shall see eye to eye, when the Lord shall bring again Zion." —Isaiah 52:8.

Here we pause for a moment to make a few remarks upon the idea of gathering to this place. It is well known that there were lands belonging to the government, to be sold to individuals; and it was understood by all, at least we believed so, that we lived in a free country, a land of liberty and of laws, guaranteeing to every man, or any company of men, the right of purchasing lands, and settling, and living upon them: therefore we thought no harm in advising the Latter Day Saints, or Mormons, as they are reproachfully called, to gather to this place, inasmuch as it was their duty, (and it was well understood so to be,) to purchase, *with money*, lands, and live upon them—not infringing upon the civil rights of any individual, or community of people: always keeping in view the saying, "Do unto others as you would wish to have others do unto you." Following also the good injunction: "Deal justly, love mercy, and walk humbly with thy God."

These were our motives in teaching the people, or Latter Day Saints, to gather together, beginning at this place. And inasmuch as there are those who have had different views from this, we feel, that it is a cause of deep regret: For, be it known unto all men, that our principles concerning this thing, have not been such as have been represented by those who, we have every reason to believe, are designing and wicked men, that have said that this was our doctrine: —to infringe upon the rights of a people who inhabit our civil and free country: such as to drive the inhabitants of Jackson county from their lands, and take possession thereof unlawfully. Far, yea, far be such a principle from our hearts: it never entered into our mind, and we only say, that God shall reward such in that day when he shall come to make up his jewels.

But to return to my subject: after having ascertained the very spot, and having the happiness of seeing quite a number of the families of my brethren, comfortably situated upon the land, I took leave of them and journeyed back to Ohio, and used every influence and argument, that lay in my power, to get those who believe in the everlasting covenant, whose circumstances woul[d] admit, and whose families were willing to remove to the place which I now designated to be the land of Zion: And thus the sound of the gathering, and of the doctrine, went abroad into the world; and many we have reason to fear, having a zeal not according to knowledge, not understanding the pure principles of the doctrine of the church, have no doubt, in the heat of enthusiasm, taught and said many things which are derogatory to the genuine character and principles of the church, and for these things we are heartily sorry, and would apologize if an apology would do any good.

But we pause here and offer a remark upon the saying which we learn has gone abroad, and has been handled in a manner detrimental to the cause of truth, by saying, "that in preaching the doctrine of gathering, we break up families, and give license for men to leave their families; women their husbands; children their parents, and slaves their masters, thereby deranging the order, and breaking up the harmony and peace of society." We shall here show our faith, and thereby, as we humbly trust, put an end to these faults, and wicked misrepresentations, which have caused, we have every reason to believe, thousands to think they were doing God's service, when they were persecuting the children of God: whereas, if they could have enjoyed the true light, and had a just understanding of our principles, they would have embraced them with all their hearts, and been rejoicing in the love of the truth.

And now to show our doctrine on this subject, we shall commence with the first principles of the gospel, which are repentance, and baptism for the remission of sins, and the gift of the Holy Ghost by the laying on of the hands. This we believe to be our duty, to teach to all mankind the doctrine of repentance, which we shall endeavor to show from the following quotations:

> "Then opened he their understanding, that they might understand the scriptures, and said unto them, thus it is written, and thus it behoved Christ to suffer, and to rise from the dead, the third day; and that repentance and remission of sins should be preached in his name among all nations, beginning at Jerusalem." —Luke 24:45, 46, 47.

By this we learn, that it behoved Christ to suffer, and to be crucified, and rise again on the third day, for the express purpose that repentance and remission of sins should be preached unto all nations.

> "Then Peter said unto them, repent, and be baptized every one of you, in the name of Jesus Christ, for the remission of sins, and ye shall receive the gift of the Holy Ghost. For the promise is unto you, and to

your children, and to all that are afar off, even as many as the Lord our God shall call." —Acts 2:38, 39.

By this we learn, that the promise of the Holy Ghost, is unto as many as the doctrine of repentance was to be preached, which was unto all nations. And we discover also, that the promise was to extend by lineage: for Peter says, "not only unto you, but unto your children, and unto all that are afar off." From this we infer that it was to continue unto their children's children, and even unto as many generations as should come after, even as many as the Lord their God should call.—We discover here that we are blending two principles together, in these quotations. The first is the principle of repentance, and the second is the principle of the remission of sins. And we learn from Peter, that remission of sins is obtained by baptism in the name of the Lord Jesus Christ; and the gift of the Holy Ghost follows inevitably: for, says Peter, "you shall receive the gift of the Holy Ghost." Therefore we believe in preaching the doctrine of repentance in all the world, both to old and young, rich and poor, bond and free, as we shall endeavor to show hereafter—how and in what manner, and how far it is binding upon the consciences of mankind, making proper distinctions between old and young men, women and children, and servants.

But we discover, in order to be benefitted by the doctrine of repentance, we must believe in obtaining the remission of sins. And in order to obtain the remission of sins, we must believe in the doctrine of baptism, in the name of the Lord Jesus Christ. And if we believe in baptism for the remission of sins, we may expect a fulfilment of the promise of the Holy Ghost: for the promise extends to all whom the Lord our God shall call. And hath he not surely said, as you will find in the last chapter of Revelations:

"And the Spirit and the bride say, Come. And let him that heareth, say, Come. And let him that is athirst, come. And whosoever will, let him take the water of life freely." Rev. 22:17.

Again the Savior says:

"Come unto me, all ye that labor, and are heavy laden, and I will give you rest. Take my yoke upon you, and learn of me; for I am meek and lowly in heart; and ye shall find rest unto your souls. For my yoke is easy, and my burden is light." —Matt. 11:28, 29, 30.

Again Isaiah says:

"Look unto me, and be ye saved, all the ends of the earth: for I am God, and there is none else. I have sworn by myself, the word is gone out of my mouth in righteousness, and shall not return, that unto me every knee shall bow, every tongue shall swear. Surely, shall one say, in the Lord have I righteousness and strength: even to him shall men come; and all that are incensed against him shall be ashamed." —Isaiah 45:22, 23, 24.

And to show further connections in proof of the doctrine above named, we quote the following scriptures:

"Him hath God exalted with his right hand, to be a Prince and a Savior, for to give repentance to Israel, and forgiveness of sins. And we are his witnesses of these things; and so is also the Holy Ghost, whom God hath given to them that obey him." —Acts 5:31, 32.

"But when they believed Philip, preaching the things concerning the kingdom of God, and the name of Jesus Christ, they were baptized, both men and women. Then Simon himself believed also; and when he was baptized, he continued with Philip, and wondered, beholding the miracles and signs which were done. Now when the apostles, which were at Jerusalem, heard that Samaria had received the word of God, they sent unto them Peter and John; who, when they were come down, prayed for them, that they might receive the Holy Ghost. (For as yet he was fallen upon none of them: only they were baptized in the name of the Lord Jesus.)—Then laid they their hands on them, and they received the Holy Ghost. ★ ★ ★ And as they went on their way, they came unto a certain water; and the eunuch said, See, here is water; what doth hinder me to be baptized?—And Philip said, If thou believest with all thine heart thou mayest. And he answered and said, I believe that Jesus Christ is the Son of God. And he commanded the chariot to stand still: and they went down both into the water, both Philip and the eunuch; and he baptized him. And, when they were come up out of the water, the Spirit of the Lord caught away Philip, that the eunuch saw him no more: and he went on his way rejoicing. But Philip was found at Azotus; and, passing through, he preached in all the cities, till he came to Cesarea." —Acts 8:12, 13, 14, 15, 16, 17,—36, to the end.

"While Peter yet spake these words, the Holy Ghost fell on all them which heard the word. And they of the circumcision, which believed, were astonished, as many as came with Peter, because that on the Gentiles also was poured out the gift of the Holy Ghost: for they heard them speak with tongues, and magnify God. Then answered Peter, Can any man forbid water, that these should not be baptized, which have received the

Holy Ghost as well as we? And he commanded them to be baptized in the name of the Lord. Then prayed they him to tarry certain days." —Acts 10:44, 45, 46, 47, 48.

"And on the Sabbath, we went out of the city, by a river side, where prayer was wont to be made; and we sat down, and spake unto the women that resorted thither. And a certain woman, named Lydia, a seller of purple, of the city of Thyatira, which worshiped God, heard us: whose heart the Lord opened, that she attended unto the things which were spoken of Paul. And when she was baptized, and her household, she besought us, saying, If ye have judged me to be faithful to the Lord, come into my house, and abide there. And she constrained us. ★ ★ ★ ★ And at midnight Paul and Silas prayed, and sang praises unto God: and the prisoners heard them. And suddenly there was a great earthquake, so that the foundations of the prison were shaken; and immediately all the doors were opened, and every one's bands were loosed. And the keeper of the prison awaking out of his sleep, and seeing the prison doors open, he drew out his sword, and would have killed himself, supposing that the prisoners had been fled. But Paul cried with a loud voice, saying, Do thyself no harm; for we are all here. Then he called for a light, and sprang in, and came trembling, and fell down before Paul and Silas; and brought them out, and said, Sirs, what must I do to be saved? And they said believe on the Lord Jesus Christ, and thou shalt be saved and thy house. And they spake unto him the word of the Lord, and to all that were in his house. And he took them the same hour of the night, and washed their stripes, and was baptized, he and all his, straightway. And when he had brought them into his house, he set meat before them, and rejoiced, believing in God with all his house." —Acts 16:13, 14, 15.—25, to 35.

"And it came to pass, that, while Apollos was at Corinth, Paul, having passed through the upper coasts, came to Ephesus; and finding certain disciples, he said unto them, Have ye received the Holy Ghost since ye believed? And they said unto him, We have not so much as heard whether there be any Holy Ghost. And he said unto them, Unto what then were ye baptized? And they said, Unto John's baptism. Then said Paul, John verily baptized with the baptism of repentance, saying unto the people, that they should believe on him which should come after him, that is, on Christ Jesus. When they heard this, they were baptized in the name of the Lord Jesus. And, when Paul had laid his hands upon them, the Holy Ghost came on them; and they spake with tongues, and prophesied." —Acts 19:1, 2, 3, 4, 5, 6.

"And one Ananias, a devout man, according to the law, having a good report of all the Jews which dwelt there, Came unto me, and stood, and said unto me, Brother Saul, receive thy sight. And the same hour I looked up upon him. And he said, the God of our fathers hath chosen thee, that thou shouldst know his will, and see that Just One, and shouldst hear the voice of his mouth. For thou shalt be his witness unto all men, of what thou hast seen and heard. And now why tarriest thou? arise, and be baptized, and wash away thy sins, calling on the name of the Lord." —Acts 22:12, 13, 14, 15, 16.

"For, when for the time ye ought to be teachers, ye have need that one teach you again which be the first principles of the oracles of God; and are become such as have need of milk, and not of strong meat. For every one that useth milk, is unskilful in the word of righteousness; for he is a babe. But strong meat belongeth to them that are of full age, even those who by reason of use, have their senses exercised to discern both good and evil." —Heb. 5:12, 13, 14.

"Therefore, leaving the principles of the doctrine of Christ, let us go on unto perfection; not laying again the foundation of repentance from dead works, and of faith towards God, of the doctrine of baptisms, and of laying on of hands, and of resurrection of the dead, and of eternal judgment. And this will we do, if God permit. For it is impossible for those who were once enlightened, and have tasted of the heavenly gift, and were made partakers of the Holy Ghost, and have tasted the good word of God, and the powers of the world to come, if they shall fall away, to renew them again unto repentance; seeing they crucify to themselves the Son of God afresh, and put him to an open shame." —Heb. 6:1, 2, 3, 4, 5, 6.

These quotations are so plain, in proving the doctrine of repentance and baptism for the remission of sins, I deem it unnecessary to enlarge this letter with comments upon them—but I shall continue the subject in my next.

In the bonds of the new and everlasting covenant,

&

At the close of my letter in the September No. of the "Messenger and Advocate," I promised to continue the subject there commenced: I do so with a hope that it may be a benefit and a means of assistance to the elders in their labors, while they are combating the prejudices of a crooked and perverse generation, by having in their possession, the facts of my religious principles, which are misrepresented by almost all those whose crafts are in danger by the same; and also to aid those who are anxiously inquiring, and have been excited to do so from rumor, to a[s]certaining correctly, what my principles are.

I have been drawn into this course of proceeding, by persecution, that is brought upon us from false rumor, and misrepresentations concerning my sentiments.

But to proceed, in the letter alluded to, the principles of repentance and baptism for the remission of sins, are not only set forth, but many passages of scripture, were quoted, clearly illucidating the subject; let me add, that I do positively rely upon the truth and veracity of those principles inculcated in the new testament; and then pass from the above named items, on to the item or subject of the gathering, and show my views upon this point: which is an item which I esteem to be of the greatest importance to those who are looking for salvation in this generation, or in these what may be called "the latter times," as all the prophets that have written, from the days of righteous Abel down to the last man, that has left any testimony on record, for our consideration, in speaking of the salvation of Israel in the last days, goes directly to show, that it consists in the work of the gathering.

Firstly, I shall begin by quoting from the prophecy of Enoch, speaking of the last days: "Righteousness will I send down out of heaven, and truth will I send forth out of the earth, to bear testimony of mine Only Begotten, his resurrection from the dead, [this resurrection I understand to be the corporeal body] yea, and also the resurrection of all men, righteousness and truth will I cause to sweep the earth as with a flood, to gather out mine own elect from the four quarters of the earth, unto a place which I shall prepare; a holy city, that my people may gird up their loins, and be looking forth for the time of my coming: for there shall be my tabernacle; and it shall be called Zion, a New Jerusalem."

Now I understand by this quotation, that God clearly manifested to Enoch, the redemption which he prepared, by offering the Messiah as a Lamb slain from before the foundation of the world: by virtue of the same, the glorious resurrection of the Savior, and the resurrection of all the human family,—even a resurrection of their corporeal bodies: and also righteousness and truth to sweep the earth as with a flood. Now I ask how righteousness and truth are agoing to sweep the earth as with a flood? I will answer. —Men and angels are to be co-workers in bringing to pass this great work: and a Zion is to be prepared; even a New Jerusalem, for the elect that are to be gathered from the four quarters of the earth, and to be established an holy city: for the tabernacle of the Lord shall be with them.

Now Enoch was in good company in his views upon this subject. See Revelations, 23:3. —"And I heard a great voice out of heaven saying, Behold the tabernacle of God is with men, and he will dwell with them, and they shall be his people, and God himself shall be with them, and be their God." I discover by this quotation, that John upon the isle of Patmos, saw the same things concerning the last days, which Enoch saw. But before the tabernacle can be with men, the elect must be gathered from the four quarters of the earth.

And to show further upon this subject of the gathering: Moses, after having pronounced the blessing and the cursing upon the children of Israel, for their obedience or disobedience, says thus: —"And it shall come to pass, when all these things are come upon thee, the blessing and the curse which I have set before thee; and thou shalt call them to mind, among all the nations whither the Lord thy God hath driven thee, and shalt return unto the Lord thy God, and shalt obey his voice, according to all that I command thee, this day, thou and thy children, with all thine heart, and with all thy soul, that then the Lord thy God, will turn thy captivity, and have compassion upon thee, and will return and gather thee from all the nations whither the Lord thy God hath scattered thee; and if any of thine be driven out unto the utmost parts of heaven; from thence will the Lord thy God gather thee; and from thence will he fetch thee."

It has been said by many of the learned, and wise men, or historians, that the Indians, or aborigines of this continent, are of the scattered tribes of Israel. It has been conjectured by many others, that the aborigines of this continent, are not of the tribes of Israel; but the ten tribes have been led away into some unknown regions of the north. Let this be as it may, the prophesy I have just quoted, "will fetch them" in the last days, and place them, in the land which their fathers possessed: and you will find in the 7th verse of the 30th chapt. quoted: —"And the Lord thy God will put all these curses upon thine enemies and on them that hate thee, which persecuted thee."

Many may say that this scripture is fulfilled, but let them mark carefully what the prophet says: "If any are driven out unto the utmost parts of heaven;" (which must mean the breadths of the earth.) Now this promise is good to any, if there should be such, that are driven out, even in the last days: therefore, the children of the fathers have claim unto this day: and if these curses are to be laid over on the heads of their enemies, wo be unto the Gentiles: See book of Mormon, page 487, Wo unto the unbelieving of the Gentiles, saith the Father. Again see book of Mormon. page 497, which says: "Behold this people will I establish in this land, unto the fulfilling of the covenant which I made with your father Jacob: and it shall be a New Jerusalem." Now we learn from the book of Mormon, the very identical continent and spot of land upon which the New Jerusalem is to stand, and it must be caught up according to the vision of John upon the isle of Patmos. Now many will be disposed to say, that this New Jerusalem spoken of, is the Jerusalem that was built by the Jews on the eastern continent: but you will see from Revelations, 21:2, there was a New Jerusalem coming down from God out of heaven, adorned as a bride for her husband. That after this the Revelator was caught away in the Spirit to a great and high mountain, and saw the great and holy city descending out of heaven from God. Now there are two cities spoken of here, and as everything cannot be had in so narrow a compass as a letter, I shall say with brevity, that there is a New Jerusalem to be established on this continent.—And also the Jerusalem shall be rebuilt on the eastern continent. See book of Mormon, page 566. Behold, Ether saw the days of Christ, and he spake also concerning the house of Israel, and the Jerusalem from whence Lehi should come: after it should be destroyed it should be built up again, a holy city unto the Lord: wherefore, it could not be a New Jerusalem, for it had been in a time of old. This may suffice upon the subject of gathering until my next.

I now proceed, at the close of my letter, to make a few remarks on the duty of elders with regard to their teaching parents and children, husbands and wives, masters and slaves, or servants, &c. as I said I would in my former letter. And firstly, it becomes an elder when he is travelling through the world, warning the inhabitants of the earth to gather together, that they may be built up an holy city unto the Lord, instead of commencing with children, or those who look up to parents or guardians, to influence their minds, thereby drawing them from their duties, which they rightfully owe to such, they should commence their labors with parents, or guardians, and their teachings should be such as are calculated to turn the hearts of the fathers to the children, and the hearts of the children to the fathers. And no influence should be used, with children contrary to the consent of their parents or guardians. —But all such as can be persuaded in a lawful and righteous manner, and with common consent, we should feel it our duty to influence them to gather with the people of God. But otherwise let the responsibility rest upon the heads of parents or guardians, and all condemnation or consequences, be upon their heads, according to the dispensation which he hath committed unto us: for God has so ordained, that his work shall be cut short in righteousness, in the last days: therefore, first teach the parents, and then, with their consent, let him persuade the children to embrace the gospel also. And if children embrace the gospel, and their parents or guardians are unbelievers, teach them to stay at home and be obedient to their parents or guardians, if they require it; but if they consent to let them gather with the people of God let them do so and there shall be no wrong and let all things be done carefully, and righteously, and God will extend his guardian care to all such.

And secondly, it should be the duty of elders, when they enter into any house, to let their labors and warning voice, be unto the master of that house: and if he receive the gospel, then he may extend his influence to his wife also, with consent, that peradventure she may receive the gospel; but if a man receive not the gospel, but gives his consent that his wife may receive it, and she believes, then let her receive it. But if the man forbid his wife, or his children before they are of age, to receive the gospel, then it should be the duty of the elder to go his way and use no influence against him: and let the responsibility be upon his head—shake off the dust of thy feet as a testimony against him, and thy skirts shall then be clear of their souls. Their sins are not to be answered upon such as God hath sent to warn them to flee the wrath to come, and save themselves from this untoward generation. The servants of God will not have gone over the nations of the Gentiles, with a warning voice, until the destroying angel will commence to waste the inhabitants of the earth; and as the prophet hath said, "It shall be a vexation to hear the report." I speak because I feel for my fellow-men: I do it in the name of the Lord, being moved upon by the Holy Spirit. O that I could snatch them from the vortex of misery, into which I behold them plunging themselves, by their sins, that I may be enabled, by the warning voice, to be an instrument of bringing them to unfeigned repentance, that they may have faith to stand in the evil day.

Thirdly, it should be the duty of an elder, when he enters into a house to salute the master of that house, and if he gain his consent, then he may preach to all that are in that house, but if he gain not his consent, let him go not unto his slaves or servants, but let the responsibility be upon the head of the master of that house, and the consequences thereof; and the guilt of that house is no longer upon thy skirts: Thou art free; therefore, shake off the dust of thy feet, and go thy way. But if the master of that house give consent, that thou mayest preach to his family, his wife, his children, and his servants, his man-servants, or his maid-servants, or his slaves, then it should be the duty of the elder to stand up boldly for the cause of Christ, and warn that people with one accord, to repent and be baptized for the remission of sins, and for the Holy Ghost, always commanding them in the name of the Lord, in the spirit of meekness to be kindly affected one towards another; that the fathers should be kind to their children, husbands to their wives; masters to their slaves or servants; children obedient to their parents, wives to their husbands, and slaves or servants to their masters:

"Wives submit yourselves unto your own husbands, as unto the Lord. For the husband is the head of the wife, even as Christ is the head of the church: and He is the Savior of the body. Therefore as the church is subject unto Christ, so let the wives be to their own husbands in every thing. Husbands, love your wives, even as Christ also loved the church and gave himself for it: that he might sanctify and cleanse it with the washing of water by the word, that he might present it to himself a glorious church, not having spot, or wrinkle, or any such thing: but that it should be holy and without blemish. So ought men to love their wives as their own bodies. He that loveth his wife loveth himself. For no man ever yet hated his own flesh; but nourisheth and cherisheth it, even as the Lord the church: for we are members of his body, of his flesh, and of his bones. —For this cause shall a man leave his father and mother, and shall be joined unto his wife, and they two shall be one flesh." —Ephesians, Chapt. V. from the 22d to the end of the 21st verse.

"Wives submit yourselves unto your own husbands, as it is fit in the Lord. Husbands, love your wives, and be not bitter against them. Children, obey your parents in all things: for this is well pleasing unto the Lord. Fathers, provoke not your children to anger, lest they be discouraged. Servants, obey in all things your masters according to the flesh: not with eye service as menpleasers; but in singleness of heart, fearing God." —Colo[s]ians, Chapt. III. from the 18th to the end of the 22d verse.

But I must close this letter and resume the subject in another number.

In the bonds of the new and everlasting covenant

I have shown unto you, in my last, that there are two Jerusalems spoken of in holy writ, in a manner I think satisfactorily to your minds. At any rate I have given my views upon the subject. I shall now proceed to make some remarks from the sayings of the Savior, recorded in the 13th chapter of his gospel according to St Matthew, which in my mind affords us as clear an understanding, upon the important subject of the gathering, as any thing recorded in the bible. At the time the Savior spoke these beautiful sayings and parables, contained in the chapter above quoted, we find him seated in a ship, on the account of the multitude that pressed upon him to hear his words, and he commenced teaching them by saying: "Behold a sower went forth to sow, and when he sowed, some seeds fell by the way side, and the fowls came and devoured them up; some fell upon stony places, where they had not much earth, and forthwith they sprang up because they had no deepness of earth, and when the sun was up, they were scorched, and because they had not root they withered away; and some fell among thorns and the thorns sprang up and choked them; but others, fell into good ground and brought forth fruit, some an hundred fold, some sixty fold, some thirty fold: who hath ears to hear let him hear. And the disciples came and said unto him, why speakest thou unto them in parables, (I would remark here, that the "*them*," made use of, in this interrogation, is a personal pronoun and refers to the multitude,) he answered and said unto them, (that is the disciples,) it is given unto *you* to know the mysteries of the kingdom of heaven, but to *them* (that is unbelievers) it is not given, for whosoever hath, to him shall be given, and he shall have more abundance; but whosoever hath not, shall be taken away, even that he hath."

We understand from this saying, that those who had previously been looking for a Messiah to come, according to the testimony of the Prophets, and were then, at that time, looking for a Messiah, but had not sufficient light on the account of their unbelief, to discern him to be their Savior; and he being the true Messiah, consequently they must be disappointed and lose even all the knowledge, or have taken away from them, all the light, understanding and faith, which they had upon this subject: therefore he that will not receive the greater light, must have taken away from him, all the light which he hath. And if the light which is in you, become darkness, behold how great is that darkness? Therefore says the Savior, speak I unto them in parables, because they, seeing, see not; and hearing, they hear not; neither do they understand: and in them is fulfilled the prophecy of Esaias, which saith: by hearing ye shall hear and shall not understand; and seeing ye shall see and not perceive.

Now we discover, that the very reasons assigned by this prophet, why they would not receive the Messiah, was, because they did or would not understand; and seeing they did not perceive: for this people's heart is waxed gross; their ears are dull of hearing; their eyes they have closed, lest at any time, they should see with their eyes, and hear with their ears, and understand with their hearts, and should be converted and I should heal them.

But what saith he to his disciples: Blessed are your eyes, for they see, and your ears, for they hear; for verily I say unto you, that many prophets and righteous men have desired to see those things which ye see, and have not seen them; and to hear those things which ye hear, and have not heard them.

We again make a remark here, for we find that the very principles upon which the disciples were accounted blessed, was because they were permitted to see with their eyes, and hear with their ears, and the condemnation which rested upon the multitude, which received not his saying, was because they were not willing to see with their eyes and hear with their ears; not because they could not and were not privileged to see, and hear, but because their hearts were full of iniquity and abomination: as your fathers did so do ye.— The prophet foreseeing that they would thus harden their hearts plainly declared it; and herein is the condemnation of the world, that light hath come into the world, and men choose darkness rather than light because their deeds are evil: This is so plainly taught by the Savior, that a wayfaring man need not mistake it.

And again hear ye the parable of the sower: Men are in the habit, when the truth is exhibited by the servants of God, of saying, all is mystery, they are spoken in parables, and, therefore, are not to be understood, it is true they have eyes to see, and see not; but none are so blind as those who will not see: And although the Savior spoke this

71

parable to such characters, yet unto his disciples he expounded it plainly; and we have reason to be truly humble before the God of our fathers, that he hath left these things on record for us, so plain that, notwithstanding the exertions and combined influence of the priests of Baal, they have not power to blind our eyes and darken our understanding, if we will but open our eyes and read with candor, for a moment. But listen to the explanation of the parable: when any one heareth the word of the kingdom, and understandeth it not, then cometh the wicked one and catcheth away that which was sown in his heart. Now mark the expression; that which was before sown in his heart; this is he which received seed by the way side; men who have no principle of righteousness in themselves, and whose hearts are full of iniquity, and have no desire for the principles of truth, do not understand the word of truth, when they hear it.—The devil taketh away the word of truth out of their hearts, because there is no desire for righteousness in them. But he that received the seed into stony places the same is he that heareth the word and, anon, with joy receiveth it, yet hath he not root in himself, but dureth for awhile; for when tribulation or persecution ariseth because of the word, by and by he is offended. He also that received seed among the thorns is he that receiveth the word, and the cares of this world, and the deceitfulness of riches choke the word, and he becometh unfruitful: but he that received seed into the good ground, is he that heareth the word and understandeth it which also beareth fruit and bringeth forth some an hundred fold, some sixty, some thirty. Thus the Savior himself explains unto his disciples the parable, which he put forth and left no mystery or darkness upon the minds of those who firmly believe on his words.

We draw the conclusion then, that the very reason why the multitude, or the world, as they were designated by the Savior, did not receive an explanation upon his parables, was, because of unbelief. To you, he says, (speaking to his disciples) it is given to know the mysteries of the kingdom of God: and why? because of the faith and confidence which they had in him. This parable was spoken to demonstrate the effects that are produced by the preaching of the word; and we believe that it has an allusion directly, to the commencement, or the setting up of the kingdom in that age: therefore, we shall continue to trace his sayings concerning this kingdom from that time forth, even unto the end of the world.

Another parable put he forth unto them, saying, (which parable has an allusion to the setting up of the kingdom, in that age of the world also) the kingdom of Heaven is likened unto a man which sowed good seed in his field, but while men slept an enemy came and sowed tares among the wheat and went his way; but when the blade was sprung up, and brought forth fruit, then appeared the tares also; so the servants of the householder came and said unto him, sir, didst not thou sow good seed in thy field? from whence then hath it tares? He said unto them, an enemy hath done this. The servants said unto him wilt thou then that we go and gather them up; but he said nay, lest while ye gather up the tares, ye root up also the wheat with them. —Let both grow together until the harvest, and in the time of harvest, I will say to the reapers, gather ye together first the tares, and bind them in bundles, to burn them; but gather the wheat into my barn.

Now we learn by this parable, not only the setting up of the kingdom in the days of the Savior, which is represented by the good seed, which produced fruit, but also the corruptions of the church, which are represented by the tares, which were sown by the enemy, which his disciples would fain have plucked up, or cleansed the church of, if their views had been favored by the Savior; but he, knowing all things, says not so; as much as to say, your views are not correct, the church is in its infancy, and if you take this rash step, you will destroy the wheat or the church with the tares: therefore it is better to let them grow together until the harvest, or the end of the world, which means the destruction of the wicked; which is not yet fulfilled; as we shall show hereafter, in the Savior's explanation of the parable, which is so plain, that there is no room left for dubiety upon the mind, notwithstanding the cry of the priests, parables, parables! figures, figures! mystery, mystery! all is mystery! but we find no room for doubt here, as the parables were all plainly elucidated.

And again, another parable put he forth unto them, having an allusion to the kingdom which should be set up, just previous or at the time of harvest, which reads as follows: —The kingdom of heaven is like to a grain of mustard seed, which a man took and sowed in his field, which indeed is the least of all seeds, but when it is grown it is the greatest among herbs, and becometh a tree, so that the birds of the air come and lodge in the branches thereof. Now we can discover plainly, that this figure is given to represent the church as it shall come forth in the last days. Behold the kingdom of heaven is likened unto it. Now what is like unto it?

Let us take the book of Mormon, which a man took and hid in his field; securing it by his faith, to spring up in the last days, or in due time: let us behold it coming forth out of the ground, which is indeed accounted the least of all seeds, but behold it branching forth; yea, even towering, with lofty branches, and God-like majesty, until it becomes the greatest of all herbs: and it is truth, and it has sprouted and come forth out of the earth; and righteousness begins to look down from heaven; and God is sending down his powers, gifts and angels, to lodge in the branches thereof: The kingdom of heaven is like unto a mustard seed. Behold, then, is not this the kingdom of heaven that is raising its head in the last days, in the majesty of its God; even the church of the Latter day saints, —like an impenetrable, immovable rock in the midst of the mighty deep, exposed to storms and tempests of satan, but has, thus far, remained steadfast and is still braving the mountain waves of opposition, which are driven by the tempestuous winds of sinking crafts, have and are still dashing with tremendous foam, across its triumphing brow, urged onward with redoubled fury by the enemy of righteousness, with his pitchfork of lies, as you will see fairly represented in a cut, contained in Mr. [Eber] Howe's "Mormonism Unveiled?"

And we hope that this adversary of truth will continue to stir up the sink of iniquity, that people may the more readily discern between the righteous and wicked. We also would notice one of the modern sons of Sceva, who would fain have made people believe that he could cast out devils, by a certain pamphlet (viz. the "Millen[n]ial Harbinger,") that went the rounds through our country, who felt so fully authorized to brand Jo Smith, with the appellation of Elymus the sorcerer, and to say with Paul, O full of all subtl[e]ty and all mischief, thou child of the devil, thou enemy of all righteousness, wilt thou not cease to pervert the right ways of the Lord! We would reply to this gentleman—Paul we know, and Christ we know, but who are ye? And with the best of feelings, we would say to him, in the language of Paul to those who said they were John's disciples, but had not so much as heard there was a Holy Ghost, to repent and be baptised for the remission of sins by those who have legal authority, and under their hands you shall receive the Holy Ghost, according to the scriptures.

Then laid they *their* hands on them, and they received the Holy Ghost. —Acts: ch. 8, v. 17.

And, when Paul had laid *his* hands upon them, the Holy Ghost came on them: and they spake with tongues, and prophesied. —Acts: ch. 19, v. 6.

Of the doctrine of baptisms, and of laying on of hands, and of resurrection of the dead, and of eternal judgment. —Heb. ch. 6, v. 2.

How then shall they call on him in whom they have not believed? and how shall they believe in him of whom they have not heard? and how shall they hear without a preacher? And how shall they preach except they be sent? as it is written, How beautiful are the feet of them that preach the gospel of peace, and bring glad tidings of good things! —Rom. ch. 10, v. 14-15.

But if this man will not take our admonition, but will persist in his wicked course, we hope that he will continue trying to cast out devils, that we may have the clearer proof that the kingdom of satan is divided against itself, and consequently cannot stand: for a kingdom divided against itself, speedily hath an end. If we were disposed to take this gentleman upon his own ground and justly heap upon him that which he so readily and unjustly heaps upon others, we might go farther; we might say that he has wickedly and maliciously lied about, vilified and traduced the characters of innocent men. We might invite the gentleman to a public investigation of these matters; yea, and we do challenge him to an investigation upon any or all principles wherein he feels opposed to us, in public or in private.

We might farther say that, we could introduce him to "Mormonism Unveiled." Also to the right honorable Doct. P[hilastus]. Hurlburt, who is the legitimate author of the same, who is not so much a doctor of physic, as of falsehood, or by name[.] We could also give him an introduction to the reverend Mr. Howe, the illegitimate author of "Mormonism Unveiled," in order to give currency to the publication, as Mr. Hurlburt, about this time, was bound over to court, for threatening life. He is also an associate of the celebrated Mr. Clapp, who has of late immortalised his name by swearing that he would not believe a Mormon under oath; and by his polite introduction to said Hurlburt's wife, which cost him (as we have been informed) a round sum. Also his son Mathew testified that, the book of Mormon had been proved false an hundred times, by How[e]'s book: and also, that he would not believe a Mormon under oath. And also we could mention the reverend Mr. Bentley, who, we believe, has been actively engaged in injuring the character of his brother-in-law, viz: Elder S[idney]. Rigdon.

Now, the above statements are according to our best information: and we believe them to be true; and this is as fair a sample of the doctrine of Campbellism, as we ask, taking the statements of these gentlemen, and judging them by their fruits. And we might add many more to the black catalogue; even the ringleaders, not of the Nazarenes, for how can any good thing come out of Nazareth, but of the far-famed Mentor mob: all sons and legitimate heirs to the same spirit of Alexander Campbell, and "Mormonism Unveiled," according to the representation in the cut spoken of above.

The above cloud of darkness has long been beating with mountain waves upon the immovable rock of the church of the Latter Day Saints, and notwithstanding all this, the mustard seed is still towering its lofty branches, higher and higher, and extending itself wider and wider, and the charriot wheels of the kingdom are still rolling on, impelled by the mighty arm of Jehovah; and in spite of all opposition will still roll on until his words are all fulfilled.

Our readers will excuse us for deviating from the subject, when they take into consideration the abuses, that have been heaped upon us heretofore, which we have tamely submitted to, until forbearance is no longer required at our hands, having frequently turned both the right and left cheek, we believe it our duty now to stand up in our own defence. With these remarks we shall proceed with the subject of the gathering.

And another parable spake he unto them: The kingdom of heaven is like unto leaven which a woman took and hid in three measures of meal, until the whole was leavened. It may be understood that the church of the Latter Day Saints, has taken its rise from a little leaven that was put into three witnesses. Behold, how much this is like the parable: it is fast leavening the lump, and will soon leaven the whole. But let us pass on.

All these things spake Jesus unto the multitudes, in parables, and without a parable spake he not unto them, that it might be fulfilled which was spoken by the prophet, saying: I will open my mouth in parables: I will utter things which have been kept secret from the foundation of the world: Then Jesus sent the multitude away and went into the house, and his disciples came unto him, saying, declare unto us the parable of the tares of the field. He answered and said unto them, he that soweth the good seed is the son of man; the field is the world; the good seed are the children of the kingdom, but the tares are the children of the wicked one. Now let our readers mark the expression, the field is the world; the tares are the children of the wicked one: the enemy that sowed them is the devil; the harvest is the end of the world. Let them carefully mark this expression also, *the end of the world*, and the reapers are the angels. Now men cannot have any possible grounds to say that this is figurative, or that it does not mean what it says; for he is now explaining what he had previously spoken in parables: and according to this language, the end of the world is the destruction of the wicked; the harvest and the end of the world have an allusion directly to the human family in the last days, instead of the earth, as many have imagined, and that which shall precede the coming of the Son of man, and the restitution of all things spoken of by the mouth of all the holy prophets since the world began; and the angels are to have something to do in this great work, for they are the reapers: as therefore the tares are gathered and burned in the fire, so shall it be in the end of this world; that is, as the servants of God go forth warning the nations, both priests and people, and as they harden their hearts and reject the light of the truth, these first being delivered over unto the buffetings of satan, and the law and the testimony being closed up, as it was with the Jews, they are left in darkness, and delivered over unto the day of burning: thus being bound up by their creeds and their bands made strong by their *priests*, are prepared for the fulfilment of the saying of the Savior: the Son of man shall send forth his angels, and gather out of his kingdom all things that offend, and them which do iniquity, and shall cast them into a furnace of fire and there shall be wailing and gnashing of teeth.

We understand, that the work of the gathering together of the wheat into barns, or garners, is to take place while the tares are being bound over, and preparing for the day of burning: that after the day of burnings, the righteous shall shine forth like the sun, in the kingdom of their Father: who hath ears to hear let him hear.

But to illustrate more clearly upon this gathering, we have another parable. Again the kingdom of heaven is like a treasure hid in a field, the which when a man hath found, he hideth and for joy thereof, goeth and selleth all that he hath and buyeth that field: for the

77

work after this pattern, see the church of the Latter Day Saints, selling all that they have and gathering themselves together unto a place tha[t] they may purchase for an inheritance, that they may be together and bear each other's afflictions in the day of calamity.

Again the kingdom of heaven is like unto a merchant man seeking goodly pearls, who when he had found one pearl of great price, went and sold all that he had, and bought it. For the work of this example, see men travelling to find places for Zion, and her stakes or remnants, who when they find the place for Zion, or the pearl of great price; straitway [sic] sell that they have and buy it.

Again the kingdom of heaven is like unto a net that was cast into the sea, and gathered of every kind, which when it was full they drew to shore, and sat down and gathered the good into vessels, but cast the bad away.—For the work of this pattern, behold the seed of Joseph, spreading forth the gospel net, upon the face of the earth, gathering of every kind, that the good may be saved in vessels prepared for that purpose, and the angels will take care of the bad: so shall it be at the end of the world, the angels shall come forth, and sever the wicked from among the just, and cast them into the furnace of fire, and there shall be wailing and gnashing of teeth.

Jesus saith unto them, have you understood all these things? they say unto him yea Lord: and we say yea Lord, and well might they say yea Lord, for these things are so plain and so glorious, that every Saint in the last days must respond with a hearty *amen* to them.

Then said he unto them, therefore every scribe which is in- structed into the kingdom of heaven, is like unto a man that is an house holder; which bringeth forth out of his treasure things that are new and old.

For the work of this example, see the book of Mormon, coming forth out of the treasure of the heart; also the covenants given to the Latter Day Saints: also the translation of the bible: thus bringing forth out of the heart, things new and old: thus answering to three measures of meal, undergoing the purifying touch by a revelation of Jesus Christ, and the ministering of angels, who have already commenced this work in the last days, which will answer to the leaven which leavened the whole lump. Amen.

So I close but shall continue the subject in another number.

In the bonds of the new and everlasting covenant.

{19}

"Br[other] William [Smith],
Having Received Your Letter
I Now Proce[e]de to Answer It,"
Joseph Smith to William Smith, 18 December 1835, and
Excerpts from Joseph Smith's Diary,
18-22 December 1835

(from Scott H. Faulring, ed., *An American Prophet's Record:
The Diaries and Journals of Joseph Smith*
[Salt Lake City: Signature Books in association
with Smith Research Associates, 1987], pp. 85-91)

Kirtland, Friday, Dec[ember] 18th 1835
Br[other] William [Smith],

Having received your letter I now proce[e]de to answer it. [I] shall first proce[e]de to give a brief nar[r]ation of my feelings and motives since the night I first came to the knowledge of your having a debating School, which was at the time I happened in with Bishop Whitney, his Father, and Mother &c. which was the first that I knew any thing about it. From that time I took an interest in them and was delighted with it and formed a determination to attend the School for the purpose of obtaining information with the idea of imparting the same through the assistance of the spirit of the Lord, if by any means I should have faith to do so. With this intent I went to the school on last Wednesday night. Not with the idea of braking up the school, neither did it enter into my heart that there was any wrangling or jealousy's in your heart against me.

Notwithstanding previous to my leaving home there were feelings of solemnity rolling across my breast which were unaccountable to me. Also these feelings continued by spells to depress my spirit and seemed to manifest that all was not right even after the school commenced and during the debate, yet I strove to believe that all would work together for good.

I was pleased with the power of the arguments that were ad[d]uced and did not feel to cast any reflections upon any one that

79

had spoken. But I felt that it was the duty of old men that set as presidents to be as grave at least as young men. That it was our duty to smile at solid arguments and sound reasoning and be impressed with solemnity which should be manifest in our countanance when folly and that which militates against truth and righteousness rears its head.

Therefore in the spirit of my calling and in view of the authority of the priesthood that has been confer[r]ed upon me, it would be my duty to reprove whatever I esteemed to be wrong. Fondly hoping in my heart that all parties would concider it right and therefore humble themselves that Satan might not take the advantage of us and hinder the progress of our School.

Now Br[other] William, I want you should bear with me not-withstanding my plainness. I would say to you that my feelings were grieved at the inter[r]uption you made upon Elder McLellen. I thought you should have concidered your relation with him in your apostle ship and not manifest any division of sentiment between you and him for a surrounding multitude to take the advantage of you. Therefore by way of entreaty on the account of the anxiety I had for your influence and wellfare, I said unto you, do not have any feeling, or something to that amount. Why I am thus particular is that if you have misconstrued my feelings toward you, you may be corrected.

But to proce[e]de. After the school was closed, Br[other] Hyrum requested the privilege of speaking, you objected. However, you said if he would not abuse the school he might speak, that you would not allow any man to abuse the school in your house. Now you had no reason to suspect that Hyrum would abuse the school. Therefore my feelings were mortifyed at those unnecessary observations. I undertook to reason with you, but you manifested an inconciderate and stub[b]ourn spirit. I then dispared [despaired] of benefiting you on the account of the spirit you manifested which drew from me the expression that you was as ugly as the Devil.

Father then commanded silence. I formed a determination to obey his mandate and was about to leave the house with the impression that you was under the influence of a wicked spirit [when] you replyed that you would say what you pleased in your own house. Father replyed, "Say what you please, but let the rest hold their toungs [tongues]."

Then a reflection rushed through my mind of the anxiety and care I had had for you and your family in doing what I did in finishing your house and providin[g] flour for your family &c. Also father had possession in the house as well as your self. When at any time have I transgressed the commandments of my father? Or sold my birthright that I should not have the privilege of speaking in my father's house, or in other words, in my father's family, or in your house (for so we will call it and so it shall be) that I should not have the privilege of reproving a younger brother.

Therefore I said "I will speak, for I built the house, and it is as much mine as yours," or something to that effect (I should have said that I helped finish the house). I said it merely to show that it could not be the right spirit that would rise up for trifling matters, and undertake to put me to silence. I saw that your indignation was kindled against me, and you made [movement] towards me. I was not then to be moved and I thought to pull off my loose coat least it should tangle me, and you be left to hurt me, but not with the intention of hurting You. But you was to[o] soon for me, and having once fallen into the hands of a mob, and been wounded in my side and now into the hands of a brother my side gave way.

After having been rescued from your grasp, I left your house with feelings that were indescriba[b]le. The scenery had changed and all those expectations that I had cherished when going to your house of brotherly kindness, charity, forbearance and natural affection, that in duty binds us not to make each others offenders for a word.

But alass! Abuse, anger, malice, hatred, and rage with a lame side with marks of violence heaped upon me by a brother, were the reflections of my disap[p]ointment, and with these I returned home not able to sit down, or rise up, without help, but through the blessings of God I am now better.

I have received your letter and purused it with care. I have not entertained a feeling of malice against you. I am older than you and have endured more suffering. [I] have been mar[r]ed by mobs, the labours of my calling, a series of persecution, and injuries, continually heaped upon me, all serve to debilitate my body, and it may be that I cannot boast of being stronger than you. If I could, or could not, would this be an honor or dishonor to me. If I could boast like David of slaying Goliath, who defied the armies of the living God, or like Paul of contending with Peter face to face, with sound arguments, it might be an honor. But to mangle the flesh or seek revenge upon one who never done you any wrong, can not be a source of sweet reflection to you, nor to me, neither to an honorable father and mother, brothers and sisters. When we reflect with what care and with what unremit[t]ing diligence our parents have strove to watch over us, and how many hours of sorrow and anxiety they have spent over our cradles and bedsides in times of sickness, how careful we ought to be of their feelings in their old age. It cannot be a source of swe[e]t reflection to us to say or do any thing that will bring their grey hairs down with sorrow to the grave.

In your letter you asked my forgiv[e]ness, which I readily grant, but it seems to me that you still retain an idea that I have given you reasons to be angry or disaffected with me. Grant me the privilege of saying then that however hasty or harsh I may have spoken at any time to you, it has been done for the express purpose of endeavouring to warn, exhort, admonish, and rescue you from falling into difficulties, and sorrows which I foresaw you plunging into by giving way to that wicked spirit, which you call your passions, which you should curbe and break down and put under your feet. Which if you do not you never can be saved, in my view, in the Kingdom of God. God requires the will of his creatures to be swallowed up in his will.

You desire to remain in the Church, but forsake your apostleship. This is a stratigem of the evil one. When he has gained one advantage he lays a plan for another, but by maintaining your apostleship in rising up and making one tremendious effort, you may overcome your passions and please God. By forsaking your apostleship is not to be willing to make that sacrifice that God requires at your hands and is to incur his displeasure. And without pleasing God do not think that it will be any better for you. When a man falls one step he must regain that step again, or fall another. He has still more to gain or eventually all is lost.

I desire Brother William that you will humble yourself. I freely forgive you and you know my unshaken and unchang[e]able disposition. I know in whom I trust. I stand upon the rock. The floods cannot, no they shall not overthrow me. You know the doctrine I teach is true and you know that God has blessed me. I brought salvation to my father's house, as an instrument in the hand of God, when they were in a miserable situation. You know that it is my duty to admonish you when you do wrong. This liberty I shall always take and you shall have the same privilege. I take the privilege to admonish you because of my birthright. I grant you the privilege because it is my duty to be humble and to receive rebuke and instruction from a brother or a friend.

As it regards what course you shall persue hereafter, I do not pretend to say. I leave you in the hands of God and his Church. Make your own desision, I will do you good altho[ugh] you mar me, or slay me, by so doing my garments shall be clear of your sins. If at any time you should concider me to be an imposter, for heaven's sake leave me in the hands of God and not think to take veng[e]ance on me your self.

Tyran[n]y, usurpation, and to take men's rights ever has and ever shall be banished from my heart. David sought not to kill Saul, although he was guilty of crimes that never entered my heart.

And now may God have mercy upon my father's house. May God take away enmity from betwe[e]n me and thee. And may all blessings be restored and the past be forgotten forever. May humble repentance bring us both to thee O God and to thy power and protection and a crown to enjoy the society of Father, Mother, Alvin, Hyrum, Sophron[i]a, Samuel, Catharine, Carloss, Lucy, the Saints and all the sanctified in peace forever, is the prayer of

Your brother,
Joseph Smith, Jun[ior]
To William Smith

&

Saturday morning the 19th [December 1835] At home. Wrote the above letter to Br[other] William Smith. I have had many solemn feelings this day Concerning my Brothe[r] William and have prayed in my heart to[o] fervently that the Lord will not cast him off, but he may return to the God of Jacob and magnify his apostleship and calling. May this be his happy lot for the Lord of Glory's Sake. Amen.

Sunday the 20th At home all day. Took solled [solid] Comfort with my Family [and] had many serious reflections. Also Brothers Palmer and Tailor Came to see me. I showed them the sacred record [the Egyptian\Book of Abraham papyri] to their Joy and sati[s]faction. O may God have mercy upon these men and keep them in the way of Everlasting life in the name of Jesus. Amen.

Monday morni[n]g, 21st At home. Spent this [day] in indeavering to treasure up know[l]edge for the be[n]ifit of my Calling. The day pas[s]ed of[f] very pleasantly for which I thank the Lord for his blessings to my soul [and] his great mercy over my Family in sparing our lives. O Continue thy Care over me and mine for Christ['s] sake.

Tu[e]sday, 22d At home. Continued my studys. O may God give

83

me learning even Language and indo[w] me with qualifycations to magnify his name while I live. I also deliv[er]ed an address to the Church this Evening. The Lord blessed my Soul.

My scribe also is unwell. O m[a]y God heal him and for his kindness to me[.] O my soul be thou greatful to him and bless him and he shall be blessed of God forever. I believe him to be a faithful friend to me therefore my soul delighteth in him. Amen.

20

"*Dear Sir*—This Place Having Recently Been Visited by a Gentleman Who Advocated the Principles or Doctrines of Those Who Are Called Abolitionists," Joseph Smith to Oliver Cowdery, 9 April 1836

(from *Latter Day Saints' Messenger and Advocate*
[Kirtland, Ohio] 2 [April 1836], 7:289-91)

Dear Sir—This place having recently been visited by a gentleman who advocated the principles or doctrines of those who are called abolitionists; if you deem the following reflections of any service, or think they will have a tendency to correct the opinions of the southern public, relative to the views and sentiments I believe, as an individual, and am able to say, from personal knowledge, are the feelings of others, you are at liberty to give them publicity in the columns of the [Messenger and] Advocate. I am prompted to this course in consequence, in one respect, of many elders having gone into the Southern States, besides, there now being many in that country who have already embraced the fulness of the gospel, as revealed through the book of Mormon,— having learned, by experience, that the enemy of truth does not slumber, nor cease his exertions to bias the minds of communities against the servants of the Lord, by stiring up the indignation of men upon all matters of importance or interest.

Thinking, perhaps, that the sound might go out, that "an abolitionist" had held forth several times to this community, and that the public feeling was not aroused to create mobs or disturbances, leaving the impression that all he said was concurred in, and received as gospel and the word of salvation. I am happy to say, that no violence or breach of the public peace was attempted, so far from this, that all except a very few, attended to their own avocations and left the gentleman to hold forth his own arguments to nearly naked walls.

I am aware, that many who profess to preach the gospel, complain against their brethren of the same faith, who reside in the south, and are ready to withdraw the hand of fellowship because they will not renounce the principle of slavery and raise their voice against every thing of the kind. This must be a tender point, and one which should call forth the candid reflection of all men, and especially before they advance in an opposition calculated to lay waste the fair States of the South, and set loose, upon the world a community of people who might peradventure, overrun our country and violate the most sacred principles of human society,— chastity and virtue.

No one will pretend to say, that the people of the free states are as capable of knowing the evils of slavery as those who hold them. If slavery is an evil, who, could we expect, would first learn it? Would the people of the free states, or would the slave states? All must readily admit, that the latter would first learn this fact. If the fact was learned first by those immediately concerned, who would be more capable than they of prescribing a remedy?

And besides, are not those who hold slaves, persons of ability, discernment and candor? Do they not expect to give an account at the bar of God for their conduct in this life? It may, no doubt, with propriety be said, that many who hold slaves live without the fear of God before their eyes, and, the same may be said of many in the free states. Then who is to be the judge in this matter?

So long, then, as those of the free states are not interested in the freedom of the slaves, any other than upon the mere principles of equal rights and of the gospel, and are ready to admit that there are men of piety who reside in the South, who are immediately concerned, and until *they* complain, and call for assistance, why not cease their clamor, and no further urge the slave to acts of murder, and the master to vigorous discipline, rendering both miserable, and unprepared to pursue that course which might otherwise lead them both to better their condition? I do not believe that the people of the North have any more right to say that the South *shall not* hold slaves, than the South have to say the North *shall*.

And further, what benefit will it ever be to the slave for persons to run over the free states, and excite indignation against their masters in the minds of thousands and tens of thousands who understand nothing relative to their circumstances or conditions? I mean particularly those who have never travelled in the South, and scarcely seen a negro in all their life. How any community can ever be excited with the chatter of such persons— boys and others who are too indolent to obtain their living by honest industry, and are incapable of pursuing any occupation of a professional nature, is unaccountable to me. And when I see persons in the free states signing documents against slavery, it is no less, in my mind, than an array of influence, and a declaration of hostilities against the people of the South! What can divide our Union sooner, God only knows!

After having expressed myself so freely upon this subject, I do not doubt but those who have been forward in raising their voice against the South, will cry out against me as being uncharitable, unfeeling and unkind—wholly unacquainted with the gospel of Christ. It is my privilege then, to name certain passages from the bible, and examine the teachings of the ancients upon this matter, as the fact is uncontrovertable that the first mention we have of slavery is found in the holy bible, pronounced by a man who was perfect in his generation and walked with God. And so far from that prediction's being averse from the mind of God it remains as a lasting monument of the decree of Jehovah, to the shame and confusion of all who have cried out against the South, in consequence of their holding the sons of Ham in servitude!

"And he said cursed *be* Canaan; a servant of servants shall he be unto his brethren. And he said, Blessed *be* the Lord God of Shem; and Canaan shall be his servant. —God shall enlarge Japheth, and he shall dwell in the tents of Shem; and Canaan shall be his servant." —Gen, 8:25, 26, 27.

Trace the history of the world from this notable event down to this day, and you will find the fulfilment of this singular prophecy. What could have been the design of the Almighty in this wonderful occurrence is not for me to say; but I can say that the curse is not yet taken off the sons of Canaan, neither will be until it is affected by as great power as caused it to come; and the people who interfere the least with the decrees and purposes of God in this matter, will come under the least condemnation before him; and those who are determined to pursue a course which shows an opposition and a feverish restlessness against the designs of the Lord, will learn, when perhaps it is too late for their own good, that God can do his own work without the aid of those who are not dictated by his counsel.

I must not pass over a notice of the history of Abraham, of whom so much is spoken in the scriptures. If we can credit the account, God conversed with him from time to time, and directed him in the way he should walk, saying, "I am the Almighty God; walk before me and be thou perfect." Paul says that the gospel was preached to this man. And it is further said, that he had sheep and oxen, men-servants and

87

maid-servants, &c. From this I conclude, that if the principle had been an evil one, in the midst of the communications made to this holy man, he would have been instructed differently. And if he was instructed against holding men-servants and maid-servants, he never ceased to do it; consequently must have incurred the displeasure of the Lord and thereby lost his blessings—which was not the fact.

Some may urge, that the names, man-servant and maid servant, only mean hired persons, who were at liberty to leave their masters or employers at any time. But we can easily settle this point by turning to the history of Abraham's descendants, when governed by a law given from the mouth of the Lord himself. I know that when an Israelite had been brought into servitude in consequence of debt, or otherwise, at the seventh year he went from the task of his former master or employer; but to no other people or nation was this granted in the law to Israel. And if, after a man had served six years, he did not wish to be free, then the master was to bring him unto the judges, boar [sic] his ear with an awl, and that man was "to serve him forever." The conclusion I draw from this, is that this people were led and governed by revelation, and if such a law was wrong God only is to be blamed, and abolitionists are not responsible.

Now, before proceeding any farther, I wish to ask one or two questions:— Were the apostles men of God, and did they preach the gospel? I have no doubt but those who believe the bible will admit these facts, and that they also knew the mind and will of God concerning what they wrote to the churches which they were instrumental in building up.

This being admitted, the matter can be put to rest without much argument, if we look at a few items in the New Testament. Paul says:

> "Servants, be obedient to them that are *your* masters according to the flesh, with fear and trembling, in singleness of your heart, as unto Christ; Not with eye service, as men-pleasers: but as the servants of Christ, doing the will of God from the heart: With good will doing service, as to the Lord, and not to men. Knowing that whatsoever good thing any man doeth, the same shall be received of the Lord, whether *he be* bond or free. And, ye masters, do the same things unto them, *for*bearing threatening: knowing that your Master also is in heaven: neither is there respect of persons with him." Eph. 6:5, 6, 7, 8, 9.

Here is a lesson which might be profitable for all to learn, and the principle upon which the church was anciently governed, is so plainly set forth, that an eye of truth might see and understand. Here, certainly are represented the master and servant; and so far from instructions to the servant to leave his master, he is commanded to be in obedience, as unto the Lord: the master in turn is required to treat them with kindness before God, understanding, at the same time that he is to give an account.— The hand of fellowship is not withdrawn from him in consequence of having servants.

The same writer, in his first epistle to Timothy, the sixth chapter, and the five first verses, says:

> "Let as many servants as are under the yoke count their own masters worthy of all honor, that the name of God and *his* doctrine be not blasphemed. And they that have believing masters, let them not despise *them*, because they are brethren; but rather do *them* service, because they are faithful and beloved, partakers of the benefit. These things teach and exhort. If any man teach otherwise, and consent not to wholesome words, *even* the words of our Lord Jesus Christ, and to the doctrine which is according to godliness: he is proud, knowing nothing but doting about questions and strifes of words, whereof cometh envy, strife, railings, evil surmisings, Perverse disputings of men of corrupt minds, and destitute of the truth, supposing that gain is godliness: from such withdraw thyself."

This is so perfectly plain, that I see no need of comment. The scripture stands for itself, and I believe that these men were better qualified to teach the will of God, than all the abolitionists in the world.

Before closing this communication, I beg leave to drop a word to the travelling elders: You know, brethren, that great responsibility rests upon you, and that you are accountable to God for all you teach the world. In my opinion, you will do well to search the book of Covenants, in which you will see the belief of the church concerning masters and servants. All men are to be taught to repent; but we have no right to interfere with slaves contrary to the mind and will of their masters. In fact, it would be much better and more prudent, not to preach at all to slaves, until after their masters are converted: and then, teach the master to use them with kindness, remembering that they are accountable to God, and that servants are bound to serve their masters, with singleness of heart, without murmuring. I do, most sincerely hope, that no one who is authorized from this church to preach the gospel, will so far depart from the scripture as to be found stirring up strife and sedition against our brethren of the South.

Having spoken frankly and freely, I leave all in the hands of God, who will direct all things for his glory and the accomplishment of his work.

Praying that God may spare you to do much good in this life, I subscribe myself your brother in the Lord.

21

"My Dear and Beloved Companion, of My Bosam"
Joseph Smith to Emma Smith, 12 November 1838

(from Library-Archives, Reorganized Church of Jesus Christ of
Latter Day Saints, Independence, Missouri)

My dear and beloved companion, of my bosam, in tribulation, and
affliction, I woud inform you that I am well, and that we are all of us
in good spirits[.] [A]s regards our own fate, we have been protected by
the Jackson County [Missouri] boys [state militia], in the most genteel
manner, and arrived here [Independence, Missouri] in the midst of a
splended perade, a little after noon, [and] instead of going to goal [jail]
we have a good house provided for us and the kindst treatment[.] I
have great anxiety about you, and my lovely children, my heart morns
and bleeds for the brotheren, and sisters, and for the slain of the people
of God[.] Colonal [George M.] Hinkle, proved to be a trator, to the
Church, he is worse than a hull [William Hull] who betraid the army
at detroit, he decoyed us unawares[.] God reward him[.] Jhon Carl
[John Corrill] told general wilson [Moses G. Wilson], that he was a
going to leave the Church, general Willson says he thinks much less
of him now then before[.] [W]hy I mention this is to have you [be]
careful not to trust them, if we are permited to stay any time here[.]
[W]e have obtained a promice that we may have our families brought
to us[.] [W]hat God may do for us I do not know but I hope for the
best always in all circumstances[.] [A]lthough I go unto death, I will
trust in God[.] [W]hat outrages may be committed by the mob I know
not, but expect there will be but little or no restraint[.] Oh may God
have mercy on us[.] [W]hen we arrived at the river last night an express
came to gene[r]al Willson from gene[r]al [John B.] Clark of Howard
County claiming the right of command ordering us back where or
what place God only knows, and there is some feelings betwen the
offercers[.] I do not know where it will end[.] [I]t is said by some that
general Clark, is determined to exterminate[.] God has spared some of
us thus far perhaps he will extend mercy in some degree toward us
yet[.] [S]ome of the people of this place have told me that some of the
mormans may settle in this county as others men do[.] I have some

hopes that some thing may turn out for good to the afilicted saints[.] I want you to stay where you are untill you here from me again[.] I may send for you to bring you to me[.] I cannot learn much for certainty in the situation that I am in, and can only pray for deliverance, untill it is meeted out, and take every thing as it comes, with patience and fortitude[.] I hope you will be faithful and true to every trust[.] I cant write much in my situa[t]ion[.] [C]onduct all matters as your circum-stances and necesities require[.] [M]ay God give you wisdom and prudance and sobriety which I have every reason to believe you will[.] [T]hose little childrens are subjects of my meditation continually[.] [T]ell them that Father is yet alive[.] God grant that he may see them again[.] Oh Emma for God sake do not forsake me nor the truth but remember me, if I do not meet you again in this life may God grant that we may meet in heaven[.] I cannot express my feelings, my heart is full[.] Farewell[.] Oh my kind and affectionate Emma I am yours forever[.] [Y]our Hu[s]band and true friend

{22}

"To the Church of Jesus Christ of Latter Day Saints," Joseph Smith to the Latter Day Saints, 16 December 1838 and 20 March 1839

(from *Times and Seasons* [Commerce, Illinois]
1 [April 1840], 6:82–86; and
"History of Joseph Smith," *Deseret News*
[Great Salt Lake City, Utah Territory]
4 [26 January 1854], 4:[1]; 4 [2 February 1854], 5:[1])

To the church of Jesus Christ of Latter Day Saints in Caldwell county, and to those who are scattered abroad, who are persecuted and made desolate, and who are afflicted in divers manners, for Christ's sake and the Gospel's, by the hands of a cruel mob, and the tyranical disposition of the authorities of this State.

We are sensible also, that your perils are greatly augmented by the wickedness and corruption of false brethren, may grace, mercy and peace be and abide with you. And notwithstanding all your sufferings we assure you that you have our prayers and fervent desire for your welfare both day and night.

We believe that, that God who sees us in this solitary place, will hear our prayers and reward you openly.

Know assuredly Dear brethren, that it is for the testimony of Jesus, that we are in *bonds* and in *prison*; but we say unto you, that we consider our condition better, notwithstanding our sufferings, than those who have persecuted and smitten us, and have borne false witness against us; and although our enemies seem to have a great triumph over us for the present, we most assuredly believe and know, that their triumph will be but short, and that God will deliver us out of their hands, notwithstanding their bearing false witness and otherwise. We want you, brethren, to remember Haman and Mordecai, you know that Haman could not be satisfied, so long as he saw Mordecai, at the kings gate, consequently he sought the life of Mordecai, and the whole Jewish people. But the Lord so ordered it, that Haman was hanged upon his own gallows: so shall it come to pass with poor Haman in the last days.

93

Those who have sought by their unbelief and wickedness; as well as by the principle of mobocracy, to destroy us and the people of God, by killing and scattering *them* abroad, and wilfully and maliciously delivering *us* into the hands of murderers, desiring us to be put to death, and having us dragged about in chains and cast into prison! and for what cause? It is because we were honest men, and were determined to defend the lives of the saints, at the expense of our own; I say unto you that those, who have thus vilely treated us, shall like Haman be hanged on their own gallows, or in other words, shall fall into their own gin and ditch, which they have prepared for us, and shall go backward and stumble, and fall, and their name shall perish, and God shall reward them according to all their abominations.

Dear Brethren, do not think that our hearts are faint, as though some strange thing had happened unto us, for we have seen these things before hand, and have an assurance of a better hope, than our persecutors, therefore God has made our shoulders broad, so that we can bear them: We glory in our tribulations, because we know that God is with us, that he is our friend, and he will save us. We do not care for those that can kill the body; knowing that they cannot harm our souls. We ask no favors at the hands of mobs, of the world, or of the devil; nor yet of any of his emmissaries, the *desenters*. We have never dissembled nor will we for the sake of our lives: inasmuch then as we know we have been endeavouring, with all our mights, minds, and strength to do the will of God in all things whatsoever he has commanded us, we feel a satisfaction which we would not part with for any wor[l]dly advantage whatever. As to our light speeches which may have escaped our lips from time to time, they have nothing to do with the fixed principles of our hearts; and those who have taken offence at any thing which may inadvertantly have escaped our lips, we would refer them to Isaiah's description of those, who make a man an offender for a word, and lay a snare for those that reprove in the gate: We have no retraction to make, we have reproved in the gate, and men have laid snares for us; we have spoken words and men have made us offenders; yet notwithstanding all this, our minds are not darkened, but we yet feel strong in the Lord. But behold the words of the Savior, "If the light which is in you became darkness, how great is that darkness: Look at the desenters. —And again." If you were of the world the world would love its own.

Look at those men, viz: [George] Hinckle [Hinkle], [John]

Corril[l] and [Reed] Peck, by whom we were led into the camp, as the Savior was led, like lambs prepared for the slaughter and as sheep before the shearers are dumb, so we opened not our mouths. But the men being greedy of gain sold us into the hands of those who loved them, for the world loved his own. —We would also remember W. W. Phelps who came to us as one of Job's comforters: God suffered such kind of beings to afflict Job, but it never entered into their hearts that Job would get out of it all.

This poor man who professes to be much of a prophet, has no other dumb ass to ride, but David Whitmer or to forbid his madness, when he goes up to curse Israel; but this not being of the same kind of Balaam's, therefore, notwithstanding the angel appeared unto him, yet he could not sufficiently penetrate his understanding, but that he brays out cursings instead of blessings. Poor ass, whoever lives, will see him and his rider perish like those who perished in the gainsaying of Core, or after the same condemnation, unless they repent. Now as for these and the rest of their company; we will not say that the world loves them, but we presume to say that they love the world; therefore we classify them in the error of Balaam, and in the gainsaying of Core: and with the company of Cora, Dathan and Abiram.

In speaking thus some of our brethren may think we are offended at those characters, if we are, it is not for a word, neither because they reproved in the gate; but because they have been the means of shed[d]ing innocent blood. —Are they not murderers then at the heart? are not their consciences seared as with a hot Iron? We confess that we are offended. The Savior said "that offences must come; but woe unto them by whom they come?" And again, "Blessed are ye when men shall revile you and speak all manner of evil against you falsely for my sake, rejoice and be exceeding glad for great is your reward in heaven, for so persecuted they the prophets which were before you."

Now dear brethren, if any men ever had reason to claim this promise we are the men, for we know that the world not only hates us, but "speak all manner of evil of us falsely," for no other reason, but because we have been endeavoring to teach the fullness of the gospel of Jesus Christ. After we were bartered away by Hinckle and were taken into the camp of the militia, we had all the evidence we could have wished, that the world hated us and that most cordially too. The priests of the different sects hated us. The Generals hated us, the colonels hated us, the officers and soldiers hated us; and the most profane blasphemers, drunkards, and [w]horemongers hated us. And why? Because of the testimony of Jesus Christ. Was it because we were liars? Was it because we had committed treason against the government, or burglary, or larc[e]ny, or arson or any other unlawful act; we know that such things have been reported by certain priests, lawyers and judges who are the instigators and abettors of a certain gang of murderers and robbers, who have been carrying on a scheme of mobocracy to uphold their priestcraft against the saints of the last days; and have tried by a well contemplated and premeditated scheme to put down by physical power, a system of religion that all the world, (by fair means,) and all their intelligence, were not able to resist. Hence mobbers were encouraged by priests and levites, by the pharisees and saducees, by essenees and herodions, and by the most abandoned and wicked characters that are suffered to live upon the earth, indeed a parallel cannot be found any where of such characters who gathered together to steal, to plunder, to starve and to *exterminate* the saints: these are the characters, who by their treasonable acts, have desolated and laid waste Daviess county. These are the characters that would fain make all the world believe that we are guilty of the above named acts; but they represent us fals[e]ly; we say that we have not committed treason, nor any other unlawful act in Daviess county.

Was it for murder in Ray county, that we were thus treated? We answer no. We were not present when the mobs came forth in that direction, who after dragging our brethren from their homes, and burning their habitations and killing several of our beloved friends, but not without the expense of, some of their own lives; retreated and after getting clothed with the authority of militia, raised the cry of murder! treason! &c. and appeared as innocent as a sheep. This suited their purpose, but if their borrowed garb had been torn off; instead of the peaceable sheep we should have found all the characteristics of the prowling wolf guilty of the murder of innocent and harmless men; therefore, on the heads of that mob with Bogard at their head be the crime and upon them rests the curse.

Was it for commit[t]ing adultery? We are aware that false and slanderous reports have gone abroad, which have reached our ears, respecting this thing, which have been started by renegadoes, and spread by the dissenters, who are extremely active in spreading foul and lib[e]lous reports concerning us; thinking thereby to gain the fellowship of the world, knowing that we are not of the world; and that the world hates us. But by so doing they only show themselves to be vile traitors and sycophants. Some have reported that we not only dedicated our property, but likewise our families to the Lord and Satan taking advantage of this has transfigured it into lasciviousness, a community of wives, which things are an abomination in the sight of God.

When we consecrate our property to the Lord, it is to administer to the wants of the poor and needy according to the laws of God, and when a man consecrates or dedicates his wife and children to the Lord, he does not give them to his brother or to his neighbor; which is contrary to the law of God, which says, "Thou shalt not commit adultery, Thou shalt not covet thy neighbors wife[.]" "He that looketh upon a woman to lust after her has committed adultery already in his heart." —Now for a man to consecrate his property, his wife and children to the Lord is nothing more nor less than to feed the hungry, cloth[e] the naked, visit the widows and fatherless, the sick and afflicted; and do all he can to administer to their relief in their afflictions, and for himself and his house to serve the Lord. In order to do this he and all his house must be virtuous and "shun every appearance of evil." Now if any person, has represented any thing other wise than what we now write they have willfully misrepresented us.

We have learned also since we have been in prison that many false and pernicious things, which were calculated to lead the saints astray and do great injury, have been taught by Dr. Avard, who has represented them as coming from the presidency; and we have no reason to fear, that many other designing and corrupt characters, like unto himself, have taught many things, which the presidency never knew of, until after they were made prisoners which, if they had known, they would have spurned them and their authors as they would a serpent.

Thus we find, that there has been frauds, secret abominations, and evil works of darkness going on leading the minds of the weak and unwary into confusion and distraction, and all of which has been endeavored to be palmed upon the presidency, who were ignorant of these things which were practised upon the church in our name. And now brethren what can we enumerate more, is not all manner of evil of every description spoken against us fals[e]ly, yea we say unto you fals[e]ly. We have been misrepresented misunderstood and belied, and the purity of our hearts have not been known. And some have gained influence by the hypocracy sanctified appearance and the *pious* dis-

97

courses which they have delivered. And our souls have been bowed down and we have suffered much distress in consequence thereof, and truly we have had to wade through an ocean of trouble.

We could enumerate the names of many who have acted in a mean and dastardly manner, some of whom we once considered our friends men whom we once thought would never condescend to such unhallowed proceedings, but their love of the world and the praise of men has overcome every feeling of virtue, and they have yielded obedience once more to their old master, consequently their last end will be worse than the first. It has happened to them according to the words of the Savior. ["]The dog has returned to his vomit, and the sow that was washed to her wallowing in the mire." If those under Moses' law died without mercy under two or three witnesses, of how much more severer punishment, suppose ye, shall those be thought worthy, who have betrayed and denied the new and everlasting covenant, by which they were sanctified, and called it an unholy thing; and have done despite to the spirit of grace. Again we would say inasmuch as their is virtue in us; and the keys of the kingdom have not been taken from us; and the holy priesthood has been confer'd upon us, (for verily thus saith the Lord, be of good cheer, for the keys I gave unto you are yet with you;) therefore we say unto you dear brethren, in the name of the Lord Jesus Christ, that we deliver these characters unto the buffetings of satan until the day of redemption that they may be dealt with according to their works and from henceforth shall their works be made manifest.

And now dear and well beloved brethren, to you who have continued faithful, both men women and children, we exhort you in the name of the Lord Jesus to be strong in the faith of the new and everlasting covenant, and nothing frightened at your enemies for what has happened to us is an token to our enemies of damnation but unto you and us of salvation, and that of God: therefore hold on, even unto death, "for he that seeks to save his life shall loose it, but he that looseth his life for my sake and the gospel shall find it" saith the Saviour[.]

Brethren from henceforth let truth and rig[hte]ousness prevail and abound in you, and in all things be temperate, abstain from drunkenness, profane language, and from every thing which is unrighteous and unholy, and from the very appearance of evil: be honest one with another; for it seemeth some have come short in this thing, and some have been uncharitable towards their brethren who were indebted to them: while they have been dragged about in chains and cast into dungeons: such persons will have their turn and sorrow in the rolling of the great wheel; for it rolleth and none can hinder; remember whatsoever measure you meet it shall be measured to you again.

Zion shall yet live: although she seemeth to be dead. We say unto you brethren: be not afraid of your adversaries: contend earnestly against mobs, and the unlawful works of dissenters, and of darkness; and the very God of peace shall be with you: and make a way for your escape from the adversaries. We commend you to God and the word of his grace; which is able to make you wise unto salvation. Amen.

ॐ

To the Church of Latter Day Saints at Quincy, Illinois, and scattered abroad, and to Bishop [Edward] Partridge in particular:

Your humble servant Joseph Smith, jr., prisoner for the Lord Jesus Christ's sake, and for the saints taken and held by the power of mobocracy under the exterminating reign of His Excellency, the Governor Lilburn W. Boggs, in company with his fellow prisoners and beloved brethren, Caleb Baldwin, Lyman Wight, Hyrum Smith, and Alexander McRae, send unto you all greeting: May the grace of God the Father and of our Lord and Savior Jesus Christ, rest upon you all, and abide with you for ever. —May knowledge be multiplied unto you by the mercy of God. And may faith, and virtue, and knowledge, and temperance, and patience, and godliness, and brotherly kindness, and charity, be in you and abound, —that you may not be barren in anything, nor unfruitful.

Forasmuch as we know that the most of you are well acquainted with the wrongs and the high toned injustice and cruelty that is practised upon us: whereas we have been taken prisoners, charged falsely with every kind of evil, and thrown into prison, enclosed with strong walls, surrounded with a strong guard, who continually watch day and night as indefatigable as the devil is in tempting and laying snares for the people of God:—

Therefore, dearly beloved brethren, we are the more ready and willing to lay claim to your fellowship and love. For our circumstances are calculated to awaken our spirits to a sacred remembrance of everything, and we think that yours are also, and that nothing therefore can separate us from the love of God and fellowship one with another; and that every species of wickedness and cruelty practised upon us will only tend to bind our hearts together and seal them together in love. We have no need to say to you, that we are held in bonds without cause, neither is it needful that you say unto us, We are driven from our homes and smitten without cause. We mutually understand that if the inhabitants of the State of Missouri had let the saints alone, and had been as desirable of peace as they were, there would have been nothing but peace and quietude in this State unto this day; we should not have been in this hell surrounded with demons; if not those who are damned, they are those who shall be damned; and where we are compelled to hear nothing but blasphemous oaths, and witness a scene of blasphemy, and drunkenness, and hypocrisy, and debaucheries of every description.

And again, the cries of orphans and widows would not have ascended up to God against them. It would not have stained the soil of Missouri. But O! the unrelenting hand! the inhumanity and murderous disposition of this people! It shocks all nature: it beggars and defies all description: it is a tale of woe; a lamentable tale; yea a sorrowful tale: too much to tell; too much for contemplation: too much to think of for a moment; too much for human beings: it cannot be found among the heathens; it cannot be found among the nations where kings and tyrants are enthroned; it cannot be found among the savages of the wilderness; yea, and I think it cannot be found among the wild and ferocious beasts of the forest, —that a man should be mangled for sport! —women be robbed of all that they have—their last morsel for subsistence—and then be violated to gratify the hellish desires of the mob, and finally left to perish, with their helpless offspring clinging around their necks.

But this is not all. After a man is dead, he must be dug up from his grave, and mangled to pieces—for no other purpose than to gratify their spleen against the religion of God.

They practice these things upon the saints, who have done them no wrong; who are innocent and virtuous; who loved the Lord their God, and were willing to forsake all things for Christ's sake. These things are awful to relate, but they are verily true. It must needs be that offences come, but wo unto them by whom they come.

O God! where art thou? And where is the pavilion that covereth thy hiding place? —How long shall thy hand be stayed, and thine eye, yea thy pure eye, behold from the eternal heavens, the wrongs of thy people, and of thy servants, and thine ear be penetrated with their cries? Yes, O Lord, how long shall they suffer these wrongs and unlawful oppressions, before thine heart shall be softened towards them, and thy bowels be moved with compassion towards them?

O Lord God Almighty, Maker of Heaven, Earth, and Seas, and of all things that in them is. and who controlleth and subjecteth the devil, and the dark and benighted dominion of Shayole! Stretch forth thy hand; let thine eye pierce: let thy pavilion be taken up: let thy hiding place no longer be covered; let thine ear be inclined: let thine heart be softened, and thy bowels moved with compassion toward us; let thine anger be kindled against our enemies; and in the fury of thine heart, with thy sword, avenge us of our wrongs; remember thy suffering saints, O our God! and thy servants will rejoice in thy name forever.

Dearly and beloved brethren, we see that perilous times have come, as was testified of. We may look then, with most perfect assurance for the rolling in of all those things that have been written, and with more confidence than ever before, lift up our eyes to the luminary of day, and say in our hearts, soon thou wilt veil thy blushing face. He that said, let there be light, and there was light, hath spoken this word. —And again, thou moon, thou dimmer light; thou luminary of night, shall turn to blood.

We see that everything is fulfilling; and the time shall soon come, when the Son of Man shall descend in the clouds of heaven. Our hearts do not shrink, neither are our spirits altogether broken, at the grievous yoke which is put upon us. We know that God will have our oppressors in derision: that he will laugh at their calamity, and mock when their fear cometh.

Oh that we could be with you, brethren, and unbosom our feelings to you! We would tell, that we should have been liberated at the time Elder Rigdon was, on the writ of habeas corpus, had not our own lawyers interpreted the law, contrary to what it reads, against us: which prevented us from introducing our evidence before the mock court.

They have done us much harm from the beginning. They have of late acknowledged that the law was misconstrued, and tantalized our feelings with it, and have entirely forsaken us, and have forfeited their oaths, and their bonds; and we have a come back on them, for they are co-workers with the mob.

As nigh as we can learn, the public mind has been for a long time turning in our favor, and the majority is now friendly: and the lawyers can no longer browbeat us by saying that this or that, is a matter of public opinion, for public opinion is not willing to brook it; for it is beginning to look with feelings of indignation against our oppressors, and to say that the Mormons were not in the fault in the least. We think that Truth, Honor, and Virtue, and Innocence, will eventually come out triumphant. We should have taken a habeas corpus before the High Judge and escaped the mob in a summary way; but unfortunately for us, the timber of the wall being very hard, our auger handles gave out, and hindered us longer than we expected; we applied to a friend, and a very slight incautious act gave rise to some suspicions, and before we could fully succeed, our plan was discovered; we had every thing in readiness, but the last stone, and we could have made our escape in one minute, and should have succeeded admirably, had it not been for a little imprudence, or over anxiety on the part of our friend.

The sheriff and jailer did not blame us for our attempt; it was a fine breach, and cost the county a round sum; but public opinion says, that we ought to have been permitted to have made our escape; that then the disgrace would have been on us, but now it must come on the State; that there cannot be any charge sustained against us, and that the conduct of the mob; the murders committed at Haun's mills, and the exterminating order of the Governor, and the one-sided, rascally proceedings of the Legislature, has damned the State of Missouri to all eternity. I would just name also that General Atchison has proved himself as contemptible as any of them.

We have tried for a long time to get our lawyers to draw us some petitions to the Supreme Judges of this State, but they utterly refused. We have examined the law, and drawn the petitions ourselves, and have obtained abundance of proof to counteract all the testimony that was against us, —so that if the Supreme Judge does not grant us our liberty, he has got to act without cause, contrary to honor, evidence, law or justice, sheerly to please the devil, but we hope better things, and trust before many days, God will so order our case, that we shall be set at liberty and take up our habitation with the saints.

We received some letters last evening; —one from Emma [Smith], one from Don C. Smith, and one from Bishop [Edward] Partridge—all breathing a kind and consoling spirit. We were much gratified with their contents. We had been a long time without information; and when we read those letters, they were to our souls as the gentle air is refreshing; but our joy was mingled with grief, because of the sufferings of the poor, and much injured Saints. And we need not say to you that the floodgates of our hearts were hoisted, and our eyes were a fountain of tears, but those who have not been enclosed in the walls of prison, without cause or provocation, can have but little idea how sweet the voice of a friend is; one token of friendship from any source whatever awakens and calls into action every sympathetic feeling; it brings up in an instant everything that is passed; it seizes the present with the avidity of lightning; it grasps after the future with the fierceness of a tiger; it retrogrades from one thing to another until finally all enmity, malice, and hatred, and past differences, misunderstandings, and mismanagements, are slain victorious at the feet of Hope; and when the heart is sufficiently contrite, then the voice of inspiration steals along, and whispers, My Son, peace be unto thy soul; thine adversity and thine afflictions shall be but a small moment; and then if thou endure it well, God shall exalt thee on high; thou shalt triumph over all thy foes; thy friends do stand by thee, and they shall hail thee again, with warm hearts and friendly hands: thou art not yet as Job; thy friends do not contend against thee, neither charge thee with transgression as they did Job; and they who do charge thee with transgression, their hope shall be blasted, and their prospects shall melt away as the hoar frost melteth before the burning rays of the rising sun; and also that God hath set to his hand and seal, to change the times and seasons, and to blind their minds that they may not understand His marvellous workings, that he may prove them also, and take them in their own craftiness; also because their hearts are corrupted, and the things which they are willing to bring upon others, and love to have others suffer, may come upon themselves, to the very uttermost; that they may be disappointed also, and their hopes may be cut off; and not many years hence, that they and their posterity shall be swept from under heaven, saith God, that not one of them is left to stand by the wall; —Cursed are all those that shall lift up the heel against mine anointed, saith the Lord, and cry they have sinned when they have not sinned before me, saith the Lord, but have done that which was meet in mine eyes, and which I commanded them; but those who cry transgression, do it; because they are the servants of sin, and are the children of disobedience themselves; and those who swear falsely against my servants, that they might bring them into bondage, and death: Wo unto them; because they have offended my little ones, they shall be severed from the ordinances of mine house; their basket shall not be full; their houses and their barns shall perish, and they themselves shall be despised by those that flattered them; they shall not have right to the priesthood, nor their posterity after them, from generation to generation; it had been better for them that a millstone had been hanged about their necks, and they drowned in the depth of the sea.

Wo unto all those that discomfort my people, and drive, and murder, and testify against them, saith the Lord of Hosts; a generation of vipers shall not escape the damnation of hell. Behold mine eyes seeth and knoweth all their works, and I have in reserve a swift judgment in the season thereof, for them all; for there is a time appointed for every man, according as his works shall be.

And now beloved brethren, we say unto you, that inasmuch as God hath said that he would have a tried people, that he would purge them as gold, now we think that this time he has chosen his own crucible, wherein we have been tried, and we think if we get through with any degree of safety, and shall have kept the faith, that it will be a sign to this generation, altogether sufficient to bear them without excuse; and we think also, it will be a trial of our faith equal to that of Abraham, and that the ancients will not have whereof to boast over us in the day of judgment, as being called to pass thro' heavier afflictions; that we may hold an even weight in the balances with them; but now after having suffered so great sacrifice, and having passed through so great a season of sorrow, we trust that a ram may be caught in the thicket speedily, to relieve the sons and daughters of Abraham from their great anxiety, and to light up the lamp of salvation upon their countenances, that they may hold on now, after having gone so far unto everlasting life.

Now brethren, concerning the places for the location of the Saints, we cannot counsel you as we would if we were present with you; and as to the things that were written heretofore, we did not consider them anything very binding, therefore we now say once for all, that we think it most proper, that the general affairs of the church, which are necessary to be considered, while your humble servant remains in bondage, should be transacted by a general conference of the most faithful, and the most respectable of the authorities of the church, and a minute of those transactions may be kept, and for-warded, from time to time, to your humble servant; and if there should be any corrections by the word of the Lord, they shall be freely transmitted, and your humble servant will approve all things whatso-ever is acceptable unto God. If anything should have been suggested by us, or any names mentioned, except by commandment, or thus saith the Lord, we do not consider it binding: therefore our hearts shall not be grieved if different arrangements should be entered into. Nevertheless we would suggest the propriety of being aware of an aspiring spirit, which spirit has oftentimes urged men forwards, to make foul speeches, and influence the church to reject milder counsels, and has eventually been the means of bringing much death, and sorrow upon the church.

We would say, be aware of pride also: for well and truly hath the wise man said, that pride goeth before destruction, and a haughty spirit before a fall. And again, outward appearance is not always a criterion for us to judge our fellow man; but the lips betray the haughty and overbearing imaginations of the heart; by his words and his deeds, let him be scanned. Flattery also is a deadly poison. A frank and an open rebuke, provoketh a good man to emulation; and in the hour of trouble he will be your best friend; but on the other hand, it will draw out all the corruptions of a corrupt heart, and lying and the poison of asps shall be under their tongues; —and they do cause the pure in heart to be cast into prison, because they want them out of their way.

A fanciful and flowery, and heated imagination be aware of; because the things of God are of deep import; and time, and experience, and careful and ponderous, and solemn thoughts, can only find them out. —Thy mind, O man! if thou wilt lead a soul unto salvation, must stretch as high as the utmost heavens, and search into and contemplate the lowest considerations of the darkest abyss, and expand upon the broad considerations of eternity's expanse; he must commune with God. How much more dignified, and noble, are the thoughts of God, than the vain imaginations of the human heart! None but fools will trifle with the souls of men.

How vain and trifling have been our spirits, our conferences, our councils, our meetings, our private as well as public conversations; too low; too mean; too vulgar; too condescending, for the dignified characters, of the called and chosen of God, according to the purposes of His will, from before the foundation of the world, to hold the keys of the mysteries of those things that have been kept hid from the foundation until now, of which some have tasted a little, and on which many of them are to be poured down from heaven upon the heads of babes; yea, the weak, obscure, and despisable ones of the earth.

Therefore we beseech of you brethren, that you bear with those who do not feel themselves more worthy than yourselves, —while we exhort one another to a reformation with one and all, both old and young, teachers and taught, both high and low, rich and poor, bond and free; male and female; let honesty, and sobriety, and candor, and solemnity, and virtue, and pureness, and meekness, and simplicity, crown our heads in every place; and in fine, become as little children, without malice, guile or hypocrisy.

And now brethren, after your tribulations, if you do these things, and exercise fervent prayer and faith in the sight of God always, he shall give unto you knowledge by his Holy Spirit, yea by the unspeakable gift of the Holy Ghost, that has not been revealed since the world was until now; —which our forefathers have waited with anxious expectation to be revealed in the last times, which their minds were pointed to, by the angels as held in reserve for the fullness of their glory, a time to come in the which nothing shall be withheld, whether there be one God or many Gods, they shall be manifest; all thrones, and dominions, principalities and powers, shall be revealed and set forth upon all who have endured valiently for the gospel of Jesus Christ; and also if there be bounds set to the heavens, or to the seas; or to the dry land, or to the sun, moon, or stars; all the times of their revolutions; all the appointed days, months, and years, and all the days of their days, months and years, and all their glories, laws, and set times, shall be revealed, in the days of the dispensation of the fullness of times, according to that which was ordained in the midst of the council of the Eternal God, of all other Gods, before this world was, that should be reserved unto the finishing and the end thereof, when every man shall enter into his eternal presence, and into his immortal rest.

But, I beg leave to say unto you brethren, that ignorance, superstition and bigotry, placing itself where it ought not, is oftentimes in the way of the prosperity of this church; like the torrent of rain from the mountains, that floods the most pure and crystal stream with mire, and dirt, and filthiness, and obscures everything that was clear before, and all hurls along in one general deluge; but time weathers tide; and notwithstanding we are rolled in for the time being by the mire of the flood, the next surge peradventure, as time rolls on, may bring us to the fountain as clear as crystal, and as pure as snow; while the filthiness, flood-wood, and rubbish is left and purged out by the way.

How long can rolling waters remain impure? What power shall stay the heavens? As well might man stretch forth his puny arm to stop the Missouri river in its decreed course, or to turn it up stream, as to hinder the Almighty from pouring down knowledge from heaven, upon the heads of the Latter Day Saints.

What is Boggs or his murderous party, but wimbling willows upon the shore to catch the flood-wood? As well might we argue that water is not water, because the mountain torrents send down mire and rolls the crystal stream, altho' afterwards renders it more pure than before; or that fire is not fire, because it is of a quenchable nature, by pouring on the flood, as to say that our cause is down because renegadoes, liars, priests, thieves, and murderers, who are all alike tenacious of their crafts and creeds, have poured down from their spiritual wickedness in high places, and from their strong holds of the devil, a flood of dirt and mire, and filthiness, and vomit, upon our heads.

No! God forbid. Hell may pour forth its rage like the burning lava of mount Vesuvius or of Etna, or of the most terrible of the burning mountains; and yet shall Mormonism stand. Water, Fire, Truth, and God, are all the same. Truth is Mormonism. —God is the author of it. He is our Shield. It is by Him we received our birth. It was by His voice that we were called to a dispensation of his gospel in the beginning of the fullness of times. It was by Him we received the Book of Mormon; and it was by him that we remain unto this day; and by him we shall remain, if it shall be for our glory; and in His Almighty name we are determined to endure tribulations as good soldiers unto the end.

But brethren, we shall continue to offer further reflections in our next Epistle. You will learn by the time you have read this, —and if you do not learn it, you may learn it, —that walls and irons, doors and creaking hinges, and half scared to death guards and jailers, grinning like some damned spirits lest an innocent man should make his escape to bring to light the damnable deeds of a murderous mob, —is calculated in its very nature, to make the soul of an honest man feel stronger than the powers of hell.

But we must bring our Epistle to a close. We send our respects to fathers, mothers, wives and children, brothers and sisters; we hold them in the most sacred remembrance.

We feel to enquire after Elder [Sidney] Rigdon, if he has not forgotten us; it has not been signified to us by his scrawl. Brother George W. Robinson also, and Elder [Reynolds] Cahoon, we re- member him, but would like to jog his memory a little on the fable of the bear and the two friends who mutually agreed to stand by each other. And perhaps it would not be amiss to mention uncle

John, and various others. A word of consolation, and a blessing would not come amiss from anybody, while we are being so closely whispered by the bear. But we feel to excuse every body and every thing, yea the more readily, when we contemplate that we are in the hands of worse than a bear, for the bear would not prey upon a dead carcass.

Our respects, and love, and fellowship to all the virtuous Saints. We are your brethren, and fellow sufferers, and prisoners of Jesus Christ for the gospel's sake, and for the hope of glory which is in us: AMEN.

JOSEPH SMITH, jr.,
HYRUM SMITH,
LYMAN WIGHT,
CALEB BALDWIN,
ALEXANDER McRAE,

ঽ&

. . . I continued my Epistle to the Church of Latter Day Saints as follows:

We continue to offer further reflections to Bishop [Edward] Partridge, and to the Church of Jesus Christ of Latter Day Saints, whom we love with a fervent love, and do always bear them in mind in all our prayers to the throne of God.

It still seams to bear heavily in our minds that the church would do well to secure to themselves the contract of the land which is proposed to them by Mr. Isaac Galland, and to cultivate the friendly feelings of that, gentleman, inasmuch as he shall prove himself to be a man of honor and a friend to humanity. We really think that his letter breathes that kind of spirit, if we can judge correctly. And Isaac Van Allen, Esq., the Attorney General of Iowa Territory, —that peradventure such men may be wrought upon by the providence of God, to do good unto his people. Governor [Samuel D.] Lucas also, —We suggest the idea of praying fervently for all men who manifest any degree of sympathy for the suffering children of God.

We think that peradventure the United States Surveyor of the Iowa Territory may be of great benefit to the church if it be the will of God, to this end, if righteousness should be manifested as the girdle of our loins.

It seems to be deeply impressed upon our minds, that the Saints ought to lay hold of every door that shall seem to be opened unto

them, to obtain foothold on the earth, and be making all the preparation that is within the power of possibles for the terrible storms that are
now gathering in the heavens, with darkness and gloominess, and
thick darkness, as spoken of by the Prophets, which cannot be now of
a long time lingering, for there seems to be a whispering that the
angels of heaven who have been entrusted with the council of these
matters for the last days, have taken counsel together and among the
rest of the general affairs that have to be transacted in there honorable
council, they have taken cognizance of the testimony of those who
were murdered at Haun's mills, and also those who were martyred
with D[avid]. W. Patten, and elsewhere, and have passed some decisions peradventure in favor of the Saints, and those who were called to
suffer without cause.

These decisions will be made known in their time; and they will
take into consideration all those things that offend.

We have a fervent desire that in your general conferences, everything should be discussed with a great deal of care and propriety lest you
grieve the Holy Spirit, which shall be poured out at all times upon your
heads when you are exercised with those principles of righteousness that
are agreeable to the mind of God, and are properly affected one toward
another, and are careful by all means to remember those who are in
bondage, and in heaviness, and in deep affliction for your sakes. And if
there are any among you who aspire after their own aggrandizement, and
seek their own opulence, while their brethren are groaning in poverty,
and are under sore trials, and temptations, they cannot be benefited by
the intercession of the Holy Spirit, which maketh intercession for us day
and night with groanings that cannot be uttered.

We ought at all times to be very careful, that such high-mindedness never have place in our hearts; but condescend to men of low
estate, and with all long suffering bear the infirmities of the weak.

Behold there are many called, but few are chosen. And why are
they not chosen? Because their hearts are set so much upon the things
of this world, and aspire to the honors of men, that they do not learn
this one lesson—that the rights of Priesthood are inseparably connected with the powers of heaven, and that the powers of heaven
cannot be controlled, nor handled only upon the principles of righteousness. That they may be conferred upon us, it is true; but when we
undertake to cover our sins, or to gratify our pride, or vain ambition,
or to exercise control, or dominion, or compulsion, upon the souls of

the children of men, in any degree of unrighteousness, behold the heavens withdraw themselves: the Spirit of the Lord is grieved; and when it has withdrawn, *amen to the Priesthood*, or the authority of that man. Behold! ere he is aware, he is left unto himself, to kick against the pricks; to persecute the Saints, and to fight against God.

We have learned by sad experience, that it is the nature and disposition of almost all men, as soon as they get a little authority, as they suppose, they will immediately begin to exercise unrighteous dominion. Hence many are called, but few are chosen.

No power or influence can or ought to be maintained by virtue of the Priesthood, only by persuasion, by long suffering, by gentleness and meekness, and by love unfeigned; by kindness, and pure knowledge, which shall greatly enlarge the soul without hypocrisy, and without guile, reproving betimes with sharpness when moved upon by the Holy Ghost and then showing forth afterwards an increase of love toward him whom thou hast reproved, lest he esteem thee to be his enemy; that he may know that thy faithfulness is stronger than the cords of death; thy bowels also being full of charity towards all men, and to the household of faith, and virtue garnish thy thoughts unceasingly, then shall thy confidence wax strong in the presence of God and the doctrine of the Priesthood shall distil upon thy soul as the dews from heaven. The Holy Ghost shall be thy constant companion, and thy sceptre an unchanging sceptre of righteousness and truth, and thy dominion shall be an everlasting dominion, and without compulsory means it shall flow unto thee forever and ever.

The ends of the earth shall enquire after thy name, and fools shall have thee in derision, and hell shall rage against thee, —while the pure in heart, and the wise and the noble, and the virtuous, shall seek counsel, and authority, and blessings constantly from under thy hand, and thy people shall never be turned against thee by the testimony of traitors; and although their influence shall cast thee into trouble, and into bars and walls, thou shalt be had in honor, and but for a small moment and thy voice shall be more terrible in the midst of thine enemies, than the fierce lion, because of thy righteousness: and thy God shall stand by thee forever and ever.

If thou art called to pass through tribulation; if thou art in perils among false brethren; if thou art in perils among robbers; if thou art in perils by land or by sea; if thou art accused with all manner of false accusations; if thine enemies fall upon thee; if they tear thee from the society of thy father and mother and brethren and sisters; —and if with a drawn sword thine enemies tear thee from the bosom of thy wife, and of thine offspring, and thine Elder Son, although but six years of age, shall cling to thy garments, and shall say, My father, my father, why can't you stay with us? —O my father! what are the men going to do with you? —and if then he shall be thrust from thee by the sword, and thou be dragged to prison, and thine enemies prowl around thee like wolves for blood of the lamb: and if thou shouldst be cast into the pit, or into the hands of murderers, and the sentence of death passed upon thee; if thou be cast into the deep; if the billowing surge conspire against thee; if the fierce winds become thine enemy; if the heavens gather blackness, and all the elements combine to hedge up the way: and above all, if the very jaws of hell shall gape open her mouth wide after thee, know thou my son, that all these things shall give thee experience, and shall be for thy good. The Son of Man hath descended below them all, —art thou greater than he?

Therefore hold on thy way, and the Priesthood shall remain with thee, for their bounds are set, they cannot pass. Thy days are known, and thy years shall not be numbered less, therefore fear not what man can do; for God shall be with you forever and ever.

Now brethren, I would suggest for the consideration of the Conference, of its being carefully and wisely understood, by the council or conferences, that our brethren scattered abroad, who understand the spirit of the gathering, that they fall into the places of refuge and safety that God shall open unto them, between Kirtland and Far West. Those from the east and from the west, and from far countries, let them fall in somewhere between those two boundaries, in the most safe and quiet places they can find; and let this be the present understanding, until God shall open a more effectual door for us for further considerations.

And again, we further suggest for the consideration of the council, that there be no organization of large bodies upon common stock principles, in property, or of large companies of firms until the Lord shall signify it in a proper manner, as it opens such a dreadful field for the avaricious, and the indolent and corrupt hearted to prey upon the innocent, and virtuous, and honest.

We have reason to believe that many things were introduced among the Saints, before God had signified the times; and notwithstanding the principles and plans, may have been good, yet aspiring men, or in other words, men who had not the substance of godliness about them, —perhaps undertook to handle edge tools. Children you know, are fond of tools, while they are not yet able to use them.

Time and experience, however, is the only safe remedy against such evils. There are many teachers, but perhaps not many fathers. There are times coming when God will signify many things which are expedient for the well-being of the Saints; but the times have not yet come, but will come, as fast as there can be found place, and receptions for them.

And again we would suggest for your consideration the propriety of all the Saints gathering up a knowledge of all the facts, and suffering and abuses put upon them by the people of this State; and also of all the property, and amount of damages which they have sustained, both of character and personal injuries, as well as real property; and also the names of all persons that have had a hand in their oppressions, as far as they can get hold of them and find them out; and perhaps a committee can be appointed to find out these things, and to take statements, and affidavits, and also to gather up the libelous publications that are afloat, and all that are in the magazines, and in the encyclopedias, and all the libelous histories that are published, and are writing, and by whom, and present the whole concatenation of diabolical rascality, and nefareous, and murderous impositions that have been practised upon this people, that we may not only publish to all the world, but present them to the heads of government in all their dark and hellish hue, as the last effort which is enjoined on us by our Heavenly Father, before we can fully and completely claim that promise which shall call him forth from his hiding place, and also the whole nation may be left without excuse before he can send forth the power of his mighty arm.

It is an imperious duty that we owe to God, to angels, with whom we shall be brought to stand, and also to ourselves, to our wives and children, who have been made to bow down with grief, sorrow, and care, under the most damning hand of murder, tyranny, and oppression, supported and urged on, and upheld by the influence of that spirit which hath so strongly riveted the creeds of the fathers, who have inherited lies upon the hearts of the children, and filled the world with confusion, and has been growing stronger and stronger, and is now the very main spring of all corruption, and the whole earth groans under the weight of its iniquity.

It is an iron yoke, it is a strong band; they are the very hand cuffs, and chains, and shackles, and fetters of hell.

Therefore, it is an imperious duty that we owe not only to our own wives and children, but to the widows and fatherless, whose husbands and fathers have been murdered under its iron hand; — which dark and blackening deeds are enough to make hell itself shudder, and to stand aghast, and pale, and the hands of the very devil tremble and palsy. And also it is an imperious duty that we owe to all the rising generation, and to all the pure in heart, which there are many yet on the earth among all sects, parties and denominations, who are blinded by the subtle craftiness of men whereby they lie in wait to deceive, and only kept from the truth because they know not where to find it; therefore that we should waste and wear out our lives in bringing to light all the hidden things of darkness, wherein we know them; and they are truly manifest from heaven.

These should then be attended to with great earnestness. Let no man count them as small things; for there is much which lieth in futurity, pertaining to the Saints, which depends upon these things. You know brethren, that a very large ship is benefited very much by a very small helm in the time of a storm, by being kept workways with the wind and the waves.

Therefore dearly beloved brethren, let us cheerfully do all things that lieth in our power, and then may we stand still with the utmost assurance, to see the salvation of God, and for his arm to be revealed.

And again, I would further suggest the impropriety of the organization of bands or companies, by covenant or oaths, by penalties or secrecies; but let the time past of our experience and sufferings by the wickedness of Doctor [Sampson] Avard suffice, and let our covenant be that of the Everlasting Covenant, as is contained in the holy writ, and the things that God hath revealed unto us. Pure friendship always becomes weakened, the very moment you undertake to make it stronger by penal oaths and secre[c]y.

Your humble servant or servants, intend from henceforth to disapprobate everything that is not in accordance with the fullness of the gospel of Jesus Christ, and is not of a bold, and frank, and upright nature. They will not hold their peace as in times past when they see iniquity beginning to rear its head, for fear of traitors, or the consequences that shall follow by reproving those who creep in unawares, that they may get something to destroy the flock. We believe that the experience of the Saints in times past has been sufficient that they will from henceforth be always ready to obey the truth without having men's persons in admiration because of advantage. It is expedient that we should be aware of such things; and we ought always to be aware of those prejudices which sometimes so strangely presented themselves, and are so congenial to human nature, against our friends, neighbors and brethren of the world, who choose to differ with us in opinion and in matters of faith. Our religion is between us and our God. Their religion is between them and their God.

There is a tie from God that should be exercised towards those of our faith, —who walk uprightly, which is peculiar to itself—but it is without prejudice, but gives scope to the mind which enables us to conduct ourselves with greater liberality towards all others that are not of our faith than what they exercise towards one another. —These principles approximate nearer to the mind of God, because it is like God, or god-like.

Here is a principle also which we are bound to be exercised with, that is in common with all men, such as governments, and laws, and regulations in the civil concerns of life. This principle guarantees to all parties, sects and denominations, and classes of religion, equal, coherent, and indefeasable rights; they are things that pertain to this life; therefore all are alike interested; they make our responsibilities one towards another in matters of corruptible things, while the former principles do not destroy the latter, but bind us stronger and make our responsibilities not only one to another, but unto God also. Hence we say, that the Constitution of the United States is a glorious standard; it is founded in the wisdom of God. It is a heavenly banner; —it is to all those who are privileged with the sweets of its liberty, like the cooling shades and refreshing waters of a great rock in a thirsty and a weary land. It is like a great tree under whose branches men from every clime can be shielded from the burning rays of an inclement sun.

We brethren, are deprived of the protection of this glorious principle, by the cruelty of the cruel, by those who only look for the time being, for pasturage like the beasts of the field, only to fill themselves; and forget that the Mormons as well as the Presbyterians; and those of every other class and description, have equal rights to partake of the fruits of the great tree of our National Liberty. But notwithstanding we see what we see, and we feel what we feel, and we know what we know, yet that fruit is no less precious and delicious to our taste; we cannot be weaned from the milk, neither can we be driven from the breast; neither will we deny our religion because of the hand of oppression; but we will hold on until death.

We say that God is true; that the Constitution of the United States is true; that the Bible is true; that the Book of Mormon is true; that the Book of Covenants are true; that Christ is true; that the ministering angels sent forth from God are true, and that we know that we have an house not made with hands eternal in the heavens, whose builder and maker is God: —a consolation which our oppressors cannot feel, when fortune, or fate, shall lay its iron hand on them as it has on us. Now we ask, What is man? Remember brethren, that time and chance happeneth to all men.

We shall continue our reflections in our next.

We subscribe ourselves, your sincere friends and brethren in the bonds of the everlasting gospel, prisoners of Jesus Christ for the sake of the gospel and the saints.

We pronounce the blessing of heaven upon the heads of the saints who seek to serve God with undivided hearts, in the name of Jesus Christ: AMEN.

"Dear—and Affectionate—Wife,"
Joseph Smith to Emma Smith, 4 April 1839

(from Beinecke Rare Book and Manuscript Library,
Yale University, New Haven, Connecticut)

Dear—and affectionate—wife.

Thursay night I set down just as the sun is going down, as we peak throw the greats [grates] of this lonesome prision [Liberty Jail, Missouri], to write to you, that I may make known to you my situation. It is I believe it is now about five months and six days since I have been under the *grimace*, of a guard night and day, and within the walls grates and screeking iron do[o]rs, of a lonesome dark durty prison. With immotions known only to God, do I write this letter[.] [T]he contemplations, of the mind under these circumstances, defies the pen, or tounge, or Angels, to discribe, or paint, to the human being, who never experiance[d] what we experience. This night we expect; is the last night we shall try our weary Joints and bones on our dirty straw couches in these walls[.] [L]et our case hereafter be as it may, as we expect to start to morrow, for Davis Co[unty], for our trial. We shall have a change of venue to some of the lower counties, for the final *trial*, as our lawyers generaly say, if law can be adheared to in Davis, as it grants us the privaliege [of a change of venue]. But you are awere what we may expect, of beings that have conducted [themselves] as they have[.] We lean on the arm of Jehovah, and none else, for our deliverance, and if he dont do it, it will not be done, you may be assured[.] [F]or there is great thirsting for our blood, in this state; not because we are guilty of any thing: but because they say these men will give an account of what has been done to them; the wrongs they have sustain[ed] if it is known, it will ruin the State. So the mob party have sworn, to have our lives, at all hasards, but God will disappoint them we trust. We shall be moved from this [place] at any rate and we are glad of it let what will become of us[.] [W]e cannot get into a worse hole then this is[.] [W]e shall not stay here but one night besides this[.] [T]hank God, we shall never cast a lingering wish after liberty in clay county Mo. [W]e have enough of it to last forever[.] [M]ay God reward fals swearers according to their works, is all I can wish them. My Dear Emma I think of you and the children continualy[.] [I]f I could tell you my tale, I think you would say it was altogether enough for once, to grattify the malice of hell that I have suffered. I want to see little Frederick, Joseph, Julia, and Alexander, [and] Joana [Carter], and old major [his horse]. And as to yourself if you want to know how much I want to see you, examine your feelings, how much you want to see me, and Judge for you[r]self. I would gladly walk from here to you barefoot, and bareheaded, and half naked, to see you and think it great pleasure, and never count it toil[.] [B]ut do not think I am babyish, for I do not feel so[.] I bare with fortitude all my oppression, so do those that are with me, not one of us have flinched yet[.] I want you should not let those little fellows, forgit me[.] [T]ell them Father loves them with a perfect love, and he is doing all he can to git away from the mob to come to them[.] [D]o teach them all you can, that they may have good minds[.] [B]e tender and kind to them[.] [D]ont be fractious to them, but listen to their wants[.] [T]ell them Father says they must be good children and mind their mother[.] My Dear Emma there is great respo[n]sibility resting upon you, in preserveing yourself in honor, and sobriety, before them, and teaching them right things, to form their young and tender minds, that they begin in right paths, and not git contaminated when young, by seeing ungodly examples[.] I soppose you see the need of my council, and help, but a combinnation of things have conspired to place me where I am, and I know it is not my fault, and further if my voice and council had been heeded I should not have been here[.] [B]ut I find no fault with you, at tall I know nothing but what you have done the best you could[.] [I]f there is any thing it is known to yourself, you must be your own Judge, on that subject: and if e[i]ther of us have done wrong it is wise in us to repent of it, and for God sake, do not be so foolish as to yield to the flattery of the Devel, falshoods, and vainty, in this hour of trouble, that our affections be drawn, away from the right objects[.] [T]hose preasious things God has given us will rise up in Judgement against us if we do not mark well our steps, and ways. My heart has often been exceding sorrowful when I have thaught of these thing[s] for many considerations[.] [O]ne thing let [me adm]onished you by way of my duty, do not [be] self willed, neither harber a spirit of revevenge: and again remember that he who is my enemy, is yours also, and never give up an old tried friend, who has waded through all manner of toil, for your sake, and throw him away becau[se] fools may tell you he has some *faults*[.] [T]hese thing[s] have accured to me [as] I have been writing[.] I do[n't] speak of them because you do not know them, but because I want to stir up your pure mind by way of *rememberance:* all feelings of diss[at]isfaction is far from my heart[.] I wish to act upon that principle of *generosity,* that will acquit myself in the preasance of [—] through the mercy of God[.] You [remainder of text missing]

{24}

"On the Doctrines of Faith,"
A Sermon Delivered on 27 June 1839

(from Willard Richards Pocket Companion,
original in archives, Historical Department,
Church of Jesus Christ of Latter-day Saints,
Salt Lake City, Utah)

On the Doctrines of Faith. Faith comes by hearing the word of God through the testimony of the Servants of God, that Testimony is always attended by the Spirit of prophecy & Revelation.

Repentance is a thing that cannot be trifled with every day. Daily transgression & daily repentance is not that which is pleasing in the sight of God—

Baptism is a holy ordinance preparatory to the reception of the Holy Ghost. It is the channel & Key by which the Holy Ghost will be administered. The gift of the Holy Ghost by the laying on of hands cannot be received through the medium of any other principle than the principle of Righteousness, for if the proposals are not complied with it is of no use but withdraws.

Tongues were given for the purpose of preaching among those whose language is not understood as on the day of Pentecost &c, & it is not necessary for tongues to be taught to the church particularly. For any man that has the Holy Ghost, can speak of the things of God in his own tongue, as well as to speak in another, for faith comes not by signs but by hearing the word of God.

The doctrine of the Resurrection of the Dead & Eternal Judgment are necessary to preach among the first principles of the gospel of Jesus Christ.—

The Doctrine of Election

St Paul exhorts us to make our Calling & Election shure. This is that sealing power spoken of by Paul in other places (See Eph I. 13.14. In whom ye also trusted, that after ye heard the work of truth; the gospel of your salvation, in whom also after that ye believed[,] ye were sealed with that Holy Spirit of promise. Which is the earnest [transaction?] of our inheritance, until the redemption of the purchased possession unto the praise of his glory.) That we may be sealed up unto the day of redemption, this principle ought (in its proper place) to be taught, for God hath not revealed any thing to Joseph [Smith], but what he will make known unto the Twelve [Apostles] & even the least Saint may know all things as fast as he is able to bear them. For the day must come when no man need say to his neighbor know ye the Lord for all shall know him (who Remain) from the least to the greatest. How is this to be done? It is to be done by this sealing power & the other comforter spoken of which will be manifest by Revelation. There is two Comforters spoken of [one of which] is the Holy Ghost the same as given on the day of pentecost and that all Saints receive after faith. Repentance & Baptism. This first comforter or Holy Ghost has no other effect than pure inteligence. It is more powerful in expanding the mind enlightening the understanding & storeing the intellect with present knowledge of a man who is of the literal Seed of Abraham than one that is a gentile though it may not have half as much visible effect upon the body[,] for as the Holy Ghost falls upon one of the Literal Seed of Abraham it is calm & serene & his whole soul & body are only exercised by the pure spirit of Inteligence; while the effect of the Holy Ghost upon a Gentile is to purge out the old blood & make him actually of the seed of Abraham. That man that has none of the blood of Abraham (naturally) must have a new creation by the Holy Ghost, in such a case there may be more of a powerful effect upon the body & visible to the eye than upon an Israelite, while the Israelite at first might be far before the Gentile in pure inteligence[.]

The other Comforter spoken of is a subject of great interest & perhaps understood by few of this generation. After a person hath faith in Christ, repents of his sins & is Baptized for the remission of his sins & received the Holy Ghost (by the laying on of hands) which is the first Comforter then let him continue to humble himself before God, hungering & thirsting after Righteousness & living by every word of God & the Lord will soon say unto him Son thou shalt be exalted &c. When the Lord has thoroughly proved him & finds that the man is determined to serve him at all hazard then the man will find his calling & Election made sure then it will be his privilege to receive the other Comforter which the Lord hath promised the saints as is recorded in the testimony of St John in the XIV ch[apter] from the 12th to the 27 verses[.] Note the 16. 17. 18. 21. 23. verses (16. vs) & I will pray the father & he shall give you another Comforter, that he may abide with you forever; (17) Even the Spirit of Truth; whom the world cannot receive because it seeth him not, neither knoweth him; but ye know him; for he dwelleth with you & shall be in you. (18) I will not leave you comfortless. I will come to you. (21) He that hath my commandments & keepeth them, he it is that loveth me & he that loveth me shall be loved of my father & I will love him & will manifest myself to him. (23) If a man Love me he will keep my words & my Father will love him & we will come unto him, & make our abode with him.

Now what is this other Comforter? It is no more or less than the Lord Jesus Christ himself & this is the sum & substance of the whole matter, that when any man obtains this last Comforter he will have the personage of Jesus Christ to attend him or appear unto him from time to time & even he will manifest the Father unto him & they will take up their abode with him, & the visions of the heavens will be opened unto him & the Lord will teach him face to face & he may have a perfect knowledge of the mysteries of the kingdom of God, & this is the state & place the Ancient Saints arrived at when they had such glorious vision[s:] Isaiah, Ezekiel, John upon the Isle of Patmos, St Paul in the third heavens, & all the Saints who held communion with the general Assembly & Church of the First Born &c.

The Spirit of Revelation is in connection with these blessings. A person may profit by noticing the first intimation of the Spirit of Revelation[,] for instance when you feel pure Inteligence flowing unto you it may give you sudden strokes of ideas that by noticeing it you may find it fulfilled the same day or Soon. (I.E.) those things that were presented unto your minds by the Spirit of God will come to pass and thus by learning the Spirit of God & understanding it you may grow into the principle of Revelation until you become perfect in Christ Jesus.

An Evangelist is a patriarch even the oldest man of the Blood of Joseph or of the seed of Abraham, wherever the Church of Christ is established in the earth, there should be a patriarch for the benefit of the posterity of the Saints as it was with Jacob. in giving his patriarchal blessing unto his Sons &c.—

{25}

"Ever Keep in Exercise the Principles of Mercy," A Sermon Delivered on 2 July 1839

(from Scott G. Kenney, ed., *Wilford Woodruff's Journal*, 9 vols. [Midvale, Utah: Signature Books, 1983-85], 1:342-44)

Joseph [Smith] arose & presented some precious things of the kingdom unto us in the power of the Holy Ghost, yea precious principles that ought to be engraven upon our hearts & practiced in our lives, some of which are as follows:

Ever keep in exercise the principles of mercy & be ready to forgive our brother on the first intimations of repentance & asking forgiveness & should we even forgive our brother or our enemy before they ask it our heavenly father would be equally as merciful unto us & also we ought to be willing to repent of & confess all of our own sins & keep nothing back, & let the Twelve [Apostles] be humble & not be exalted & beware of pride & not seek to excell one above another but act for each others good & honerably make mention of each others name in our prayrs before the Lord & before our fellow men, & not backbite & devour our brother.

Why will not man learn wisdom by precept & example at this late age of the world & not be oblieged to learn every thing we know by sad experiance? Must the new ones that are chosen to fill the places of those that are fallen of the quorum of the Twelve, begin to exhalt themselves untill they get so high that they will tumble over & have a great fall & go wallowing through the mud, mire, & darkness Judas like to the buffating of Satan as several of the Twelve have done, or will they learn wisdom & be wise? (O God give them wisdom & keep them humble I pray.)

When the Twelve or any other witness of Jesus Christ stands befor the Congregations of the earth & they preach in the power & demonstration of the Holy Ghost & the people are asstonished & confounded at the doctrin & say that that man has preached a power-ful discours a great sermon then let that man or those men take care that they do not asscribe the glory unto themselves but be careful that they are humble & asscribe the praise & glory to God & the Lamb for it is by the power of the Holy Priesthood & the Holy Ghost that they have power thus to speak. What art thou O man but dust & from whom dost thou receive thy power & blessings but from God?

Then O ye Twelve notice this key & be wise for Christ sake & your own souls sake. Ye are not sent out to be taught but to teach. Let every man be Sober be vigilent & let all his words be seasoned with grace & keep in mind that it is a day of warning & not of many words.

Act honest before God & man. Beware of gentile sophestry such as bowing & scraping unto men in whom you have no Confidence. Be honest open & frank in all your intercourse with mankind.

O ye Twelve and all Saints, profit by this important Key that in all your trials, troubles, & temptations, afflictions bonds imprisionment & death see to it that you do not betray heaven, that you do not betray Jesus Christ, that you do not betray your Brethren, & that you do not betray the revelations of God whether in the bible, Book of Mormon, or Doctrine & Covenants or any of the word of God. Yea in all your kicking, & floundering see to it that you do not this thing lest innocent blood be found in your skirts & you go down to *hell*.

We may ever know by this sign that there is danger of our being led to a fall & aposticy, when we give way to the devil so as to neglect the first known duty. But whatever you do do not betray your *Friend*.

"The Priesthood Was First Given to Adam," A Sermon Delivered Prior to 8 August 1839

(from Willard Richards Pocket Companion, original in archives, Historical Department, Church of Jesus Christ of Latter-day Saints, Salt Lake City, Utah)

The Priesthood was first given to Adam: he obtained the first Presidency & held the Keys of it, from generation to Generation; he obtained it in the creation before the world was formed as in Gen. 1, 26:28, —he had dominion given him over every living Creature. He is Michael, the Archangel, spoken of in the Scriptures, —Then to Noah who is Gabriel, he stands next in authority to Adam in the Priesthood; he was called of God to this office & was the Father of all living in his day, & To him was given the Dominion. These men held keys, first on earth, & then in Heaven. —The Priesthood is an everlasting principle & Existed with God from Eternity & will to Eternity, without beginning of days or end of years. The Keys have to be brought from heaven whenever the Gospel is sent. —When they are revealed from Heaven it is by Adams Authority.

Dan[iel] VII Speaks of the Ancient of days, he means the oldest man our Father Adam, Michael; he will call his children together, & hold a council with them to prepare them for the coming of the Son of Man. He, (Adam) is the Father of the human family & presides over the Spirits of all men, & all that have had the Keys must stand before him in this great Council. This may take place before some of us leave this stage of action. The Son of Man stands before him & there is given him glory & dominion. —Adam delivers up his Stewardship to Christ, that which was deliverd to him as holding the Keys of the Universe, but retains his standing as head of the human family.

The Spirit of Man is not a created being: it existed from Eternity & will exist to eternity. Anything created cannot be Eternal & earth, water &c —all these had their existence in an elementary State from

Eternity. Our Savior speaks of Children & Says their angels always stand before my father.

The Father called all spirits before him at the creation of Man & organized them. He (Adam) is the head, was told to multiply. The Keys were given to him, and by him to others & he will have to give an account of his Stewardship, & they to him. The Priesthood is everlasting. The Savior, Moses, & Elias gave the Keys to Peter, James & John on the Mount when they were transfigured before him. The Priesthood is everlasting, without beginning of days or end of years, without Father, Mother &c, —

If there is no change of ordinances there is no change of Priesthood. Wherever the ordinances of the Gospel are administered there is the priesthood. How have we come at the priesthood in the last days? The[n] it came down, down in regular succession. Peter James & John had it given to them & they gave it up. Christ is the Great High priest; Adam next. —Paul speaks of the Church coming to an innumerable company of Angels, to God the Judge of all, the Spirits of Just men made perfect, to Jesus the mediator of the New Covenant, &c. Heb XII, 23. I saw Adam in the valley of Ah-dam-ondi-Ahman—he called together his children & blessed them with a Patriarchal blessing. The Lord appeared in their midst, & he (Adam) blessed them all, & foretold what should befall them to the latest generation—See D.C. See III 28, 29 par- This is why Abraham blessed his posterity. He wanted to bring them into the presence of God. They looked for a city, &c. —Moses sought to bring the children of Israel into the presence of God, through the power of the Pri[e]sthood, but he could not. In the first ages of the world they tried to establish the same thing— & there were Elias's raised up who tried to restore these very glories but did not obtain them. But (Enoch did for himself & those that were with Him, but not for the world. J[ohn]. T[aylor].) they prophesied of a day when this Glory would be revealed. —Paul spoke of the Dispensation of the fulness of times, when God would gather together all things in one &c &c. Those men to whom these Keys have been given will have to be there. (I.E. when Adam ["the Ancient of Days"] shall again assemble his children of the Priesthood, & Christ be in their midst) the Ancient of Days come &c &c J[ohn]. T[aylor].) And they without us cannot not be made perfect. These men are in heaven, but their children are on Earth. Their bowels yearn over us. God sends down men for this reason, Mat. 13.41. & the Son of man shall send forth his Angels &c— All these authoritative characters will come down & join hand in hand in bringing about this work— The Kingdom of heaven is like a grain of mustard seed. The mustard seed is small but brings forth a large tree, and the fowls lodge in the branches. The fowls are the Angels, the Book of Mormon perhaps, these Angels come down combined together to gather their children, & gather them. We cannot be made perfect without them, nor they without us[.] when these things are done the Son of man will descend, the ancient of Days sit.— We may come to an innumerable company of Angels[,] have communion with & receive instruction from them.— Paul told about Moses's proceedings. Spoke of the Children of Israel being baptized, &c, he knew this & that all the ordinances, & blessings were in the Church. Paul had these things: & we may have the fowls of the heaven lodge in the branches &c. The horn made war with the Saints, & overcame them &c, until the Ancient of Days came, judgment was given to the Saints of the Most High, from the Ancient of Days— the time came that the Saints possessed the kingdom— this not only makes us ministers here but in Eternity. Salvation cannot come without revelation, it is in vain for anyone to minister without it.

No man is a minister of Jesus Christ, without being a Prophet. No man can be the minister of Jesus Christ, except he has the testimony of Jesus & this is the Spirit of Prophecy. Whenever Salvation has been administered it has been by Testimony. Men at the present time testify of Heaven & of hell, & have never seen either— & I will say that no man knows these things without this. Men profess to prophecy. I will prophecy that the signs of the coming of the Son of Man are already commenced, one pestilence will dessolate after another, we shall soon have war & bloodshed. The Moon will be turned to blood. I testify of these things, & that the coming of the Son of Man is nigh even at your doors.— If our Souls & our bodies are not looking forth for the coming of the Son of Man, & after we are dead if we are not looking forth, &c we shall be among those who are calling for the rocks to fall upon us &c— The hearts of the children will have to be turned to the fathers, & the fathers to the children living or dead to prepare them for the coming of the Son of Man. If Elijah did not come the whole earth would be smitten. There will be here & there a stake &c. For the gathering of the Saints[.] Some may have cried peace, but the Saints & the world will have little peace from henceforth. Let this not hinder us from going to the Stakes, for God has told us to flee not dallying, or we shall be scattered, one here, another there. There your children shall be blessed & you in the midst of friends where you may be blessed &c The Gospel net gathers of every kind. I prophecy that the man who tarries after he has an opportunity of going will be aflicted by the Devil. Wars are at hand we must not delay, but we are not required to Sacrifice. We ought to have the building up of Zion as our greatest object.— When wars come we shall have to flee to Zion, the cry is to make haste. The last revelation says ye shall not have time to have gone over the Earth until these things come. It will come as did the cholera, war, & fires burning[,] earthquake, one pestilence after another &c the Ancient of Days come then judgment will be given to the Saints.

Whatever you may hear about me or Kirtland [Ohio], take no notice of, for if it be a place of refuge the Devil will use his greatest efforts to trap the Saints. You must make yourselves acquainted with those men, who, like Daniel pray three times a day to the house of the Lord.— Look to the Presidency & receive instruction. Every man who is afraid, covetous &c will be taken in a snare.— The time is soon coming when no man will have any peace but in Zion & her Stakes. I saw men hunting the lives of their own sons, & brother murdering brother, women killing their own daughters & daughters seeking the lives of their mothers. I saw armies arrayed against armies I saw blood, desolations, fires &c— The Son of Man has said that the mother shall be against the daughter, & the daughter against the mother &c, &,— these things are at our doors. They will follow the Saints of God from City to City— Satan will rage & The Spirit of the Devil is now enraged, I know not how soon these things will take place, and with a view of them shall I cry peace? No! I will lift up my voice & testify of them. How long you will have good crops & the famine be kept off I do not know. When the fig tree leaves, know then that the summer is nigh at hand. We may look for Angels & recieve their ministering but we are to try the spirits & prove them. For it is often the case that men make a mistake in regard to these things.

God has so ordained that when he has communicated[,] no vision [is] to be taken but what you see by the seeing of the eye or what you hear by the hearing of the ear— When you see a vision pray for the interpretation[;] if you get not this, shut it up.— There must be certainty in this matter. An open vision will manifest that which is more important. Lying Spirits are going forth in the Earth.

There will be great manifestation of Spirit both false & true &c. Being born again comes by the Spirit of God through ordinances. An

127

angel of God never has wings. Some will say that they have seen a Spirit, that he offered them his hand, but they did not touch it. This is a lie. First it is contrary to the plan of God. A Spirit cannot come but in glory. An angel has flesh and bones, we see not their glory. The Devil may appear as an angel of light. Ask God to reveal it, if it be of the Devil, he will flee from you, if of God he will manifest himself or make it manifest, we may come to Jesus & ask him. he will know all about it.— If he comes to a little child, he will adapt himself to the Language & capacity of a little child.— There is no Gold nor Silver &c. it is false, all is plain in heaven; every Spirit or vision or Singing is not of God. The Devil is an orator, he is powerful: he took our Savior onto a pinnacle of the temple, & kept him in the wilderness for forty days. The gift of discerning spirits will be given to the presiding Elder, pray for him that he may have this gift. Speak not in the Gift of tongues without understanding it, or without interpretation, The Devil can speak in Tongues. The Adversary will come with his work, he can tempt all classes, Can speak in English or Dutch.— Let no one speak in tongues unless he interpret except by the consent of the one who is placed to preside, then he may discern or interpret or another may. Let us seek for the Glory of Abraham, Noah, Adam, the Apostles[,] have communion with these things[,] and then we shall be among that number when Christ comes.

{27}

"Extract, from the Private Journal of Joseph Smith Jr.," 1839

(from *Times and Seasons* [Commerce, Illinois] 1 [November 1839], 1:2-9)

On the fourteenth day of March, in the year of our Lord one thousand eight hundred and thirty eight, I with my family, arrived in Far West, Caldwell county Missouri, after a journey of more than one thousand miles, in the winter season, and being about eight weeks on our Journey; during which we suffered great affliction, and met with considerable persecution on the road. However, the prospect of meeting my friends in the west, and anticipating the pleasure of dwelling in peace, and enjoying the blessings thereof, buoyed me up under the difficulties and trials which I had then to endure. However, I had not been there long before I was given to understand that plots were laid, by wicked and designing men for my destruction, who sought every opportunity to take my life; and that a company on the Grindstone forks of Grand river, in the county of Daviess, had offered the sum of one thousand dollars for my scalp: persons of whom I had no knowledge whatever, and who, I suppose, were entire strangers to me; and in order to accomplish their wicked design, I was frequently waylaid &c.; consequently, my life was continually in jeopardy.

I could hardly have given credit to such statements, had they not been corroborated by testimony, the most strong and convincing; as shortly after my arrival at Far West, while watering my horse in Shoal Creek, I distinctly heard three or four guns snap, which were un-doubtedly intended for my destruction; however, I was mercifully preserved from those who sought to destroy me, by their lurking in the woods and hiding places, for this purpose.

My enemies were not confined alone, to the ignorant and obscure, but men in office, and holding situations under the Governor of the State [Lilburn Boggs], proclaimed themselves my enemies, and gave encour-agement to others to destroy me; amongst whom, was Judge [Austin A.] King, of the fifth Judicial circuit, who has frequently been heard to say that I ought to be beheaded on account of my religion— Expressions such as these, from individuals holding such important offices as Judge King's, could not fail to produce, and encourage persecution against me, and the people with whom I was connected. And in consequence of the prejudice which existed in the mind of this Judge, which he did not endeavor to keep secret, but made it as public as he could, the people took every advantage they possibly could, in abusing me, and threatening my life; regardless of the laws, which promise protection to every religious society, without distinction.

During this state of things I do not recollect that either myself, or the people with whom I was associated, had done any thing to deserve such treatment, but felt a desire to live at peace, and on friendly terms, with the citizens of that, and the adjoining counties, as well as with all men; and I can truly say, "for my love they were my enemies," and "sought to slay me without any cause," or the least shadow of a pretext.

My family was kept in a continual state of alarm, not knowing, when I went from home, that I should ever return again; or what would befall me from day to day. But notwithstanding these manifestations of enmity, I hoped that the citizens would eventually cease from their abusive and murderous purposes, and would reflect with sorrow upon their conduct in endeavoring to destroy me, whose only crime was in worshipping the God of heaven, and keeping his commandments; and that they would soon desist from harrassing a people who were as good citizens as the majority of this vast republic—who labored almost night and day, to cultivate the ground; and whose industry, during the time they were in that neighborhood, was proverbial.

In the latter part of September, A.D. 1838, I took a journey, in company with some others, to the lower part of the county of Caldwell, for the purpose of selecting a location for a Town. While on my journey, I was met by one of our brethren from Dewitt, in Carroll county, who stated that our people, who had settled in that place, were, and had been for some time, surrounded by a mob, who had threatened their lives, and had shot at them several times; and that he was on his way to Far West, to inform the brethren there, of the facts. I was surprised on receiving this intelligence, although there had, previous to this time, been some manifestations of mobs, but I had hoped that the good sense of the majority of the people, and their respect for the constitution, would have put down any spirit of persecution, which might have been manifested in that neighborhood.

Immediately on receiving this intelligence, I made preparations to go to that place, and endeavor if possible, to allay the feelings of the citizens, and save the lives of my brethren who were thus exposed to their wrath. I arrived at Dewitt, about the first of October, and found that the accounts of the situation of that place were correct, for it was with much difficulty, and by travelling unfrequented roads, that I was able to get there; all the principal roads being strongly guarded by the mob, who refused all ingress as well as egress. I found my brethren, (who were only a handfull, in comparison to the mob, by which they were surrounded,) in this situation, and their provisions nearly exhausted, and no prospect of obtaining any more.

We thought it necessary to send immediately to the Governor, to inform him of the circumstances; hoping, from the Executive, to receive the protection which we needed, and which was guaranteed to us, in common with other citizens. Several Gentlemen of standing and respectability, who lived in the immediate vicinity, (who were not in any wise connected with the church of Latter Day Saints,) who had witnessed the proceedings of our enemies; came forward and made affidavits to the treatment we had received, and concerning our perilous situation; and offered their services to go and present the case to the Governor themselves. A messenger was accordingly despatched to his Excellency, who made known to him our situation. But instead of receiving any aid whatever, or even sympathy from his Excellency, we were told that "the quarrel was between the Mormons and the mob," and that "we might fight it out." In the mean time, we had petitioned the Judges to protect us. They sent out about one hundred of the militia, under the command of Brigadier General [Hiram G.] Parks; but almost immediately on their arrival, General Parks informed us that the greater part of his men under Capt. [Samuel] Bogart had mutinied, and that he should be obliged to draw them off from the place, for fear they would join the mob; consequently he could afford us no assistance.

We had now, no hopes whatever, of successfully resisting the mob, who kept constantly increasing: our provisions were entirely exhausted and we being wearied out, by continually standing on guard, and watching the movements of our enemies; who, during the time I was there, fired at us a great many times. Some of the brethren died, for want of the common necessaries of life, and perished from starvation; and for once in my life, I had the pain of beholding some of my fellow creatures fall victims to the spirit of persecution, which did then, and has since prevailed to such an extent in Upper Missouri—men too, who were virtuous, and against whom, no legal process could for one moment, be sustained; but who, in consequence of their love to God—attachment to his cause—and their determination to keep the *faith*, were thus brought to an untimely grave.

Many houses belonging to my brethren, were burned; their cattle driven away, and a great quantity of their property destroyed by the mob. Seeing no prospect of relief, the Governor having turned a deaf ear to our entreaties, the militia having mutinied, and the greater part of them ready to join the mob; the brethren came to the conclusion to leave that place, and seek a shelter elsewhere; they consequently took their departure, with about seventy waggons, with the remnant of the property they had been able to save from their matchless foes, and proceeded to Caldwell. During our journey, we were continually harrassed and threatened by the mob, who shot at us several times; whilst several of our brethren died from the fatigue and privations which they had to endure, and we had to inter them by the wayside, without a coffin, and under circumstances the most distressing.

On my arrival in Caldwell I was informed by General [Alexander W.] Doniphan of Clay county, that a company of mobbers eight hundred strong, were marching towards a settlement of our people's in Daviess county. He ordered out one of the officers to raise a force and march immediately to what he called Wight's town and defend our people from the attacks of the mob, until he should raise the militia in his, and the adjoining counties to put them down. A small company of militia who were on their route to Daviess county, and who had passed through Far West, he ordered back again, stating that they were not to be depended upon, as many of them were disposed to join the mob; and to use his own expression, were "damned rotten hearted." According to orders [Mormon militia] Lieut. Colonel [George M.] Hinkle marched with a number of our people to Daviess county to afford what assistance they could to their brethren. Having some property in that county and having a house building there, I went up at the same time. While I was there a number of houses belonging to our people were burned by the mob, who committed many other depredations, such as driving off horses, sheep, cattle hogs &c. A number, whose houses were burned down as well as those who lived in scattered and lonely situations, fled into the town for safety, and for shelter from the inclemency of the weather, as a considerable snow storm had taken place just about that time; women and children, some in the most delicate situations, were thus obliged to leave their homes, and travel several miles in order to effect their escape. My feelings were such as I cannot describe when I saw them flock into the village, almost entirely destitute of clothes, and only escaping with their lives. During this state of affairs General Parks arrived at Daviess county, and was at the house of Colonel Lyman Wight, when the intelligence was brought, that the mob were burning houses; and also when women and children were fleeing for safety. Colonel Wight who held a commission in the 59th regiment under his (General Parks) command, asked what was to be done. He told him that he must immediately, call out his men and go and put them down. Accordingly, a force was immediately raised for the purpose of quelling the mob, and in a short time were on their march with a determination to drive the mob, or die in the attempt; as they could bear such treatment no longer. The mob having learned the orders of General Parks, and likewise being aware of the determination of the oppressed, they broke up their encampments and fled. The mob seeing that they could not succeed by force, now resorted to stratagem; and after removing their property out of their houses, which were nothing but log cabins, they actually set fire to their own houses, and then reported to the authorities of the state that the Mormons were burning and destroying all before them.

On the retreat of the mob from Daviess, I returned to Caldwell, hoping to have some respite from our enemies, at least for a short time; but upon my arrival there, I was informed that a mob had commenced hostilities on the borders of that county, adjoining to Ray co. and that they had taken some of our brethren prisoners, burned some houses and had committed depredations on the peaceable inhabitants. A company under the command of [Mormon militia] Capt. [David W.] Patten, was ordered out by Lieutenant Col. Hinckle to go against them, and stop their depredations, and drive them out of the county. Upon the approach of our people, the mob fired upon them, and after discharging their pieces, fled with great precipitation, with the loss of one killed and several wounded. In the engagement Capt Patten, (a man beloved by all who had the pleasure of his acquaintance,) was wounded and died shortly after. Two others were likewise killed and several wounded. Great excitement now prevailed, and mobs were heard of in every direction who seemed determined on our destruction. They burned the houses in the country and took off all the cattle they could find. They destroyed cornfields, took many prisoners, and threatened death to all the Mormons. On the 28 of Oct. a large company of armed soldiery were seen ap[p]roaching Far West. They came up near to the town and then drew back about a mile and encamped for the night. We were informed that they were Militia, ordered out by the Governor for the purpose of stopping our proceedings; it having been represented to his excellency, by wicked and designing men from Daviess, that we were the aggressors, and had committed outrages in Daviess &c They had not yet got the Governors orders of *extermination*, which I believe did not arrive until the next day. On the following morning, a flag was sent, which was met by several of our people, and it was hoped that matters would be satisfactorily arranged after the officers had heard a true statement of all the circumstances. Towards evening, I was waited upon by Colonel Hinckle who stated that the officers of the Militia desired to have an interview with me, and some others, hoping that the difficulties might be settled without having occasion to carry into effect the exterminating orders, which they had received from the Governor. I immediately complied with the request, and in company with Elders [Sidney] Rigdon and [Parley P.] Pratt, Colonel [Lyman] Wight, and Geo. W. Robinson, went into the camp of the militia. But judge of my surprise, when instead of being treated with that respect which is due from one citizen to another, we were taken as prisoners of war, and were treated with the utmost contempt. The officers would not converse with us, and the soldiers, almost to a man, insulted us as much as they felt disposed, breathing out threats against me and my companions. I cannot begin to tell the scene which I there witnessed. The loud cries and yells of more than one thousand voices, which rent the air and could be heard for miles; and the horrid and blasphemous threats and curses which were poured upon us in torrents, were enough to appal[l] the stoutest heart. in the evening we had to lie down on the cold ground surrounded by a strong guard, who were only kept back by the power of God from depriving us of life. We petitioned the officers to know why we were thus treated, but they utterly refused to give us any answer, or to converse with us. The next day they held a court martial, and sentenced us to be shot, on Friday morning, on the public square, as an ensample to the Mormons. However notwithstanding their sentence, and determination, they were not permitted to carry their murderous sentence into execution.

Having an opportunity of speaking to General Wilson, I inquired of him the cause why I was thus treated, I told him I was not sensible of having done any thing worthy of such treatment; that I had always been a supporter of the constitution and of Democracy. His answer was "I know it, and that is the reason why I want to kill you or have you killed." The militia then went into the town and without any restraint whatever, plundered the houses, and abused the innocent and unoffending inhabitants. They went to my house and drove my family out of doors. They carried away most of my property and left many destitute. —We were taken to the town, into the public square; and before our departure from Far West, we, after much entreaties, were suffered to see our families, being attended all the while with a strong guard; I found my wife and children in tears, who expected we were shot by those who had sworn to take our lives, and that they should see me no more. When I entered my house, they clung to my garments, their eyes streaming with tears, while mingled emotions of joy and sorrow were manifest in their countenances. I requested to have a private interview with them a few minutes, but this privilege was denied me. I was then obliged to take my departure, but who can realize my feelings which I experienced at that time; to be torn from my companion, and leaving her surrounded with monsters in the shape of men, and my children too, not knowing how their wants would be supplied; to be taken far from them in order that my enemies might destroy me when they thought proper to do so. My partner wept, my children clung to me and were only thrust from me by the swords of the guard who guarded me. I felt overwhelmed while I witnessed the scene, and could only recommend them to the care of that God, whose kindness had followed me to the present time; and who alone could protect them and deliver me from the hands of my enemies and restore me to my family.

I was then taken back to the camp and then I with the rest of my brethren, viz: Sidney Rigdon, Hyr[u]m Smith, Parley P. Pratt, Lyman Wight, Amasa Lyman, and George W. Robinson, were removed to Independence, Jackson county. They did not make known what their intention or designs were in taking us there; but knowing that some of our most bitter enemies resided in that county, we came to the conclusion that their design was to shoot us, which from the testimony of others, I do think was a correct conclusion. While there, we were under the care of Generals Lucas and Wilson, we had to find our own board, and had to sleep on the floor with nothing but a mantle for our covering, and a stick of wood for our pillow. After remaining there a few days we were ordered by General Clark to return; we were accordingly taken back as far as Richmond, and there we were thrust into prison and our feet bound with fetters. While in Richmond, we were under the charge of Colonel [Ebenezer] Price from Chariton county, who suffered all manner of abuse to be heaped upon us. During this time my afflictions were great, and our situation was truly painful. After remaining there a few days we were taken before the court of inquiry, but were not prepared with witnesses, in co[n]sequence of the cruelty of the mob, who threatened destruction to all who had any thing to say in our favor: but notwithstanding their threats there were a few who did not think their lives dear so that they might testify to the truth, and in our behalf, knowing we were unlawfully confined; but the court who was predjudiced against us, would not suffer them to be examined according to law, but suffered the State's Attorney to abuse them as he thought proper. We were then removed to Liberty jail in Clay county, and there kept in close confinement in that place for more than four months. While there, we petitioned Judge Turnham for a writ of habeas corpus, but on account of the predjudice of the jailor all communication was cut off; at length however, we succeeded in getting a petition conveyed to him, but for fourteen days we received no answer. We likewise petitioned the other Judges but with no success. After the expiration of fourteen days Judge Turnham ordered us to appear before him, we went and took a number of witnesses, which caused us considerable expense and trouble; but he altogether refused to hear any of our witnesses. The lawyers which we had employed refused to act; being afraid of the people. This being the case, we of course could not succeed, and were consequently remanded back to our prison house. —We were sometimes visited by our friends whose kindness and attention, I shall ever remember with feelings of lively gratitude, but frequently we were not suffered to have that privilege. Our vi[c]tuals were of the coarsest kind, and served up in a manner which was disgusting. We continued in this situation, bearing up under the injuries and cruelties we suffered as well as we could, until we were removed to Daviess county, where we were taken in order to be tried for the crimes with which we had been charged. The grand jury (who were mostly intoxicated,) indicted us for treason, &c. &c.

While there, we got a change of venue to Boon county, and were conducted on our way to that place by a strong guard. The second evening after our departure the guard got intoxicated, we thought it a favorable opportunity to make our escape; knowing that the only object of our enemies was our destruction; and likewise knowing that a number of our brethren had been massacred by them on Shoal creek, amongst whom were two children; and that they sought every opportunity to abuse others who were left in that state; and that they were never brought to an account for their barbarous proceedings, but were winked at, and encouraged, by those in authority. We thought that it was necessary for us, inasmuch as we loved our lives, and did not wish to die by the hand of murderers and assas[s]ins; and inasmuch, as we loved our families and friends, to deliver ourselves from our enemies, and from that land of tyran[n]y and oppression, and again take our stand among a people in whose bosoms dwell those feelings of republicanism and liberty which gave rise to our nation: —Feelings which the inhabitants of the state of Missouri were strangers to. —Accordingly we took the advantage of the situation of our guard and took our departure, and that night we trav[e]led a considerable distance. We continued on our journey both by night and by day, and after suffering much fatigue and hunger, I arrived in Quincy, Illinois, amidst the congratulations of my friends and the embraces of my family.

I have now resided in this neighborhood for several weeks as it is known to thousands of the citizens of Illinois, as well as of the State of Missouri, but the authorities of Mo., knowing that they had no justice in their crusade against me, and the people with whom I was associated, have not yet to my knowledge, taken the first step towards having me arrested.

Amongst those who have been the chief instruments, and leading characters, in the unparallelled persecutions against the church of Latter Day Saints; the following stand conspicuous, viz: Generals Clark, Wilson, and Lucas, Colonel Price, and Cornelius Guilliam. Captain Bogart also, whose zeal in the cause of oppression and injustice, was unequalled, and whose delight has been to rob, murder, and spread devastation amongst the Saints. He stole a valuable horse, saddle and bridle from me; which cost two hundred dollars, and then sold the same to General Wilson. On understanding this I applied to General Wilson for the horse, who assured me, upon the honor of a gentleman, and an officer, that I should have the horse returned to me; but this promise has not been fulfilled.

All the threats, murders, and robberies which these, officers have been guilty of, are entirely looked over by the Executive of the state; who, to hide his own iniquity, must of course shield and protect those whom he employed, to car[r]y into effect his murderous purposes.

I was in their hands as a prisoner about six months, but notwithstanding their determination to destroy me, with the rest of my brethren who were with me; and although at three different times (as I was informed) we were sentenced to be shot, without the least shadow of law, (as we were not military men,) and had the time, and place appointed for that purpose; yet, through the mercy of God, in answer to the prayers of the saints, I have been preserved, and delivered out of their hands, and can again enjoy the society of my friends and brethren, whom I love: and to whom I feel united in bonds that are stronger than death: and in a state where I believe the laws are respected, and whose citizens, are humane and charitable.

During the time I was in the hands of my enemies; I must say, that although I felt great anxiety, respecting my family and friends; who were so inhumanly treated and abused; and who had to mourn the loss of their husbands and children, who had been slain; and after having been robbed of nearly all that they possessed be driven from their homes, and forced to wander as strangers in a strange country, in order, that they might save themselves and their little ones, from the destructions they were threatened with in Missouri; yet, as far as I was concerned, I felt perfectly calm, and resigned to the will of my heavenly Father. I knew my innocency, as well as that of the saints; and that we had done nothing to deserve such treatment from the hands of our oppressors: consequently, I could look to that God, who has the hearts of all men in his hands, and who had saved me frequently from the gates of death for deliverance: and notwithstanding that every avenue of escape seemed to be entirely closed, and death stared me in the face, and that my destruction was determined upon, as far as man was concerned; yet, from my first entrance into the camp, I felt an assurance, that I with my brethren and our families should be delivered. Yes, that still small voice, which has so often whispered consolation to my soul, in the de[p]th of sorrow and distress, bade me be of good cheer, and promised deliverance, which gave me great comfort: and although the heathen raged, and the people imagined vain things, yet the Lord of hosts, the God of Jacob, was my refuge; and when I cried unto him in the day of trouble, he delivered me; for which I call upon my soul, and all that is within me, to bless and praise his holy name: For although I was "troubled on every side, yet not distressed; perplexed, but not in d[e]spair, persecuted, but not forsaken; cast down, but not destroyed."

The conduct of the saints under their accumulated wrongs and sufferings, has been praise-worthy; their courage, in defending their brethren from the ravages of mobs; their attachment to the cause of truth, under circumstances the most trying and distressing, which humanity can possibly endure; their love to each other; their readiness to afford assistance to me, and my brethren who were confined in a dungeon; their sacrifices in leaving the state of Missouri, and assisting the poor widows and orphans, and securing them houses in a more hospitable land; all conspire to raise them in the estimation of all good and virtuous men; and has secured them the favor and approbation of Jehovah; and a name, as imperishable as eternity. And their virtuous deeds, and heroic actions, while in defence of truth and their brethren: will be fresh and blooming; when the names of their oppressors shall either be entirely forgotten, or only remembered, for their barbarity and cruelty. Their attention and affection to me, while in prison, will ever be remembered by me; and when I have seen them thrust away, and abused by the jailor and guard, when they came to do any kind offices, and to cheer our minds while we were in the gloomy prison house, gave me feelings, which I cannot describe, while those who wished to insult and abuse us, by their threats and blasphemous language, were applauded and had every encouragement given them.

However, thank God, we have been delivered; and although, some of our beloved brethren, have had to seal their testimony with their blood; and have died martyrs to the cause of truth; yet,

> Short, though bitter was their pain,
> Everlasting is their joy.

Let us not sorrow as "those without hope," the time is fast approaching, when we shall see them again, and rejoice together, without being affraid of wicked men: Yes, those who have slept in Christ, shall he bring with him, when he shall come to be glorified in his saints, and admired by all those who believe: but to take vengeance upon his enemies, and all those who obey not the gospel. At that time, the hearts of the widow and fatherless shall be comforted, and every tear shall be wiped from off their faces.

The trials they have had to pass through, shall work together for their good, and prepare them for the society of those, who have come up out of great tribulation; and have washed their robes, and made them white in the blood of the Lamb. Marvel not then, if you are persecuted, but remember the words of the Savior, "The servant is not above his Lord, if they have persecuted, me, they will persecute you also;" and that all the afflictions through which the saints have to pass, are in fulfillment of the words of the prophets, which have spoken since the world began. We shall ther[e]fore do well to discern the signs of the times, as we pass along, that the day of the Lord may not "overtake us as a thief in the night." Afflictions, persecutions, imprisonments and deaths, we must expect according to the scriptures, which tell us, that the blood of those whose souls were under the alter, could not be avenged on them that dwell on the earth, untill their brethren should be slain, as they were.

If these transactions had taken place among barbarrians, under the authority of a despot; or in a nation, where a certain religion is established according to law, and all others proscribed; then there might have been some shadow of defence offered. But can we realize that in a land which is the cradle of Liberty and equal rights, and where the voice of the conquerors, who had vanquished our foes, had scarcely died away upon our ears, where we frequently mingled with those who had stood amidst the "battle and the breeze," and whose arms have been nerved in the defence of their country and liberty: whose institutions are the theme of philosophers and poets, and held up to the admiration of the whole civilized world. In the midst of all these scenes, with which we were surrounded, a persecution, the most unwarrantable, was commenced; and a tragedy, the most dreadful, was enacted, by a large portion of the inhabitants, of one of those free and independent States, which comprise this vast republic; and a deadly blow was struck at the institutions, for which our Fathers had fought many a hard battle, and for which, many a Patriot had shed his blood; and suddenly, was heard, amidst the voice of joy and gratitude for our national liberty, the voice of mourning, lamentation and woe. Yes, in this land, a mob, regardless of those laws, for which so much blood had been spilled, dead to every feeling of virtue and patriotism, which animated the bosom of freemen; fell upon a people whose religious faith was different from their own; and not only destroyed their homes, drove them away, and carried off their property, but murder[e]d many a free born son of America. A tragedy, which has no parrallel in modern, and hardly in ancient times; even the face of the Red man would be ready to turn pale at the recital of it.

It would have been some consolation, if the authorities of the State had been innocent in this affair, but they are involved in the guilt thereof; and the blood of innocence, even of *children*, cry for vengeance upon them. I ask the citizens of this vast republic, whether such a state of things is to be suffered to pass unnoticed, and the hearts of widows, orphans and patriots, to be broken, and their wrongs left without redress? No! I invoke the genius of our constitution, I appeal to the patriotism of Americans, to stop this unlawful and unholy procedure; and pray that God may defend this nation from the dreadful effects of such outrages. Is there not virtue in the body politic? Will not the people rise up in their majesty, and with that promptitude and zeal, which is so character[i]stic of them, discountenance such proceedings, by bringing the offenders to that punishment which they so richly deserve; and save the nation from that disgrace and ultimate ruin, which otherwise must inevitably fall upon it?

{28}

"In Order to Investigate
the Subject of the Priesthood,"
A Sermon Delivered on 5 October 1840

(from a manuscript by Robert B. Thompson,
original in archives, Historical Department,
Church of Jesus Christ of Latter-day Saints,
Salt Lake City, Utah)

In order to investigate the subject of the Priesthood so important to
this as well as every succeeding generation, I shall proceed to trace the
subject as far as I possibly can from the Old and new Testament.

There are two Priesthoods spoken of in the Scriptures, viz the
Melchisadeck and the Aaronic or Levitical. Altho there are two
Priesthoods, yet the Melchisadeck Priesthood comprehends the
Aaronic or Levitical Priesthood and is the Grand head, and holds the
highest Authority which pertains to the Priesthood the keys of the
Kingdom of God in all ages of the world to the latest posterity on the
earth and is the channel through which all knowledge, doctrine, the
plan of salvation and every important matter is revealed from heaven.
Its institution was prior to "the foundation of this earth or the
morning stars sang together or the Sons of God shouted for joy" and
is the highest and holiest Priesthood and is after the order of the Son
[of] God, and all other Priesthoods are only parts, ramifications,
powers and blessings belonging to the same and are held controlled
and directed by it. It is the channel through which the Almighty
commenced revealing his glory at the beginning of the creation of this
earth and through which he has continued to reveal himself to the
children of men to the present time and through which he will make
known his purposes to the end of time Commencing with Adam who
was the first man who is spoken of in Daniel as being the "Antient of
days" or in other words the first and oldest of all, the great grand
progenitor of whom it is said in another place he is Michael because
he was the first and father of all, not only by progeny, but he was the
first to hold the spiritual blessings, to whom was made known the plan

142

of ordinances for the Salvation of his posterity unto the end, and to whom Christ was first revealed, and through whom Christ has been revealed from heaven and will continue to be revealed from henceforth. Adam holds the Keys of the dispensation of the fulness of times, i.e. the dispensation of all the times have been and will be revealed through him from the begining to Christ and from Christ to the end of all the dispensations that have [and] are to be revealed.

Ephesians 1st Chap 9 & 10 verses. "Having made known unto us the mystery of his will, according to his good pleasure which he has purposed in himself that in the dispensation of the fulness of times he might gather together in one all things in Christ both which are in heaven and which are on earth in him." Now the purpose in himself in the winding up scene of the last dispensation is that all things pertaining to that dispensation should be conducted precisely in accordance with the preceeding dispensations. And again, God purposed in himself that there should not be an eternal fulness until every dispensation should be fulfilled and gathered together in one and that all things whatsoever that should be gathered together in one in those dispensations unto the same fulness and eternal glory should be in Christ Jesus, therefore he set the ordinances to be the same for Ever and ever and set Adam to watch over them to reveal them from heaven to man or to send Angels to reveal them. Heb 1 Chap. 16 verse. Are they not all ministring spirits sent forth to minister to those who shall be heirs of Salvation. These angels are under the direction of Michael or Adam who acts under the direction of Christ.

From the above quotation we learn that Paul perfectly understood the purpose of God in relation to his connexion with man, and that glorious and perfect order which he established in himself whereby he sent forth power revelations and glory. God will not acknowledge that which he has not called, ordained, and chosen. In the begining God called Adam by his own voice. See Genesis 3 Chap 9 & 10 verses. And the Lord called unto Adam and said unto him where art thou, and he said I heard thy voice in the garden and I was afraid because I was naked and hid myself. Adam received commandments and instruction from God. This was the order from the begining: that he received revelations, commandments, and ordinances at the begining is beyond the power of controversy, else, how did they begin to offer Sacrifices to God in an acceptable manner? And if they offered sacrifices they must be authorized by ordination. We read in Gen 4th

Chap. v. 4 that Abel brought of the firstlings of the flock and the fat thereof and the Lord had respect to Abel and to his offring. And again Heb II Chap 4 verse. By Faith Abel offered unto God a more excellent Sacrifice than Cain by which he obtained witness that he was righteous God testifying of his gifts[,] and by it he being dead yet speaketh. How doth ye yet speak? Why he magnified the Priesthood which was confired upon him and died a righteous man, and therefore has become an angel of God by receiving his body from the dead, therefore holding still the keys of his dispensation[,] and was sent down from heaven unto Paul to minister consoling words & to commit unto him a knowledge of the mysteries of Godliness[;] and if this was not the case I would ask how did Paul know so much about Abel and why should he talk about his speaking after he was dead. How that he spoke after he was dead must be, by being sent down out of heaven, to administer. This then is the nature of the priesthood, every man holding the presidency of his dispensation[;] and one man holding the presidency of them all even Adam, and Adam receiving his presidency and authority from Christ, but cannot receive a fulness, untill Christ shall present the kingdom to the Father which shall be at the end of the last dispensation. The power, glory, and blessings of the priesthood could not continue with those who received ordination only as their righteousness continued, for Cain also being authorized to offer sacrifice but not offering it in righteousness[,] therefore he was cursed. It signifies then that the ordinances must be kept in the very way God has appointed, otherwise their priesthood will prove a cursing instead of a blessing. If Cain had fulfilled the law of righteousness as did Enoch he could have walked with God all the days of his life and never failed of a blessing. Gen [5:22] And Enock walked with God after he begat Mathusalah 300 years and begat Sons and Daughters and all the days of Enoch were 365 years and Enoch walked with God and he was not for God took him. Now this Enoch God reserved unto himself that he should not die at that time and appointed unto him a ministry unto terrestiral bodies of whom there has been but little revealed. He is reserved also unto the presidency of a dispensation and more shall be said of him and terrestrial bodies in another treaties. He is a ministring Angel to minister to those who shall be heirs of Salvation and appered unto Jude as Abel did unto Paul. Therefore Jude spoke of him 14 & 15 verses in Jude and Enoch the seventh revealed these sayings. Behold the Lord cometh with ten thousand of his saints[.] Paul was also aquainted with this character and received instructions from him. Heb 11 Chap. 5 ver[se] By Faith Enoch was translated that he should not see death, and was not found because God had translated him for before his translation he had this testimony that he pleased God. But without faith it is impossible to please God, for he that cometh to God must believe that he is, and that he is a revealer to those who diligently seek him.

Now the doctrine of translation is a power which belongs to this priesthood, there are many things which belong to the powers of the priesthood and the keys thereof that have been kept hid from before the foundation of the world. They are hid from the wise and prudent to be revealed in the last times[.] many may have supposed that the doctrine of translation was a doctrine whereby men were taken immediately into the presence of God and into an Eternal fulness but this is a mistaken idea. There place of habitation is that of the terrestrial order and a place prepared for such characters, he held in reserve to be ministring angels unto many planets, and who as yet have not entered into so great a fulness as those who are resurrected from the dead. See Heb 11 Chap part of the 35 verse "others were tortured not accepting deliverance that they might obtain a better resurrection." Now it was evident, that there was a better resurrection or else God would not have revealed it unto Paul[;] wherein then can it be said a better ressurrection? This distinction is made between the doctrine of the actual ressurrection and the doctrine of translation, the doctrine of translation obtains deliverance from the tortures and sufferings of the body[;] but their existence will prolong as to their labors and toils of the ministry before they can enter into so great a rest and glory, but on the other hand those who were tortured not accepting deliverance received an immediate rest from their labors. See Rev [14:13] And I heard a voice from heaven saying blessed are the dead who die in the Lord for from henceforth they do rest from their labors and their works do follow them.— They rest from their labors for a long time and yet their work is held in reserve for them, that they are permitted to do the same works after they receive a ressurection for their bodies, but we shall leave this subject and the subject of the terresteal bodies for another time in order to treat upon them more fully. The next great grand patriarch who held the Keys of the priesthood was Lamech. See Gen 5 Chap 28 & 29 verse— And Lamech lived 182 years and begat a Son and he called his name Noah saying this same shall comfort us concerning our work and the toil of our hands because of the ground which the Lord has curst. "The priesthood continued from Lamech to Noah Gen 6 Chap 13 verse. And God said unto Noah the end of all flesh is before me, for the earth is filled with violence through them, and behold I will destroy them with the earth," thus we behold the Keys of this priesthood consisted in obtaining the voice of Jehovah that he talked with him in a familiar and friendly manner, that he continued to him the Keys, the Covenants, the power and the glory with which he blessed Adam at the beginning and the offring of Sacrifice which also shall be continued at the last time, for all the ordinances and duties that ever have been required by the priesthood under the direction and commandments of the Almighty in any of the dispensations, shall all be had in the last dispensation. Therefore all things had under the Authority of the Priesthood at any former period shall be had again— bringing to pass the restoration spoken of by the mouth of all the Holy Prophets. Then shall the sons of Levi offer an acceptable sacrifice to the Lord Se[e] Malichi 3 Chap. 3 & 4. And he shall sit as a refiner and purifier of Silver; and he shall purify the sons of Levi, and purge them as gold and silver, that they may offer unto the Lord.

It will be necessary here to make a few observations on the doctrine, set forth in the above quotation. As it is generally supposed that Sacrifice was entirely done away when the great sacrif[ic]e was offered up and that there will be no necessity for the ordinance of Sacrifice in future, but those who assert this are certainly not aquainted with the duties, privileges and authority of the priesthood or with the prophets. The offering of Sacrifice has ever been connected and forms a part of the duties of the priesthood. It began with the prieshood and will be continued untill after the coming of Christ from generation to generation— We freequently have mention made of the offering of Sacrifice by the servants of the most high in antient days prior to the law of moses. See which ordinances will be continued when the priesthood is restored with all its authority power and blessings. Elijah was the last prophet that held the keys of this priesthood, and who will, before the last dispensation, restore the authority and delive[r] the Keys of this priesthood in order that all the ordinances may be attended to in righteousness.

It is true that the Savior had authoritity and power to bestow this blessing but the Sons of Levi were too predjudi[ced].

And I will send Elijah the Prophet before the great and terrible day of the Lord &c &c.

Why send Elijah[?] because he holds the Keys of the Authority to administer in all the ordinances of the priesthood and without the authority is given[,] the ordinances could not be administered in righteousness.

It is a very prevalent opinion that in the sacrifices which were offered were entirely consumed, [but] this was not the case[.] if you read Leviticus [2] Chap 12-31 verses you will observe that the priests took a part as a memorial and offered it up before the Lord, while the remainder was kept for the maintenance of the priests. So that the offerings and sacrifices are not all consumed upon the Alter, but the blood is sprinkled and the fat and certain other portions are consumed. These sacrifices as well as every ordinance belonging to the priesthood will when the temple of the Lord shall be built and the Sons Levi be purified[,] be fully restored and attended to[,] then all their powers ramifications and blessings— This ever was and will exist when the powers of the Melchisid Priesthood are sufficiently manifest. Else how can the restitution of all things spoken of by all the Holy Prophets be brought to pass. It is not to be understood that, the law of moses will be established again with all it rights and variety of ceremonies, this had never been spoken off by the prophets but those things which existed prior [to] Mose's day viz Sacrifice will be continued— It may be asked by some what necessity for Sacrifice since the great Sacrifice was offered? In answer to which if Repentance Baptism and faith existed prior to the days of Christ what necessity for them since that time—

The priesthood has descended in a regular line from Father to Son through their succeeding generations[.]

See Book of Doctrine & Covenants [107:40-52].

{29}

"Satan Was Generally Blamed for the Evils which We Did," A Sermon Delivered on 16 May 1841

(from *Times and Seasons* [Nauvoo, Illinois] 2 [1 June 1841], 15:429-30)

At 10 o'clock A.M. a large concourse of the saints assembled on the meeting ground and were addressed by Pres. Joseph Smith, who spoke at considerable length. He commenced his observations by remarking that the kindness of our Heavenly Father, called for our heartfelt gratitude. He then observed that satan was generally blamed for the evils which we did, but if he was the cause of all our wickedness, men could not be condemned. The devil cannot compel mankind to evil, all was voluntary.— Those who resist the spirit of God, are liable to be led into temptation, and then the association of heaven is withdrawn from those who refuse to be made partakers of such great glory— God would not exert any compulsory means and the Devil could not; and such ideas as were entertained by many were absurd. The creature was made subject to vanity, not willingly, but Christ subjected the same in hope— we are all subject to vanity while we travel through the crooked paths, and difficulties which surround us. Where is the man that is free from vanity? None ever were perfect but Jesus, and why was he perfect? because he was the son of God, and had the fulness of the Spirit, and greater power than any man.— But, notwithstanding our vanity we look forward with hope, (because "we are subjected, in hope,") to the time of our deliverance.

He then made some observations on the first principles of the gospel, observing that many of the saints who had come from different States and Nations, had only a very superficial knowledge of these principles, not having heard them fully investigated. He then briefly stated the principles of faith, repentance, and baptism for the remission of sins which were believed by some of the religious societies of the day, but the doctrine of laying on of hands for the gift of the holy ghost, was discarded by them.

The speaker then referred them to the 6th chap. of Heb. 1. and 2. verses, "not laying again the foundation of repentance from dead works &c., but of the doctrines of baptism, laying on of hands, the resurrection and eternal judgment &c." The doctrine of eternal judgment was perfectly understood by the apostle, is evident from several passages of scripture. Peter preached repentance and baptism for the remission of sins to the Jews, who had been led to acts of violence and blood, by their leaders, but to the Rulers he said, "I would that through ignorance ye did it, as did also those ye ruled."— ["]Repent, therefore, and be converted that your sins may be blotted out, when the times of refreshing (redemption), shall come from the presence of the Lord, for he shall send Jesus Christ, who before was preached unto you &c." The time of redemption here had reference to the time, when Christ should come: then and not till then would their sins be blotted out. Why? Because they were murderers, and no murderer hath eternal life. Even David, must wait for those times of refreshing, before he can come forth and his sins be blotted out; for Peter speaking of him says, "David hath not yet ascended into heaven, for his sepulchre is with us to this day:" his remains were then in the tomb. Now we read that many bodies of the saints arose, at Christ's resurrection, probably all the saints, but it seems that David did not. Why? because he had been a murderer.

If the ministers of religion had a proper understanding of the doctrine of eternal judgment, they would not be found attending the man who had forfeited his life to the injured laws of his country by shedding innocent blood; for such characters cannot be forgiven, until they have paid the last farthing. The prayers of all the ministers in the world could never close the gates of hell against a murderer.

The speaker then spoke on the subject of election, and read the 9th chap[ter]. in Romans, from which it was evident that the election there spoken of was pertaining to the flesh, and had reference to the seed of Abraham, according to the promise God made to Abraham, saying, "In thee and in thy seed all, the families of the earth shall be blessed." To them belonged the adoption, and the covenants &c. Paul said, when he saw their unbelief I wish myself accursed—according to the flesh—not according to the spirit.

Why did God say to Pharoah, "for this cause have I raised thee up?" Because Pharoah was a fit instrument—a wicked man, and had committed acts of cruelty of the most atrocious nature.

The election of the promised seed still continues, and in the last days, they shall have the priesthood restored unto them, and they shall be the "Saviors on mount Zion" the "ministers of our God," if it were not for the remnant which was left, then might we be as Sodom and as Gomorah.

The whole of the chapter had reference to the priesthood and the house of Israel; and unconditional election of individuals to eternal life was not taught by the apostles.

God did elect or predestinate, that all those who would be saved, should be saved in Christ Jesus, and through obedience to the gospel; but he passes over no man's sins, but visits them with correction, and if his children will not repent of their sins, he will discard them.

{30}

"The Doctrine of Baptism for the Dead,"
A Sermon Delivered on 3 October 1841

(from *Times and Seasons* [Nauvoo, Illinois]
2 [15 October 1841], 24:577-78)

President Joseph Smith, by request of some of the Twelve, gave instructions on the doctrine of Baptism for the Dead: which was listened to with intense interest by the large assembly. The speaker presented "Baptism for the Dead" as the only way that men can appear as saviors on mount Zion. The proclamation of the first principles of the gospel was a means of salvation to men individually, and it was the truth, not men that saved them; but men, by actively engaging in rites of salvation substitutionally, became instrumental in bringing multitudes of their kin into the kingdom of God. He explained a difference between an angel and a ministering spirit; the one a resurrected or translated body, with its spirit, ministering to embodied spirits the other a disembodied spirit, visiting and ministering to disembodied spirits. Jesus Christ became a ministering spirit, while his body [was] laying in the sepulchre, to the spirits in prison; to fulfil an important part of his mission, without which he could not have perfected his work or entered into his rest. After his resurrection, he appeared as an angel to his disciples &c. Translated bodies cannot enter into rest until they have undergone a change equivalent to death. Translated bodies are designed for future missions. The angel that appeared to John on the Isle of Patmos was a translated or resurrected body.— Jesus Christ went in body, after his resurrection, to minister to translated and resurrected bodies. There has been a chain of authority and power from Adam down to the present time. The only way to obtain truth and wisdom, is not to ask it from books, but to go to God in prayer and obtain divine teaching. It is no more incredible that God should save the dead, than that he should raise the dead. There is never a time when the spirit is too old to approach God. All are within the reach of pardoning mercy, who have not committed the unpardonable sin, which hath no forgiveness, neither in this world, nor in the world to come. There is a way to release the spirit of the dead; that is, by the

151

power and authority of the Priesthood—by binding and loosing on earth.

This doctrine appears glorious, inasmuch as it exhibits the greatness of divine compassion and benevolence in the extent of the plan of human salvation. This glorious truth is well calculated to enlarge the understanding, and to sustain the soul under troubles, difficulties, and distresses.

For illustration the speaker presented, by supposition, the case of two men, brothers, equally intelligent, learned, virtuous and lovely walking in uprightness and in all good conscience, so far as, they had been able to discern duty from the muddy stream of tradition, or from the blotted page of the book of nature. One dies, and is buried, having never heard the gospel of reconciliation, to the other the message of salvation is sent, he hears and embraces it, and is made the heir of eternal life. Shall the one become a partaker of glory, and the other be consigned to hopeless perdition? Is there no chance for his escape? Sectarianism answers, "none! none!! none!!!" Such an idea is worse than atheism. The truth shall break down and dash in pieces all such bigoted Pharisaism; the sects shall be sifted, the honest in heart brought out, and their priests left in the midst of their corruption. The speaker then answered the objections urged against the Latter Day Saints for not admitting the validity of sectarian baptism, and for withholding fellowship from sectarian churches. It was like putting new wine into old bottles and putting old wine into new bottles. What, new revelations in the old churches! New revelations knock out the bottom of their bottomless pit. New wine into old bottles!— the bottles burst and the wine runs out. What, Sadducees in the new church! Old wine in new leather bottles will leak through the pores and escape; so the Sadducee saints mock at authority, kick out of the traces, and run to the mountains of perdition, leaving the long echo of their braying behind them.

The speaker then contrasted the charity of the sects, in denouncing all who disagree with them in opinion, and in joining in persecuting the saints, with the faith of the saints, who believe that even such may be saved in this world and in the world to come, (murderers and apostates excepted.)

This doctrine, he said, presented in a clear light, the wisdom and mercy of God, in preparing an ordinance for the salvation of the dead, being baptized by proxy, their names recorded in heaven, and they judged according to the deeds done in the body. This doctrine was the burden of the scriptures. Those saints who neglect it, in behalf of their deceased relatives, do it at the peril of their own salvation.

The dispensation of the fulness of times will bring to light the things that have been revealed in all former dispensations, also other things that have not been before revealed. He shall send Elijah the prophet &c., and restore all things in Christ.

The speaker then announced, "There shall be no more baptisms for the dead, until the ordinance can be attended to in the font of the Lord's House; and the church shall not hold another general conference, until they can meet in said house. For thus saith the Lord!"

{31}

"We Have again the Warning Voice Sounded in Our Midst," A Sermon Delivered on 20 March 1842

(from Scott G. Kenney, ed., *Wilford Woodruff's Journal*, 9 vols. [Midvale, Utah: Signature Books, 1983-85], 2:159-63)

The Speaker [Joseph Smith] read the 14 ch[apter]. Revelations, And sayes "we have again the warning voice sounded in our midst which shows the uncertainty of human life. And in my leisure moments I have meditated upon the subject, & asked the question[,] Why is it that infant innocent Children are taken away from us, esspecially those that seem to be most intelligent beings?"

Answer. "This world is a vary wicked world & it is a proverb that the world grow weaker & wiser, but if it is the case the world grows more wicked & corrupt. In the early ages of the world[,] A richeous man & a man of God & intelligence had a better chance to do good to be received & believed than at the present day. But in these days such a man is much opposed & persecuted by most of the inhabitants of the earth & he has much sorrow to pass through. Hence the Lord takes many away even in infancy that they may escape the envy of man, the sorrows & evils of this present world & they were two pure & to[o] lovly to live on Earth. Therefore if rightly considered, instead of morning we have reason to rejoice, as they are deliverd from evil & we shall soon have them again.

What chance is their for infidelity when we are parting with our friends almost daily? None at all. The infidel will grasp at evry straw for help untill death stares him in the face & then his infidelity takes its flight[;] for the realities of the eternal world are resting upon him in mighty power & when evry earthly support & prop fails him, he then sensibly feels the eternal truths of the immortality of the Soul.

Also the doctrin of Baptizing Children or sprinkling them or they must welter in Hell is a doctrin not true not supported in Holy writ & is not consistant with the character of God. The moment that Children leave this world they are taken to the bosom of Abraham. The ownly difference between the old & young dying is one lives longer in heaven & Eternal light & glory than the other & was freed a little sooner from this miserable wicked world. Notwithstanding all this glory we for a moment loose sight of it & mourn the loss but we do not mourn as those without hope.

(We should take warning & not wait for the death bed to repent.) As we see the infant taken away by death, so may the youth & middle aged as well as the infant suddenly be called into eternity. Let this then proove as a warning to all not to procrastinate repentance or wait till a death bed, for it is the will of God that man should repent & serve him in health & in the strength & power of his mind in order to secure his blessings & not wait untill he is called to die.

"My intention (says the speaker) was to have treated upon the subject of Baptism. But having a case of death before us, I thought it proper to refer to that subject. I will now however say a few words upon Baptism as intended.["]

God has made certain decreas which are fixed & unalterable. For instance God set the sun, the moon, the stars in the heavens, & [has] given them their laws conditions, & bounds which they cannot pass except by his command. They all move in perfect harmony in there sphere & order & are as wonders, lights & signs unto us. The sea also has its bounds which it cannot pass. God has set many signs in the earth as well as in heaven. For instance the oaks of the forest the fruit of the tree, the herd of the field all bear a sign that seed hath been planted there. For it is a decree of the Lord that evry tree fruit or herb bearing seed should bring forth after its kind & cannot Come forth after any other law or principle.

Upon the same principle do I contend that Baptism is a sign, ordained of God for the believer in Christ to take upon himself in order to enter into the kingdom of God. "For except you are born of the water & the spirit you cannot enter into the kingdom of God,["] saith the Savior. As It is a sign or command which God hath set for man to enter into this[,] those who seek to enter in any other way will seek in vain, for God will not receive them neither will the angels acknowledge their works as accepted, for they have not taken upon themselves those ordinances & signs which God ordained for man to receive in order to receive a celestial glory, & God has decreed that all who will not obey his voice shall not escape the damnation of hell. What is the damnation of hell? To go with that society who have not obeyed his commands.

Baptism is a sign to God, to Angels to heaven that we do the will of God & their is no other way beneath the heavens whareby God hath ordained for man to come & any other cource is in vain. God hath decreed & ordained that man should repent of all his sins & Be Baptized for the remission of his sins. Then he can come to God in the name of Jesus Christ in faith. Then we have the promise of the Holy Ghost.

What is the sign of the healing of the sick? The laying on of hands is the sign or way marked out by James & the custom of the ancient saints as ordered by the Lord & we Should not obtain the blessing by persuing any other course except the way which God has marked out.

What if we should attempt to get the Holy Ghost through any other means except the sign or way which God hath appointed? Should we obtain it? Certainly not. All other means would fail. The Lord says do so & so & I will bless so & so. Their is certain key words & signs belonging to the priesthood which must be observed in order to obtaine the Blessings.

The sign of Peter was, to repent & be baptized for the remission of Sins, with the promise of the gift of the Holy Ghost & in no other way is the gift of the Holy Ghost obtained.

Their is a difference between the Holy Ghost & the gift of the Holy Ghost. Cornelius received the Holy Ghost before he was Baptized which was the convincing power of God unto him of the truth of the gospel. But he could not receive the gift of the Holy Ghost untill after he was Baptized, & had he not taken this sign or [or]dinances upon him the Holy Ghost which convinced him of the truth of God would have left him untill he obeyed these ordinances & received the gift of the Holy Ghost by the laying on of hands according to the order of God. He could not have healed the sick or command an evil spirit to come out of a man & it obey him for the spirit might say to him as he did to the sons of Seavy[,] Peter I know & Christ I know but who are ye?

It matereth not whether we live long or short after we come to a knowledge of the principles & obey them. I know that all men will be damned if they do not come in the way which God has appointed.

As Concerning the resurrection I will merly say that all men will come from the grave as they lie down, whether old or young. Their will not be added unto ther stature one cubit neither taken from it All being raised by the power of God having the spirit of God in their bodies & not Blood. Children will be enthroned in the presence of

God & the Lamb with bodies of the same stature that were on earth. Having been redeemed by the Blood of the Lamb they will there enjoy a fulness of that light Glory & intelligence which is received in the celestial kingdom of God. "Blessed are the dead who die in the Lord, for they rest from their labours & their works do follow them.["]

{32}

"Happiness Is the Object
and Design of Our Existence,"
Joseph Smith to Nancy Rigdon, circa 11 April 1842

(from *Sangamo Journal* [Springfield, Illinois], 19 August 1842)

Happiness is the object and design of our existence, and will be the end thereof if we pursue the path that leads to it; and this path is virtue, uprightness, faithfulness, holiness, and keeping all the commandments of God. But we cannot keep all the commandments without first knowing them, and we cannot expect to know all, or more than we now know unless we comply with or keep those we have already received. That which is wrong under one circumstance, may be and often is, right under another. God said thou shalt not kill,— at another time he said thou shalt utterly destroy. This is the principle on which the government of heaven is conducted—by revelation adapted to the circumstances in which the children of the kingdom are placed. Whatever God requires is right, no matter what it is, although we may not see the reason thereof till long after the events transpire. If we seek first the kingdom of God, all good things will be added. So with Solomon—first he asked wisdom, and God gave it him, and with it every desire of his heart, even things which may be considered abominable to all who do not understand the order of heaven only in part, but which, in reality were right, because God gave and sanctioned by special revelation. A parent may whip a child, and justly too, because he stole an apple; whereas, if the child had asked for the apple, and the parent had given it, the child would have eaten it with a better appetite, there would have been no stripes—all the pleasures of the apple would have been received, all the misery of stealing lost. This principle will justly apply to all of God's dealings with his children. Everything that God gives us is lawful and right, and 'tis proper that we should enjoy his gifts and blessings whenever and wherever he is disposed to bestow; but if we should seize upon these same blessings and enjoyments without law, without revelation, without commandment, those blessings and enjoyments would prove cursings and vexations in the end, and we should have to go down in sorrow and wailings of everlasting regret. But in obedience there is joy and peace unspotted, unalloyed, and as God has designed our happiness, the happiness of all his creatures, he never has, he never will institute an ordinance, or give a commandment to his people that is not calculated in its nature to promote that happiness which he has designed, and which will not end in the greatest amount of good and glory to those who become the recipients of his laws and ordinances. Blessings offered, but rejected are no longer blessings, but become like the talent hid in the earth by the wicked and slothful servant—the proffered good returns of the giver, the blessing is bestowed on those who will receive, and occupy; for unto him that hath shall be given, and he shall have abundantly; but unto him that hath not, or will not receive, shall be taken away that which he hath, or might have had.

> "Be wise to-day, 'tis madness to defer.
> Next day the fatal precedent may plead;
> Thus on till wisdom is pushed out of time," Into eternity.

Our heavenly father is more liberal in his views, and boundless in his mercies and blessings, than we are ready to believe or receive, and at the same time is as terrible to the workers of iniquity, more awful in the executions of his punishments, and more ready to detect every false way than we are apt to suppose him to be. He will be enquired of by his children—he says ask and ye shall receive, seek and ye shall find; but if ye will take that which is not your own, or which I have not given you, you shall be rewarded according to your deeds, but no good thing will I withhold from them who walk uprightly before me, and do my will in all things, who will listen to my voice, and to the voice of my servant whom I have sent, for I delight in those who seek diligently to know my precepts, and abide by the laws of my kingdom, for all things shall be made known unto them in mine own due time, and in the end they shall have joy.

{33}

"Observations Respecting the Priesthood,"
A Sermon Delivered on 28 April 1842

(from the Minutes of the Nauvoo [Illinois] Relief Society,
original in archives, Historical Department,
Church of Jesus Christ of Latter-day Saints,
Salt Lake City, Utah)

President [Joseph] Smith arose and said that the purport of his being present on the occasion was, to make observations respecting the priesthood, and give instructions for the benefit of the Society that as his instructions were intended only for the Society; he requested that a vote should be taken on those present who were not members, to ascertain whether they should be admitted.— He exhorted the meeting to act honestly and uprightly in all their proceedings inasmuch as they would be call'd to give an account to Jehovah. All hearts must repent—be pure and God will regard them and bless them in a manner that could not be bless'd in any other way—

 . . . Prest. J[oseph]. Smith arose and call'd the attention of the meeting to the 12th chap of 1st Co[rinthians]. "Now concerning spiritual gifts" &C.— said that the passage which reads "No man can say that Jesus is the Lord but by the holy ghost," should be translated, No man can know &C.

He continued to read the Chap[ter] and give instructions respecting the different offices, and the necessity of every individual acting in the sphere allotted him or her; and filling the several offices to which they were appointed— Spoke of the disposition of man, to consider the lower offices in the church dishonorable and to look with jealous eyes upon the standing of others— that it was the nonsense of the human heart, for a person to be aspiring to other stations than appointed of God— that it was better for individuals to magnify their respective callings, and wait patiently till God shall say to them come up higher.

He said the reason of these remarks being made was, that some little things was circulating in the Society, that some persons were not going right in laying hands on the sick, &C. Said if he had common sympathies, would rejoice that the sick could be heal'd, that the time had not been before, that these things could be in their proper order— that the Church is not now organiz'd in its proper order, and cannot be until the Temple is completed. Prest. Smith continued the subject by adverting to the commission given to the ancient apostles "Go ye into all the world" &C. No matter who believeth; these signs such as healing the sick, casting out devils &C. Should follow all that believe whether male or female. He ask'd the Society if they could not see by this sweeping stroke that w[h]erein they are ordained, it is the privilege of those set apart to administer in that authority which is conferr'd on them— and if the sisters should have faith to heal the sick, let all hold their tongues, and let every thing roll on.

He said if God has appointed him, and chosen him as an instrument to lead the church, why not let him lead it through? why stand in the way when he is appointed to do a thing? Who knows the mind of God? Does he not reveal things differently from what we expect? He remarked that he was continually rising—altho' he had every thing bearing him down, standing in his way and opposing—after all he always comes out right in the end.

Respecting the females laying on hands, he further remark'd, there could be no devil in it if God gave his sanction by healing that there could be no more sin in any female laying hands on the sick than in wetting the face with water. It is no sin for any body to do it that has faith, or if the sick has faith to be heal'd by the administration.

He reproved those that were dispos'd to find fault with the management of concern saying that if he undertook to lead the church he would lead it right—that he calculat[e]s to organize the church in proper order &C.

President Smith continued by speaking of the difficulties he had to surmount ever since the commencement of the work in consequence of aspiring men, "great big Elders" as he called them who had caused him much trouble, whom he had taught in the private counsel; and they would go forth into the world and proclaim the things he had taught them as their own revelation— said the same aspiring disposition will be in this Society, and must be guarded against—that every person should stand and act in the place appointed, and thus sanctify the Society and get it pure—

He said he had been trampled under foot by aspiring Elders, for all were infected with that spirit, for instance P[arley]. Pratt O[rson].

Pratt, O[rson]. Hyde and J[ohn]. Page had been aspiring— They could not be exhalted but must run away as though the care and authority of the church were vested with them— He said we had a subtle devil to deal with and could only curb him by being humble.

He said as he had this opportunity, he was going to instruct the Society and point out the way for them to conduct, that they might act according to the will of God— that he did not know as he should have many opportunities of teaching them— that they were going to be left to themselve— they would not long have him to instruct them— that the church would not have his instruction long, and the world would not be troubled with him a great while, and would not have his teachings— He spoke of delivering the keys to this society and to the Church— that according to his prayers God had appointed him elsewhere.

He exhorted the sisters always to concentrate their faith and prayers for, and place confidence in those whom God has appointed to honor, whom God has plac'd at the head to lead— that we should arm them with our prayers— that the keys of the kingdom are about to be given to them, that they may be able to detect every thing false—as well as to the Elders.

He said if one member become corrupt and you know it; you must immediately put it away. The sympathies of the heads of the church have induc'd them to bear with those that were corrupt in consequence of which all become contaminated— you must put down iniquity and by your good example provoke the Elders to good works— if you do right no danger of going too fast; he said he did not care how fast we run in the path of virtue. Resist evil and there is no danger. God, man, angels and devils can't condemn those that resist every thing that is evil as well might the devil seek to dethrone Jehovah, as that soul that resists every thing that is evil.

The charitable Society—this is according to your natures—it is natural for females to have feelings of charity— you are now placed in a situation where you can act according to those sympathies which God has planted in your bosoms. If you live up to these principles how great and glorious— if you live up to your privilege the angels cannot be restrain'd from being your associates—

Females, if they are pure and innocent can come into the presence of God, for what is more pleasing to God than innocence; you must be innocent or you cannot come up before God. If we would come before

God let us be pure ourselves. The devil has great power— he will so transform things as to make one gape at those who are doing the will of God— You need not be teasing men for their deeds, but let the weight of innocence be felt which is more mighty than a millstone hung about the neck. Not war, not jangle, not contradiction, but meekness, love purity, these are the things that should magnify us. Action must be brough[t] to light— iniquity must be purged out— then the vail will be rent and the blessings of heaven will flow down— they will roll down like the Mississippi river. This Society shall have power to command Queens in their midst— I now deliver it as a prophecy that before ten years shall roll around, the queens of the earth shall come and pay their respects to this Society— they shall come with their millions and shall contribute of their abundance for the relief of the poor— If you will be pure, nothing can hinder.

After this instruction, you will be responsible for your own sins. It is an honor to save yourselves— all are responsible to save themselves.

Prest. Smith, after reading from the above mentioned chapter, Continued to give instruction respecting the order of God, as established in the church; saying every one should aspir[e] only to magnify his own office &C.

He then commenc'd reading the 13 chapter, "Though I speak, with the tongues of men" &C. and said don't be limited in your views with regard to your neighbors' virtues, but be limited towards your own virtues, and not think yourselves more righteous than others; you must enlarge your souls toward others if you [w]ould do like Jesus, and carry your fellow creatures to Abrams bosom. He said he had manifested long suffering and we must do so too— Prest. Smith then read, "Though I have the gift of prophecy" &C. He then said though one should become mighty— do great things— over turn mountains &C should then turn to eat and drink with the drunken; all former deeds would not save him— but he would go to destruction!

As you increase in innocence and virtue, as you increase in goodness, let your hearts expand— let them be enlarged towards others— you must be longsuffering and bear with the faults and errors of mankind. How precious are the souls of man! The female part of community are apt to be contracted, in their views. You must not be contracted but you must be liberal in your feelings.

Let this Society teach how to act towards husbands, to treat them with mildness and affection. When a man is borne down with trouble— when he is perplexed, if he can meet a smile, an argument— if he can meet with mildness, it will calm down his soul and smoothe his feelings. When the mind is going to despair it needs a solace.

This Society is to get instruction through the order which God has established— thro' the medium of those appointed to lead— and I now turn the key to you in the name of God and this Society shall rejoice and knowledge and intelligence shall flow down from this time— this is the beginning of better days to this Society.

When you go home never give a cross word, but let kindness, charity and love, crown your works henceforward. Don't envy sinners— have mercy on them, God will destroy them— Let your labors be confined mostly to those around you to your own circle, as far as knowledge is concerned, it may extend to all the world, but your administrations, should be confin'd to the circle of your immediate acquaintances and more especially to the members of the society.

Those ordain'd to lead the Society, are authoriz'd to appoint to different offices as the circumstances shall require.

If any have a matter to reveal, let it be in your own tongue. Do not indulge too much in the gift of tongues, or the devil will take advantage of the innocent. You may speak in tongues for your own comfort but I lay this down for a rule that if any thing is taught by the gift of tongues, it is not to be received for doctrine.

Prest. S[mith]. then offered instruction respecting the propriety of females administering to the sick by the laying on of hands— said it was according to revelation— &C. Said he never was placed in similar circumstances, and never had given the same instruction.

He clos'd his instruction by expressing his satisfaction in improving the opportunity.

{34}

"Verily Thus Saith the Lord, unto My Servant N[ewel]. K. Whitney" A Revelation to Newel K. Whitney, 27 July 1842, and Joseph Smith to Newel K. Whitney, Elizabeth Ann Whitney, and Sarah Ann Whitney, 18 August 1842

(from copies in archives, Historical Department, Church of Jesus Christ of Latter-day Saints, Salt Lake City, Utah)

Verily thus saith the Lord unto my servant N[ewel]. K. Whitney, the thing that my servant Joseph Smith has made known unto you and your Family [his plural marriage to Sarah Ann Whitney] and which you have agreed upon is right in mine eyes and shall be rewarded upon your heads with honor and immortality and eternal life to all your house both old & young because of the lineage of my Preast Hood saith the Lord it shall be upon you and upon your children after you from generation to generation, by virtue of the Holy promise which I now make unto you saith the Lord. These are the words which you shall pronounce upon my servant Joseph and your Daughter S[arah]. A[nn]. Whitney they shall take each other by the hand and you shall say you both mutually agree calling them by name to be each other's companion so long as you both shall live preserving yourselves for each other and from all others and also throughout all eternity reserving only those rights which have been given to my servant Joseph by revelation and commandment and by legal Authority in times passed. If you both agree to covenant and do this then I give you S[arah]. A[nn]. Whitney my Daughter to Joseph Smith to be his wife to observe all the rights between you both that belong to that condition. I do it in my own name and in the name of my wife your mother and in the name of my Holy Progenitors by the right of birth which is of Preast Hood vested in me by revelation and commandment and promise of the living God obtained by the Holy Melchisedeck Gethrow and other of the Holy Fathers commanding in the name of the Lord all those Powers to concentrate in you and through to your posterity forever all these things I do in the name of the Lord Jesus Christ that through this order he may be glorified and that through the power of anointing David may reign King over Israel which shall hereafter be revealed let immortality and eternal life henceforth be sealed upon your heads forever and ever.

≥≈

Dear, and Beloved, Brother
and Sister, Whitney, and &c.—

I take this oppertunity to communi[c]ate, some of my feelings, privetely at this time, which I want you three Eternaly to keep in your own bosams; for my feelings are so strong for you since what has pased lately between us, that the time of my abscence from you seems so long, and dreary, that it seems, as if I could not live long in this way: and if you three would come and see me in this my lonely retreat, it would afford me great relief, of mind, if those with whom I am alied, do love me, now is the time to afford me succour, in the days of exile, for you know I foretold you of these things. I am now at Carlos Graingers, Just back of Brother Hyrams farm, it is only one mile from town, the nights are very pleasant indeed, all three of you can come and See me in the fore part of the night, let Brother Whitney come a little a head, and nock at the south East corner of the house at the window; it is next to the cornfield, I have a room intirely by myself, the whole matter can be attended to with most perfect safty, I know it is the will of God that you should comfort me now in this time of afiliction, or not at [al]l[;] now is the time or never, but I hav[e] no kneed of saying any such thing, to you, for I know the goodness of your hearts, and that you will do the will of the Lord, when it is made known to you; the only thing to be careful of; is to find out when Emma [Smith] comes then you cannot be safe, but when she is not here, there is the most perfect safty: only be careful to escape observation, as much as possible, I know it is a heroick undertakeing; but so much the greater frendship, and the more Joy, when I see you I will tell you all my plans, I cannot write them on paper, burn this letter as soon as you read it; keep all locked up in your breasts, my life depends upon it. one thing I want to see you for it is to git the fulness of my blessings sealed upon our heads, &c. you will pardon me for my earnestness on this subject when you consider how lonesome I must be, your good feelings know how to make every allowance for me, I

166

close my letter, I think Emma [Smith, his first wife] wont come tonight[,] if she dont dont fail to come to night. I subscribe myself your most obedient, and affectionate, companion, and friend.

{35}

"Some Say the Kingdom of God Was Not Set upon Earth," A Sermon Delivered on 22 January 1843

(from Scott G. Kenney, ed., *Wilford Woodruff's Journal,* 9 vols., [Midvale, Utah: Signature Books, 1983-85], 2:213-17)

President Joseph Smith deliverd an interesting discourse at the Temple to a large congregation. Among other things he treated upon the kingdom of God & the baptism of John. He remarked some say the kingdom of God was not set up on earth untill the day of pentecost & that John did not preach the Baptism of repentance for the remission of sins. But I say in the name of the Lord that the kingdom of God was set upon earth from the days of Adam to the present time whenever there has been a righteous man on earth unto whom God revealed his word & gave power & authority to administer in his name:

And whare their is a Priest of God, A minister who has power & Authority from God to administer in the ordinances of the Gospel & officiate in the Priesthood of God, theire is the kingdom of God & in consequence of rejecting the gospel of Jesus Christ & the Prophets whom God hath sent, the judgments of God hath rested upon people, cities & nations in various ages of the world, which was the case with the cities of Sodom & gomoroah who were destroyed for rejecting the Prophets.

Now I will give my testimony. I care not for man. I speak boldly & faithfully & with authority. How is it with the kingdom of God? Whare did the kingdom of God begin? Whare their is no kingdom of God their is no salvation. What constitutes the kingdom of God? Whare there is a prophet, a priest, or a righteous man unto whom God gives his oracles there is the kingdom of God, & whare the oracles of God are not there the kingdom of God is not.

In these remarks I have no allusion to the kingdoms of the earth. We will keep the Laws of the Land. We do not speak against them. We never have & we can hardly make mention of the state of Missouri of our persecutions there &c but what the cry goes forth that we are guilty of larceny, Burglary, arson treason & murder &c &c which is fals. We speak of the kingdom of God on the earth not the kingdoms of men.

The plea of many in this day is that we have no right to receive revelations. But if we do not get revelations we do not have the oracles of God & if they have not the oracles of God they are not the people of God. But say you what will become of the world or the various professors of religion who do not believe in revelation & the oracles of God as continued to his Church in all ages of the world when he has a people on earth? I Tell you in the name of Jesus Christ they will be damned & when you get into the eternal world you will find it to be so. They cannot escape the damnation of hell.

As touching the gospel & Baptism that John preached I would say that John came preaching the gospel for the remission of Sins. He had his authority from God & the oricles of God were with him & the kingdom of [God] for a season seemed to be with John alone. The Lord promised Zecheriah that he should have a son, which was a desendant of Aaron & the Lord promised that the priesthood should continue with Aaron & his seed throughout their generations. Let No man take this honour upon himself except he be Called of God as was Aaron, & Aaron received his Call by Revelation. An angel of God Also appeared unto Zecheriah while in the Temple [and said] that he should have a son whose name should be John & he should be filled with the Holy Ghost. Zechariah was a priest of God & officiating in the Temple & John was a priest after his father & held the keys of the aronic priesthood & was Called of God to preache the Gospel & the kingdom of God[,] & the Jews as a nation having departed from the Law of God & the gospel[,] the Lord prepared the way for transfering it to the gentiles.

But says one the kingdom of God Could not be set up in the days of John for John said the Kingdom was at hand. But I would ask if it could be any nearer to them than to be in the hands of John. The people need not wait for the days of Pentecost to find the kingdom of God for John had it with him, & he came forth from the wilderness crying out repent ye for the kingdom of heaven is at hand as much as to bawl out[,] here[,] I have got the kingdom of God & I am coming after you. Ive got the kingdom of God & you can get it & I am Coming after you & if you dont receive it you will be damned & the Scriptures represent that all Jerrusalem went out unto Johns Baptism. Here was a legal administrator, & those that were baptized were subjects for a king & also the laws & oracles of God were there. Therefore the kingdom of God was there, for no man could have better authority to Administer than John & our Savior submitted to that authority himself by being Baptized By John. Therefore the kingdom of God was set up upon the earth even in the days of John. Their is a difference between the kingdom of God & the fruits & blessings that flow from that kingdom becaus their was more miracles, gifts, visions healings, tongues &c in the days of Jesus Christ & the Apostles & on the day of pentecost than under Johns Administration. It does not prove by any means that John had not the kingdom of God; any more than it would that a woman had not a milk pan because she had not a pan of milk. For while the pan might be Compared to the kingdom the milk might be Compared to the blessings of the kingdom.

John was a priest after the order of Aaron & had the keys of that priesthood & came forth preaching repentance & Baptism for the remission of sins but at the same time crys out there cometh one after me more mighter than I the latches of whose shoes I am not worthy to unlose, & christ came according to the words of John, & he was greater than John because he held the keys of Melchisedic Priesthood & the kingdom of God & had before revealed the priesthood to Moses. Yet christ was baptized by John to fulfill all righteousness & Jesus in his teaching says upon this rock I will build my Church & the gates of hell shall not prevail against it. What rock? Revelation.

Again he says except ye are born of the water & the spirit ye cannot inter into the kingdom of God, And though the heavens & earth should pass away my words shall not pass away. If a man is born of the water & the spirit he can get into the kingdom of God. It is evident the kingdom of God was on the earth & John prepared subject for kingdom by preaching the gospel to them & Baptising them & he prepared the way before the savior or came as a fore runner & prepared subject[s] for the preaching of Christ, & Christ preached through Jerrusalem on the same ground whare John had preached & when the Apostles were raised up they worked in Jerrusalem & Jesus commanded them to tarry there untill they were endowed with power from on high. Had they not work to do in Jerrusalem? They did work & prepared a people for the pentecost. The kingdom of God was with them before the day of pentecost as well as afterwords & it was also with John & he preached the same gospel & Baptism that Jesus & the Apostles preached after him.

The endowment was to prepare the desiples for their mission into the world. Whenever men can find out the will of God & find an Administrator legally authorized from God there is the kingdom of God. But whare these are not, the kingdom of God is not. All the ordinances Systems, & Administrations on the earth is of no use to the Children of men unless they are ordained & authorized of God for nothing will save a man but a legal Administrator for none others will be acknowledge[d] either by God or Angels.

I know what I say. I understand my mishion & business. God Almighty is my shield & what Can man do if God is my friend? I shall not be sacrafised untill my time comes. Then I shall be offered freely. All flesh is as grass & a governor is no better than other men. When he dies he is but a bag of dung.

I thank God for preserving me from my enemies. I have no enmity. I have no desire but to do all men good. I feel to pray for all men. We dont ask any people to throw away any good they have got. We ownly ask them to Come & get more. What if all the world should embrace this gospel? They would then see eye to eye & the blessings of God would Be poured out upon the people which is my whol[e] Soul ['s desire] Amen.

{36}

"I Was Once Praying Very Ernestly,"
Remarks Delivered on 2 April 1843

(from George D. Smith, ed.,
An Intimate Chronicle: The Journals of William Clayton
[Salt Lake City: Signature Books in association with
Smith Research Associates, 1991], pp. 95-98)

Joseph [Smith] preached on Revelations Chap[ter] 5. He called on me [William Clayton] to open the meeting. He also preached on the same subject in the evening.

During the day President Joseph made the following remarks on doctrine. "I was once praying very ernestly to know the time of the coming of the son of man when I heard a voice repeat the following. 'Joseph my son, if thou livest until thou art 84 years old thou shalt see the face of the son of man, therefore let this suffice and trouble me no more on this matter.' I was left thus without being able to decide w[h]ether this coming referred to the beginning of the Millenium, or to some previous appearing or w[h]ether I should die and thus see his face. I believe the coming of the son of man will not be any sooner than that time."

In correcting two points in Elder [Orson] Hydes discourse he observed as follows. "The meaning of that passage where it reads 'When he shall appear we shall be like him for we shall see him as he is' is this. When the savior appears we shall see that he is a man like unto ourselves, and that same sociality which exists amongst us here will exist among us there only it will be coupled with eternal glory which we do not enjoy now. Also the appearing of the father and the son in John c[hapter] 14 v[erse] 23 is a personal appearing and the idea that they will dwell in a mans heart is a sectarian doctrine and is false."

In answer to a question which I proposed to him as follows, "Is not the reckoning of gods time, angels time, prophets time and mans time according to the planet on which they reside[?"] he answered yes. "But there is no angel ministers to this earth[;] only what either does belong or has belonged to this earth and the angels do not reside on a planet like our earth but they dwell with God and the planet where he dwells is like crystal, and like a sea of glass before the throne. This is the great Urim and Thummim[;] whereon all things are manifest both things past, present and future and are continually before the Lord. The Urim and Thummim is a small representation of this globe. The earth when it is purified will be made like unto crystal and will be a Urim and Thummim whereby all things pertaining to an inferior kingdom on all kingdoms of a lower order will be manifest to those who dwell on it. And this earth will be with Christ. Then the white stone mentioned in Rev[elation] c[hapter] 2 v[erse] 17 is the Urim and Thummim whereby all things pertaining to an higher order of kingdoms even all kingdoms will be made known[;] and a white stone is given to each of those who come into this celestial kingdom whereon is a new name written which no man knoweth save he that receiveth it. The new name is the key word.

"Whatever principle of intelligence we obtain in this life will rise with us in the resurrection: and if a person gains more knowledge in this life through his diligence and obedience than another, he will have so much the advantage in the world to come. There is a law irrevocably decreed in heaven before the foundation of this world upon which all blessings are predicated; and when we obtain any blessing from God, it is by obedience to that law upon which it is predicated.

"The Holy Ghost is a personage, and a person cannot have the personage of the H[oly] G[host] in his heart. A man receive the gifts of the H[oly] G[host] and the H[oly] G[host] may descend upon a man but not to tarry with him."

He also related the following dream. "I dreamed that a silver-headed old man came to see me and said he was invaded by a gang of robbers, who were plundering his neighbors and threatening destruction to all his subjects. He had heard that I always sought to defend the oppressed, and he had come to hear with his own ears what answer I would give him. I answered, if you will make out the papers and shew that you are not the aggressor I will call out the [Nauvoo] Legion and defend you while I have a man to stand by me. The old man then turned to go away. When he got a little distance he turned suddenly round and said I must call out the Legion and go and he would have the papers ready when I arrived, and says he I have any amount of men which you can have under your command. . . .["]

Once when President Joseph was praying ernestly to know concerning the wars which are to preceed the coming of the son of man, he heard a voice proclaim that the first outbreak of general bloodshed would commence at South Carolina (see Revelation [D&C 87]).

The sealing of the 144,000 was the number of priests who should be anointed to administer in the daily sacrifice &c. During President Joseph's remarks he said there was a nice distinction between the vision which John saw as spoken of in Revelations and the vision which Daniel saw, the former relating only to things as they actually existed in heaven, the latter being a figure representing things on the earth. God never made use of the figure of a beast to represent the kingdom of heaven, when they were made use of it was to represent an apostate church.

"I Have Three Requests to Make
of the Congregation,"
A Sermon Delivered on 8 April 1843

(from a manuscript by William Clayton,
original in archives, Historical Department,
Church of Jesus Christ of Latter-day Saints,
Salt Lake City, Utah)

Pres't Joseph [Smith] called upon the choir to sing a him [hymn] and remarked that "tenor charms the ear—bass the heart." After sing[ing] the President spoke in substance as follows.

I have three requests to make of the congregation the first is that all who have faith will exercise it, that the Lord may be willing to calm the wind. The next is, that I may have your prayers that the Lord may strengthen my lungs so that, I may be able to make you all hear. And the next is, that I may have the Holy Ghost to rest upon me so as to enable me to declare those things that are true.

The subject I intend to speak upon this morning is one that I have seldom touched upon since I commenced as an Elder of the Church. It is a subject of great speculation as well amongst the Elders of the church as amongst the divines of the day; it is in relation to the beast spoken of in Revelations. The reason why it has been a subject of speculation amongst the Elders, is in consequence of a division of sentiment and opinion in relation to it. My object is to do away with this difference of opinion. To have knowledge in relation to the meaning of beasts and heads and horns and other figure[s] made use of in the revelations is not very essential to the Elders. If we get puffed up by thinking that we have much knowledge, we are apt to get a contentious spirit, and knowledge is necessary to do away [with] contention. The evil of being puffed up is not so great as the evil of contention. Knowledge does away darkness, su[s]pense and doubt, for where Knowledge is there is no doubt nor suspense nor darkness. There is no pain so awful as the pain of suspense. This is the condemnation of the wicked; their doubt and anxiety and suspense causes weeping, wailing and gnashing of teeth. In knowledge there is power. God has more power than all other beings, because he has greater Knowledge, and hence he knows how to subject all other beings to him. I will endeavour to instruct you in relation to the meaning of the beasts and figures spoken of. E[lde]r (Pelatiah) Browns has been the cause of this subject being now presented before you. He, one of the wisest old heads we have among us, has been called up before the High Council on account of the beast. The old man has preached concerning the beast which was full of eyes before and behind and for this he was hauled up for trial. I never thought it was right to call up a man and try him because he erred in doctrine, it looks too much like methodism and not like Latter day Saintism. Methodists have creeds which a man must believe or be kicked out of their church. I want the liberty of believing as I please, it feels so good not to be tramelled. It dont prove that a man is not a good man, because he errs in doctrine. The High Council undertook to censure and correct E[lde]r Brown because of his teachings in relation to the beasts, and he came to me to know what he should do about it. The subject particularly referred to, was the four beasts and four and twenty Elders mentioned in Rev. ch[apter] 5 v. 8. The old man has confounded all Christendom by speaking out that the four beasts represented the Kingdom of God; the wise men of the day could not do any thing with him, and why should we find fault, anything to whip sectarianism and put down priestcraft; a club is better than no weapon for a poor man to fight with, but I could not keep laughing at the idea of God making use of the figure of a beast to represent the Kingdom of God on the earth, when he could as well have used a far more noble and consistent figure. What? The Lord make use of the figure of a creature of the brute creation to represent that which is much more noble and important. The glories of his Kingdom? You missed it that time, old man, but the sectarians did not know enough to detect you.

When God made use of the figure of a beast in visions to the prophets, he did it to represent those Kingdoms who had degenerated and become corrupt—the Kingdoms of the world, but he never made use of the figure of a beast nor any of the brute kind to represent his kingdom. Daniel says when he saw the vision of the four beasts "I came near unto one of them that stood by, and asked him the truth of all this." The angel interpreted the vision to Daniel, but we find by the interpretation that the figures of beasts had no allusion to the Kingdom of God.

You there see that the beasts are spoken of to represent the Kingdoms of the world the inhabitants whereof were beastly and abominable characters, they were murderous, corrupt, carnivourous and brutal in their dispositions. I make mention of the prophets to qualify my declaration which I am about to make so that the young Elders who know so much may not rise up and choke me like hornets. There is a grand difference and distinction between the visions and figures spoken of by the prophets and those spoken of in the Revelations of John. None of the things John saw had any allusion to the scenes of the days of Adam or of Enoch or of Abraham or Jesus, only as far as is plainly represented by John and clearly set forth. John only saw that which was "shortly to come to pass" and that which was yet in futurity (He read Rev. ch. 1 v. 1)[.] Now I make this declaration, that those things which John saw in heaven, had no allusion to any thing that had been on the earth, because John says "he saw what was shortly to come to pass" and not what had already transpired. John saw beasts that had to do with things on the earth, but not in past ages; the beasts which he saw had to devour the inhabitants of the earth in days to come. The revelations do not give us to understand any thing of the past in relation to the Kingdom of God. What John saw and speaks of were things which were in heaven, what the prophets saw and speak of where things pertaining to the earth. I am now going to take exception to the present translation of the bible in relation to these matters. There is a grand distinction between the actual meaning of the Prophets and the Present translation. The Prophets do not declare that the[y] saw a beast or beasts, but that the[y] saw the image or figure of a beast. They did not see an actual bear or Lion but the images or figures of those beasts. The translation should have been rendered "image" instead of "beast" in every instance where beasts are mentioned by the Prophets. But John saw the actual beast in heaven, to show to John [they] did actually exist there. When the Prophets speak of seeing beasts in their visions, they saw the images; types to represent certain things and at the same time they received the interpretation as to what those images or types were designed to represent. I make this broad declaration, that where God ever gives a vision of an image, or beast or figure of any kind he always holds himself responsible to give a revelation or interpretation of the meaning thereof, otherwise we are not responsible or accountable for our belief in it. Dont be afraid of being damned for not knowing the meaning of a vision or figure where God has not given a revelation or interpretation on the subject (He here read Rev. ch 5 v 11 to 13)[.] John saw curious

177

looking beasts in heaven, he saw every creature that was in heaven, all the beasts, fowls, & fish in heaven, actually there, giving glory to God. I suppose John saw beings there, that had been saved from ten thousand times ten thousand earths like this, strange beasts of which we have no conception all might be seen in heaven. John learned that God glorified himself by saving all that his hands had made whether beasts, fowl fishes or man. Any man who would tell you that this could not be, would tell you that the revelations are not true. John heard the words of the beasts giving glory to God and understood them. God who made the beasts could understand every language spoken by them; the beasts were intelligent beings and were seen and heard by John praising and glorifying God.

The popular religionsts of the day say that the beasts spoken of in the revelations represent Kingdoms. Very well, on the same principle we can say that the twenty four Elders spoken of represent beasts, for they are all spoken of at the same time, and represented as all uniting in the same acts of praise and devotion. Deacon Homespun said the earth was flat as a pan cake, but science has proved to the contrary. The world is full of technicalities and misrepresentation, but I calculate to overthrow the technicalities of the world and speak of things as they actually exist. Again there is no revelation to prove that things do not exist in heaven as I have set forth, and we never can comprehend the things of God and of heaven but by revelation. We may spiritualize and express opinions to all eternity but that is no authority.

Ye Elders of Israel hearken to my voice and when ye are sent into the world to preach, preach and cry aloud "repent ye for the Kingdom of heaven is at hand repent and believe the gospel." Never meddle with the visions of beasts and subjects you do not understand. E[lde]r Brown when you go to Palmyra dont say any thing about the beast, but preach those things the Lord has told you to preach about, repentance and baptism for the remission of sins.

(He here read Rev. ch 13 v 1 to 8.) The spiritualizers say the beast that received the wound was Nebuchadnezzar, but we will look at what John saw in relation to this beast. The translators have used the term "dragon" for "devil". Now it was a beast that John saw in heaven, and he was then speaking of "things that were shortly to come to pass." And consequently the beast John saw could not be Nebuchadnezzar. The beast John saw was an actual beast to whom power was to be given. An actual intelligent being in heaven and this beast

178

was to have power given him. John saw "one of the heads of the beast as it were wounded to death; and his deadly wound was healed; and all the world wondered after the beast." Nebuchadnezzar and Constantine the great not excepted; it must have been a wonderful beast that all human beings wondered after it, and I will venture to say that when God gives power to the beast to destroy the inhabitants of the earth, all will wonder. Verse 4 reads "And they worshipped the dragon which gave power unto the beast; and they worshipped the beast saying, who is like unto the beast? who is able to make war with him?["] Some say it means the kingdom of the world. One thing is sure, it dont mean the kingdoms of the saints. Suppose we admit that it means the kingdoms of the world, what propriety would there be in saying who is able to make war with myself. If these spiritualizing interpretations are true, the book contradicts itself in almost every verse, but they are not true. There is a mistranslation of the word dragon in the second verse. The original hebrew word signifies the devil and not dragon as translated. Read ch 12 v 9[,] it there reads "that, old serpent called the devil,["] and it, ought to be translated devil in this case and not dragon. Everything that we have not a key word to[,] we will take it as it reads. The beasts which John saw and speaks of as being in heaven were actually living in heaven, and were actually to have power given to them over the inhabitants of the earth precisely according to the plain reading of the revelations. I give this as a key to the Elders of Israel.

{38}

"There Were Some People Who Thought
It a Terrible Thing that Any Body
Should Exercise a Little Power,"
A Sermon Delivered on 21 May 1843

(from Scott H. Faulring, ed., *An American Prophet's Record:
The Diaries and Journals of Joseph Smith*
[Salt Lake City: Signature Books in association
with Smith Research Associates, 1987], pp. 378-80)

Joseph [Smith] arrived and after pressing his way through the crowd
and getting on the stand said there were some people who thought it
a terrible thing that any body should exercise a little power. [He] said
he thought it a pity that any body should give occasion to have power
exercised.

[Joseph] requested the people to get out of their alleys and if they
did not keep them clear he might some time run up and down and
might hit some of them and called on Bro[ther] Morey to constable to
keep the alleys clear. After singing Joseph read 1st chap[ter] 2d Epistle
of Peter. . . .

When I shall have the opportunity of speaking in a house I know
not. I find my lungs failing. It has always been my fortune almost to
speak in the open air to large assemblies.

I have not an idea there has been a great many very good men
since Adam. There was one good man, Jesus. Many think a prophet
must be a great deal better than any body else. Suppose I would
condescend. Yes, I will call it condescend to be a great deal better than
any of you, I would be raised up to the highest heaven, and who
should I have to accompany me. I love that man better who swears a
stream as long as my arm and [is attentive to] administering to the poor
and dividing his substance, than the long smoothed faced hypocrites.

I don't want you to think I am very righteous, for I am not very
righteous. God judgeth men according to the light he gives them. We
have a more sure word of prophecy, where unto you [would] do well
to take heed, as unto a light that shineth in a dark place.

We were eyewitnesses of his majesty and heard the voice of his excellent glory, and what could be more sure? Transfigured on the mount &c. and what could be more sure? Divines have been quarreling for ages about the meaning of this.

[I am like a] Rough stone rol[l]ing down [a] hill.

Three grand secrets [are] lying in this chapter [2 Peter 1] which no man can dig out which unlocks the whole chapter. What is written are only hints of things which existed in the prophet's mind which are not written concerning eternal glory.

I am going to take up this subject by virtue of the knowledge of God in me which I have received from heaven.

The opinions of men, so far as I am concerned, are to me as the crackling of the thorns under the pot, or the whistling of the wind.

Columbus and the eggs. Ladder and rainbow. Like precious faith with us. Add to your faith, virtue, &c. Another point after having all these qualifications he lays this inju[nc]tion, but rather make your calling and election sure. After adding all this virtue, knowledge, and make your calling sure. What is the secret? The starting point? According as his divine power which [he] hath given unto all things that pertain to life and Godliness.

How did he obtain all things? Through the knowledge of him who hath called him. There could not any[thing] be given pertaining to life and Godliness without knowledge.

Wo, wo, wo to Christendom, the divine spirits, &c. If this be true, *Salvation* is for a man to be saved from all his enemies. Until a man can triumph over death he is not saved. Knowledge will do this.

Organization of spirits in the Eternal World. Spirits in the Eternal world are like spirits in this world. When those spirits have come into this [world] risin and received glorified bodies, they will have an ascendency over spirits who have no bodies, or kept not their first estate like the devil. Devil's punishment, should not have a habitation like the other men. Devil's retaliation [was to] come into this world, bind up men's bodies and occupy [them] himself. Authorities come along and eject him from a stolen habitation.

Design of the Great God in sending us into this world and organizing us to prepare us for the Eternal World. I shall keep [my spirit] in my own bosom. We have no claim in our eternal comfort in relation to Eternal things unless our actions and contracts and all things tend to this end.

After all this make your calling and election sure. If this in-juncti[o]n would lay largely on those to whom it was spoken, [then] How much more there [is in this] to them of the 19[th] century.

1[st] Key—Knowledge in the power of Salvation.

2[nd] Key—Make his calling and Election sure.

3[rd] It is one thing to be on the mount and hear the excellent voice &c., &c. and another to hear the voice declare to you, "You have a part and lot in the kingdom."

{39}

"How Oft Would I Have Gathered You Together," A Sermon Delivered on 11 June 1843

(from Scott G. Kenney, ed., *Wilford Woodruff's Journal,*
9 vols. [Midvale, Utah: Signature Books, 1983-85], 2:240-42)

A large assembly of Saints met at the Temple & were addressed by president Joseph Smith. He took for the foundation of his discourse the words of Jesus to the Jews how oft would I have gathered you together as a hen gathereth her chickens under wings But ye would not &c.

He then asked what was the object of Gathering the Jews together or the people of God in any age of the world. The main object was to build unto the Lord an house whereby he Could reveal unto his people the ordinances of his house and glories of his kingdom & teach the people the ways of salvation. For their are certain ordinances & principles that when they are taught and practized, must be done in a place or house built for that purpose. This was purposed in the mind of God before the world was & it was for this purpose that God designed to gather together the Jews oft but they would not. It is for the same purpose that God gathers together the people in the last days to build unto the Lord an house to prepare them for the ordinances & endowments washings & anointings &c.

One of the ordinances of the house of the Lord is Baptism for the dead. God decreed before the foundation of the world that that ordinance should be administered in a house prepared for that purpose. If a man gets the fulness of God he has to get [it] in the same way that Jesus Christ obtained it & that was by keeping all the ordinances of the house of the Lord.

Men will say I will never forsake you, but will stand by you at all times. But the moment you teach them some of the mysteries of God that are retained in the heavens and are to be revealed to the children of men when they are prepared, They will be the first to stone you & put you to death. It was the same principle that crusified the Lord Jesus Christ.

I will say something about the spirits in prision. Their has been much said about the sayings of Jesus on the cross to the thief saying this day thou shalt be with me in paradise. The commentators or translators make it out to say Paradise. But what is Paradise? It is a modern word. It does not answer at all to the original that Jesus made use of. Their is nothing in the original in any language that signifies Paradise. But it was this day I will be with thee in the world of spirits & will teach thee or answer thy inquiries. The thief on the Cross was to be with Jesus Christ in the world of spirits. He did not say Paradise or heaven.

The doctrin of Baptism for the dead is clearly shown in the new testament. And if the doctrin is not good then throw away the new testament. But if it is the word of God then let the doctrin be acknowledged & it was one reason why Jesus said how oft would I have gathered you (the Jews) together that they might attend to the ordinance of the baptism for the dead as well as the other ordinances, the Priesthood Revelations &c. This was the case on the day of Pentecost. These Blessings were poured out upon the deciples on that occasion.

Their has been Also much said about the word Hell & the sectarian world have preached much about it. But what is hell? It is annother modern term. It is taken from hades the greek or shaole, the (hebrew) & the true signification is a world of spirits.

Hades shaole paradise, spirits in prison is all one. It is a world of spirits. The righteous & the wicked all go to the same world of spirits. But says one I believe in one hell & one heaven. All are equally miserable or equally happy. But St Paul informs us of three glories & three heavens. He knew a man caught up to the third heavens, & Jesus said their were many mansions in my Fathers kingdom.

Any man may believe Jesus Christ is good & be happy in it & yet not obey his commands & at last be cut down by his righteous commandments. A man of God should be endowed with all wisdom knowledge & understanding in order to teach & lead people. The blind may lead the blind & both fall into the death together.

Their is much said concerning God the Godhead &c. The scripture says their is Gods many & Lords many. The teachers of the day say that the father is God the Son is God & the Holy Ghost is God & that they are all in one body & one God. Jesus says or prays that those that the father had given him out of the world might be made one in us as we are one. But if they were to be stuffed into one person they would make a great God.

184

If I were to testify that the world was wrong on this point it would be true. Peter says that Jesus Christ sat on the right hand of God. Any person that has seen the heavens opened knows that their is three personages in the heavens holding the keys of power. As the father hath power in himself so the Son hath power in himself. Then the father has some day laid down his body & taken it again. So he has a bo[d]y of his own. So has his Son a body of his own. So each one will be in their own body.

Many of the sects cry out O I have the testimony of Jesus. I have the spirit of God. But away with Jo Smith. He says he is a Prophet But their is to be no Prophets nor revelations in the last days; But stop sir the Revelator says that the testimony of Jesus is the spirit of Prophecy. So by your own mouth you are condemned.

But to the text. Why gather the people together in this place? For the same purpose that Jesus wanted to gather the Jews. To receive the ordinances, the blessings & the glories that God has in store for his Saints. And I would now ask this assembly and all the Saints if they will now build this house & receive the ordinances & Blessings which God has in store for you, or will you not build unto the Lord this house & let him pass by & bestow these blessings upon another? I pause for a reply.

40

"I Require Attention,"
A Sermon Delivered on 30 June 1843

(from Scott G. Kenney, ed., *Wilford Woodruff's Journal,*
9 vols. [Midvale, Utah: Signature Books, 1983-85], 2:248-55)

I require attention. I discoverd what the emotions of the people were
on my arival to this city [after being arrested, taken away, and then
returned], & I have come here to say how do you do to all parties & I
do now say How do you do at this time. I meet you with a heart full
of gratitude to Almighty God & I presume you all feel the same. I hardly
know how to express my feelings. I feel as strong as a Giant. I pulled
sticks with the men Coming along & I pulled up the strongest man
theire was on the road with one hand & two could not pull me up &
I continued to pull untill I pulled them to Nauvoo. I will pass from
that subject then.

There has been great excitement in the country & since those
men took me I have been cool & dispassionate through the whole:
thank God I am now in the hands of the Municipal Court of Nauvoo
& not in the hands of Missourians.

It has been discussed by the great & wise men lawyiers &c. O your
Powers & legal tribunals are not to be sanctioned & here we will [not]
make it lawful to drag away inocent men from their families & friends &
have them unlawfully put to death by ungodly men for ther religion.

Relative to our [Nauvoo City] Charter court[']s right of Habeas
Corpus &c we have all power: And if any man from this time forth
says any thing contrary, cast it into his teeth. Their is a secret in this; if
their is not power in our Charter and Courts, then there is not power
in the State of Illinois, nor in the Congress or Constitution of the
United States. For the United States gave unto Illinois her constitution
& Charter & Illinois gave unto Nauvoo her Charters which have
ceded unto us our vested rights & has no right or power to take them
from us. All the power their was in Illinois she gave to Nauvoo. And
any man that says to the contrary is a fool.

I want you to learn O Israel what is for the happiness & peace of this city & people. If our enemies are determined to oppress us & deprive us of our rights & privileges as they have done & if the Authorities that be on the earth will not assist us in our rights nor give us that protection which the Laws & Constitution of the United States & of this State garrentees unto us: then we will claim them from higher power from heaven & from God Almighty & the Constitution &c. I SWEAR I will not deal so mildly with them again for the time has come when forbearance is no longer a virtue. And if you are again taken unlawfully you are at liberty to give loose to Blood and Thunder. But act with Almighty Power.

But good luck for me as it always has been in evry time of trouble. Friends though strangers were raised up unto me & assisted me. The time has come when the veil is torn of[f] from the State of Illinois & they have deliverd me from the State of Missouri: friends that were raised up unto me would have spilt their Blood for me to have delivered me. Then I told them not. I would be delivered By the power of God & Generalship & I have brought them to Nauvoo & treated them kindly. I have had the privilege of rewarding them good for evil. They took me unlawfully treated me rigorously, strove to deprive me of my rights & would have run me to Missouri to have been murdered if providence had not interposed: but now they are in my hands. I took them into my house set them at the head of my table & set the best before them my house afforded & they were waited upon by my wife whome they deprived of seeing me when I was taken.

I shall be discharged by the Municipal Court of Nauvoo. Were I before any good tribunal I should be discharged. But Befor I will bear this unhallowed persecution any longer I will spill my Blood. Their is a time when bearing it longer is a sin. I will not bear it longer. I will spil the last drop of Blood I have and all that will not bear it longer say AH. And the cry of AH rung throughout the Congregation.

We must stop paying the lawyiers money. For I have learned they dont know any thing. For I know more than they all. Whosoever believeth that there is power in the Charters of Nauvoo shall be saved. He that believeth not shall not come here. If a lawyer shall say their is more power in other places & Charters than in Nauvoo believeth it not. I have converted this canditate for congress Mr Walker. I suppose when I see him Converted I will vote for him & not before. I have been with these lawyers & they have treated me well. But I am here in Nauvoo & the Missourian[s] to[o] & when they will get out I dont know perhaps when some others may.

However you may feel about the high hand of oppression, I wish you to restrain your hand from violence against these men who arestd me. My word is at stake. A hair of their heads shall not be harmed.

My life is pledged to carry out this great work. I know how readily you are to do right. You have done great things & manifested your love in flying to my assistance on this occasion. I could not have done better myself. And I Bless you in the name of the Lord with all Blessings. May you not have to suffer as you have heretofore. I know the Almighty will bless all good men. He will bless you: and the time has come when their shall be such a flocking to the standard of Liberty as never has been Nor never shall be hereafter.

What an erie [array] of things has commenced. Shall the Prophecys be esstablished by the Swords? Shall we allways bear? NO. Will not the State of Missouri stay her hand and in her unhallowed persecutions against the Saints? If not, I restrain you not any longer. I say in the name of Jesus Christ I this day turn the key that opens the heavens to restrain you no longer from this time forth. I will lead you to battle & if you are not afraid to die & feel disposed to spill your Blood in your own defence you will not offend me. Be not the aggressor. Bear untill they strike on the one cheek. Offer the other & they will be sure to strike that. Then defend yourselves & God shall bear you off.

Will any part of Illinois say we shall not have our rights? Treat them as strangers & not friends & let them go to Hell. Say some we will mob you. Mob & be damned: If I [am] under the necessity of giving up our charted rights, privileges & freedom which our fathers fought bled & died for & which the constitution of the United States & this State garrentee unto us, I will do it at the point of the Bayonet & Sword.

Many Lawyiers contend for those thing[s] which are against the rights of men & I can ownly excuse them because of ther ignorance. Go forth & Advocate the laws & rights of the people ye lawyiers. If not dont get into my hands or under the lash of my tongue.

Lawyiers say the powers of the Nauvoo Charters are dangerous. But I ask is the constitution of the United States or of this State dangerous? No. Neither are the charters granted unto Nauvoo by the legislator of Illinois dangerous & those that say they are are fools. We have not our rights. Those which the constitution of the U.S.A. grant & which our Charters grant we have not enjoyed unmolested. Missouri & all wicked men will raise the hugh & cry against us and are not satisfyed.

But how are you going to help yourselves? What will mobocrats do in the midst of this people? If mobs come upon you any more here, dung your gardings [gardens] with them. But says one you will get up excitement. We will get up no excitement except what we can find an escape from. We will rise up Washington like & break of the wait [weight] that bears us down & we will not be mobed.

To give you an account of my Journey, I will give you an anecdote that may be pleasing. A day before I was taken I rode with my wife through a Neighborhood to visit some friends & I said to Mrs Smith here is a good people. I felt this by the spirit of God. The next day I was in their hands a prisioner with Wilson who Said as he drove up ha ha ha By God we have got the prophet. He gloried much in it But he is now our prisioner.

When Reynolds of Missouri & Wilson of Carthage came to take me the first salutation was (instead of taping me on the shoulder & saying you are my prisioner) with two Cocked pistols to my head God damn you I will shoot you. I will shoot you God damn you I will shoot you nearly 50 times first & last[.] I asked them what they wanted to shoot me for. If you make any resistance. O vary well says I[,] I have no resistance to make.

They then dragged me away & while on the road I asked them by what authority they did these things. They said by a writ from the Governors of Missouri & Illinois. I then told them I wanted a writ of Habeas Corpus. The reply was God damn you you shant have it. I told a man to Go to Dixon & get me a writ of Habeas Corpus. The reply was by Willson. God dam you you shant have it. I will shoot you. I sent for a lawyier to come. One came & Reynolds shut the door in his face & would not let me speak to him & said again God damn you I will shoot you. I turned to him opened my bosom & told him to shoot away & I did it freequently. I told Mr Reynolds that I would have council to speak to & the Lawyers came to me & I got a writ of Habeas Corpus for myself & got a writ for Reynolds & Wilson for unlawful procedings towards me & cruel treatment. They Could not get out of town that night. I pleged my honor to my council that the Nauvoo Charter had power to investigate the subject & we came to Nauvoo by common consent & I am now a prisoner of higher authority. Yes higher Authority before yourselves.

The Charter expressly says that the City Council shall have power to enact all laws for the benefit & convenience of said City not contrary to the Constitutions of the United States or of this State & the City ordinance says the Municipal Court shall have power to give writs of Habeas Corpus arising under the ordinances of the City. Their is nothing but what we have power over excepted restricted by the constitution of the United States or of this state. It is in accordance wi[t]h the constitution of the U.S.A.

But says the mob what dangerous powers. But the constitution of the United States nor of this state is not dangerous against good men but bad men the breakers of the law. So with the laws of the country & so with the laws of Nauvoo. They are dangerous to mobs but not good men that wish to keep the law.

We do not go out of Nauvoo to disturb any body or any city town or place. Why need they be troubled about us? Let them not meddle with our affairs but let us alone. After we have been deprived of our rights & privileges as citizenship driven from town to town place to place state to state with the sacrifice of our homes & lands & our Blood been shed & many murdered & all this becaus of our religion because we worship Almighty God according to the dictates of our own consience. Shall we longer bear these cruelties which have been bearing upon us for the last ten years in the face of heaven & in open violation of the constitution & laws of these United States & of this State? May God forbid. I will not bear it. If they take away my rights I will fight for my rights, manfully & Righteously untill I am used up with Blood & thunder sword & pistol. We have done nothing against law or right.

As touching our City Charter & laws their is a secret in it. What is it? Our laws go behind the writ & investigate the subject ie of Habeas Corpus while other laws do not go behind the writ. You speak of Lawyiers, I am a Lawyier to[o] But the Almighty God has taught me the principle of law & the true meaning of the writ of Habeas Corpus is to defend the Innocent & investigat the subject. Go behind the writ & if the form of a writ is wright that is issued against an innocent man He should not be dragged to another state & there put to death or in jeapordy life or limb because of prejudice when he is innocent. The benefits of the constitution & law is for all alike & the great [E]loheem God has given me the privilege of having the benefits of the constitution & the writ of Habeas Corpus & I am bold to ask for this privilege this day & to ask you to carry out this privilege principle. And all who are in favor of carrying out this great principle make it manifest by raising the right hand & their was a sea of hands A universal vote. Here is truly the Committy of the whole.

In speaking of my Journey to Nauvoo I will relate a circumstance. When Mr Cyrus Walker first came to me they said I should not speak to any man & they would shoot any man that should speak to me. An old man came up & said I should have council & said he was not afraid of their pistols & they took me from him, & I had an opportunity to have killed him but I had no temptation to do it to him nor any other man, my worst enemy not even Boggs. In fact he would have more hell to live in the reflection of his past life than to die. My freedom commenced from the time the old man came to me & would talk to me. We came direct from Papa grove to Nauvoo. We got our writ directed to the nearest court having authority to try the case & we came to Nauvoo.

It did my soul good to see your feelings & love manifest towards me. I thank God that I have the honor to lead so virtuous & honest a people to be your leader & lawyier as Moses to the children of Israel. Hosannah Hosannah Hosannah Hosannah to the name of the Most High God. I commend you to his grace & may the Blessings of heaven rest upon you in the name of Jesus Christ Amen.

Furthermore if Missouri continues her warfare & continues to Issue her writs against me & this people unlawfully & unjustly as they have done & our rights are trampled upon & they take away my rights I sware with uplifted hands to Heaven I will spill my Blood in its defence. They shall not take away our rights, & if they dont stop leading me by the nose I will lead them by the nose & if they dont let me alone I will turn up the world. I will make war.

When we shake our own bushes we want to ketch our own fruit. The Lawyiers themselves acknowledge that we have all power granted us in our Charters that we Could ask for, that we had more power than any other court in the state for all other courts were restricted while ours was not & I thank God Almighty for it & I will not be rode down to Hell by the Missourians any longer, & it is my privilege to speak in my own defence & appeal to your honor.

41

"The Principle and Doctrine
of Having Many Wives and Concubines,"
A Revelation to Joseph Smith, Jr., 12 July 1843

(from *Deseret News Extra,*
[Great Salt Lake City, Utah Territory]
14 September 1852, pp. 25-27)

Verily thus saith the Lord, unto you my servant Joseph, that inasmuch as you have Enquired of my hand, to know and understand wherein I the Lord justified my servants Abraham, Isaac, and Jacob; as also Moses, David, and Solomon, my servants, as touching the principle and doctrine of their having many wives, and concubines: Behold! and lo, I am the Lord thy God, and will answer thee as touching this matter. Therefore, prepare thy heart to receive and obey the instructions which I am about to give unto you; for all those, who have this law revealed unto them, must obey the same; for behold! I reveal unto you a new and an everlasting covenant, and if ye abide not that covenant, then are ye damned; for no one can reject this covenant, and be permitted to enter into my glory; for all who will have a blessing at my hands, shall abide the law which was appointed for that blessing, and the conditions thereof, as was instituted from before the foundations of the world: and as pertaining to the new and everlasting covenant, it was instituted for the fulness of my glory; and he that receiveth a fulness thereof, must, and shall abide the law, or he shall be damned, saith the Lord God.

And verily I say unto you, that the conditions of this law are these: All covenants, contracts, bonds, obligations, oaths, vows, perform-ances, connections, associations, or expectations, that are not made, and entered into, and sealed, by the Holy Spirit of promise, of him who is anointed, both as well for time and for all eternity, and that too most holy, by revelation and commandment, through the medium of mine anointed, whom I have appointed on the earth to hold this power, (and I have appointed unto my servant Joseph to hold this power in the last days, and there is never but one on the earth at a time, on whom this power and the keys of this priesthood are conferred,) are of no efficacy, virtue, or force, in and after the resurrection from the dead; for all contracts that are not made unto this end, have an end when men are dead.

Behold! mine house is a house of order, saith the Lord God, and not a house of confusion. Will I accept of an offering, saith the Lord, that is not made in my name! Or, will I receive at your hands, that which I have not appointed! And will I appoint unto you, saith the Lord, except it be by law, even as I and my Father ordained unto you, before the world was! I am the Lord thy God, and I give unto you this commandment, that no man shall come unto the Father, but by me, or by my word, which is my law, saith the Lord; and every thing that is in the world, whether it be ordained of men, by thrones, or principalities, or powers, or things of name, whatsoever they may be, that are not by me, or by my word, saith the Lord, shall be thrown down, and shall not remain after men are dead, neither in nor after the resurrection, saith the Lord your God: for whatsoever things re-maineth, are by me; and whatsoever things are not by me, shall be shaken and destroyed.

Therefore, if a man marry him a wife in the world, and he marry her not by me, nor by my word; and he covenant with her, so long as he is in the world, and she with him, their covenant and marriage is not of force when they are dead, and when they are out of the world; therefore, they are not bound by any law when they are out of the world; therefore, when they are out of the world, they neither marry, nor are given in marriage, but are appointed angels in heaven, which angels are ministering servants, to minister for those, who are worthy of a far more, and an exceeding, and an eternal weight of glory; for these angels did not abide my law, therefore they cannot be enlarged, but remain separately, and singly, without exaltation, in their saved condition, to all eternity, and from henceforth are not Gods, but are angels of God forever and ever.

And again, verily I say unto you, if a man marry a wife, and make a covenant with her for time, and for all eternity, if that covenant is not by me, or by my word, which is my law, and is not sealed by the Holy Spirit of promise, through him whom I have anointed and appointed unto this power, then it is not valid, neither of force, when they are out of the world, because they are not joined by me, saith the Lord, neither by my word; when they are out of the world, it cannot be received there, because the angels and the Gods are appointed there, by whom they cannot pass; they cannot, therefore, inherit my glory, for my house is a house of order, saith the Lord God.

And again, verily I say unto you, if a man marry a wife by my word, which is my law, and by the new and everlasting covenant, and it is sealed unto them by the Holy Spirit of promise, by him who is anointed, unto whom I have appointed this power, and the keys of this priesthood, and it shall be said unto them, ye shall come forth in the first resurrection; and if it be after the first resurrection, in the next resurrection; and shall inherit thrones, kingdoms, principalities, and powers, dominions, all heights, and depths, then shall it be written in the Lamb's Book of Life, that he shall commit no murder, whereby to shed innocent blood; and if ye abide in my covenant, and commit no murder whereby to shed innocent blood, it shall be done unto them in all things whatsoever my servant hath put upon them, in time, and through all eternity; and shall be of full force when they are out of the world, and they shall pass by the angels, and the Gods, which are set there, to their exaltation and glory in all things, as hath been sealed upon their heads, which glory shall be a fulness and a continuation of the seeds forever and ever.

Then shall they be Gods, because they have no end; therefore shall they be from everlasting to everlasting, because they continue; then shall they be above all, because all things are subject unto them. Then shall they be Gods, because they have all power, and the angels are subject unto them.

Verily, verily I say unto you, except ye abide my law, ye cannot attain to this glory; for strait is the gate, and narrow the way, that leadeth unto the exaltation and continuation of the lives, and few there be that find it, because ye receive me not in the world, neither do ye know me. But if ye receive me in the world, then shall ye know me, and shall receive your exaltation; that where I am ye shall be also. This is eternal lives, to know the only wise and true God, and Jesus Christ whom he hath sent. I am He. Receive ye, therefore, my law. Broad is the gate, and wide the way that leadeth to the death; and many there are that go in thereat; because they receive me not, neither do they abide in my law.

Verily, verily I say unto you, if a man marry a wife according to my word, and they are sealed by the Holy Spirit of promise, according to mine appointment, and he or she shall commit any sin or transgression of the new and everlasting covenant whatever, and all manner of blasphemies, and if they commit no murder, wherein they shed innocent blood, —yet they shall come forth in the first resurrection, and enter into their exaltation; but they shall be destroyed in the flesh, and shall be delivered unto the buffetings of Satan, unto the day of redemption, saith the Lord God.

The blasphemy against the Holy Ghost, which shall not be forgiven in the world, nor out of the world, is in that ye commit murder, wherein ye shed innocent blood, and assent unto my death, after ye have received my new and everlasting covenant, saith the Lord God; and he that abideth not this law, can in no wise enter into my glory, but shall be damned, saith the Lord.

I am the Lord thy God, and will give unto thee the law of my Holy Priesthood, as was ordained by me, and my Father, before the world was. Abraham received all things, whatsoever he received, by revelation and commandment, by my word, saith the Lord, and hath entered into his exaltation, and sitteth upon his throne.

Abraham received promises concerning his seed, and of the fruit of his loins, —from whose loins ye are, viz, my servant Joseph, —which were to continue, so long as they were in the world; and as touching Abraham and his seed, out of the world, they should continue; both in the world and out of the world should they continue as innumerable as the stars; or, if ye were to count the sand upon the sea-shore, ye could not number them. This promise is yours, also, because ye are of Abraham, and the promise was made unto Abraham, and by this law are the continuation of the works of my Father, wherein he glorifieth himself. Go ye, therefore, and do the works of Abraham; —enter ye into my law, and ye shall be saved. But if ye enter not into my law, ye cannot receive the promise of my Father, which he made unto Abraham.

God commanded Abraham, and Sarah gave Hagar to Abraham, to wife. And why did she do it? Because this was the law, and from Hagar sprang many people. This, therefore, was fulfilling, among other things, the promises. Was Abraham, therefore, under condemnation? Verily, I say unto you, *Nay*; for I the Lord commanded it. Abraham was commanded to offer his son Isaac; nevertheless, it was written, thou shalt not kill. Abraham however, did not refuse, and it was accounted unto him for righteousness.

Abraham received concubines, and they bare him children, and it was accounted unto him for righteousness, because they were given unto him, and he abode in my law: as Isaac also, and Jacob did none other things than that which they were commanded; and because they did none other things than that which they were commanded, they have entered into their exaltation, according to the promises, and sit upon thrones; and are not angels, but are Gods. David also received many wives and concubines, as also Solomon, and Moses my servant; as also many others of my servants, from the beginning of creation until this time; and in nothing did they sin, save in those things which they received not of me.

David's wives and concubines were given unto him, of me, by the hand of Nathan, my servant, and others of the prophets who had the keys of this power; and in none of these things did he sin against me, save in the case of Uriah and his wife; and, therefore, he hath fallen from his exaltation, and received his portion; and he shall not inherit them out of the world; for I gave them unto another, saith the Lord.

I am the Lord thy God, and I gave unto thee, my servant Joseph, an appointment, and restore all things; ask what ye will, and it shall be given unto you, according to my word; and as ye have asked concerning adultery, —verily, verily I say unto you, if a man receiveth a wife in the new and everlasting covenant, and if she be with another man, and I have not appointed unto her by the holy anointing, she hath committed adultery, and shall be destroyed. If she be not in the new and everlasting covenant, and she be with another man, she has committed adultery; and if her husband be with another woman, and he was under a vow, he hath broken his vow, and hath committed adultery; and if she hath not committed adultery, but is innocent, and hath not broken her vow, and she knoweth it, and I reveal it unto you, my servant Joseph, then shall you have power, by the power of my Holy Priesthood, to take her, and give her unto him that hath not committed adultery, but hath been faithful; for he shall be made ruler over many; for I have conferred upon you the keys and power of the priesthood, wherein I restore all things, and make known unto you, all things, in due time.

And verily, verily I say unto you, that whatsoever you seal on earth, shall be sealed in heaven; and whatsoever you bind on earth, in my name, and by my word, saith the Lord, it shall be eternally bound in the heavens; and whosesoever sins you remit on earth, shall be remitted eternally in the heavens; and whosesoever sins you retain on earth, shall be retained in heaven.

And again, verily I say, whomsoever you bless, I will bless; and whomsoever you curse, I will curse, saith the Lord; for I the Lord am thy God.

And again, verily I say unto you, my servant Joseph, that whatsoever you give on earth, and to whomsoever you give any one on earth, by my word, and according to my law, it shall be visited with blessings, and not cursings, and with my power, saith the Lord, and shall be without condemnation on earth, and in heaven; for I am the Lord thy God, and will be with thee even unto the end of the world, and through all eternity: for verily, I seal upon you, your exaltation, and prepare a throne for you in the kingdom of my Father, with Abraham, your father. Behold, I have seen your sacrifices, and will forgive all your sins; I have seen your sacrifices, in obedience to that which I have told you: go, therefore, and I make a way for your escape, as I accepted the offering of Abraham, of his son Isaac.

Verily I say unto you, a commandment I give unto mine handmaid, Emma Smith, your wife, whom I have given unto you, that she stay herself, and partake not of that which I commanded you to offer unto her; for I did it, saith the Lord, to prove you all, as I did Abraham; and that I might require an offering at your hand, by covenant and sacrifice: and let mine handmaid, Emma Smith, receive all those that have been given unto my servant Joseph, and who are virtuous and pure before me; and those who are not pure, and have said they were pure, shall be destroyed, saith the Lord God: for I am the Lord thy God, and ye shall obey my voice; and I give unto my servant Joseph, that he shall be made ruler over many things, for he hath been faithful over a few things; and from henceforth I will strengthen him.

And I command mine handmaid, Emma Smith, to abide and cleave unto my servant Joseph, and to none else. But if she will not abide this commandment, she shall be destroyed, saith the Lord; for I am the Lord thy God, and will destroy her, if she abide not in my law; but if she will not abide this commandment, then shall my servant Joseph do all things for her, even as he hath said; and I will bless him, and multiply him, and give unto him an hundred fold in this world, of fathers and mothers, brothers and sisters, houses and lands, wives and children, and crowns of eternal lives in the eternal worlds. And again, verily I say, let mine handmaid forgive my servant Joseph his trespasses, and then shall she be forgiven her trespasses, wherein she hath trespassed against me; and I the Lord thy God will bless her, and multiply her, and make her heart to rejoice.

And again, I say, let not my servant Joseph put his property out of his hands, lest an enemy come and destroy him, for Satan seeketh to destroy; for I am the Lord thy God, and he is my servant; and behold! and lo, I am with him, as I was with Abraham, thy father, even unto his exaltation and glory.

Now as touching the law of the priesthood, there are many things pertaining thereunto. Verily, if a man be called of my Father, as was Aaron, by mine own voice, and by the voice of him that sent me, and I have endowed him with the keys of the power of this priesthood, if he do anything in my name, and according to my law, and by my word, he will not commit sin, and I will justify him. Let no one, therefore, set on my servant Joseph; for I will justify him; for he shall do the sacrifice which I require at his hands, for his transgressions, saith the Lord your God.

And again, as pertaining to the law of the Priesthood; —if any man espouse a virgin, and desire to espouse another, and the first give her consent; and if he espouse the second, and they are virgins, and have vowed to no other man, then is he justified; he cannot commit adultery, for they are given unto him; for he cannot commit adultery with that, that belongeth unto him, and to none else: and if he have ten virgins given unto him by this law, he cannot commit adultery; for they belong to him; and they are given unto him; —therefore is he justified. But if one, or either of the ten virgins, after she is espoused, shall be with another man, she has committed adultery, and shall be destroyed; for they are given unto him to multiply and replenish the earth, according to my commandment, and to fulfil the promise which was given by my Father before the foundation of the world; and for their exaltation in the eternal worlds, that they may bear the souls of men; for herein is the work of my Father continued, that he may be glorified.

And again, verily, verily I say unto you, if any man have a wife who holds the keys of this power, and he teaches unto her the law of my Priesthood, as pertaining to these things; then shall she believe, and administer unto him, or she shall be destroyed, saith the Lord your God; for I will destroy her; for I will magnify my name upon all those who receive and abide in my law. Therefore, it shall be lawful in me if she receive not this law, for him to receive all things, whatsoever I the Lord his God will give unto him, because she did not believe and administer unto him, according to my word; and she then becomes the transgressor, and he is exempt from the law of Sarah, who administ[er]ed unto Abraham according to the law, when I commanded Abraham to take Hagar to wife. —And now, as pertaining to this law, —verily, verily I say unto you, I will reveal more unto you, hereafter; therefore, let this suffice for the present. —Behold, I am Alpha and Omega: —AMEN.

{42}

"It Has Gone Abroad that I Was No Longer a Prophet," A Sermon Delivered on 23 July 1843

(from Scott H. Faulring, ed., *An American Prophet's Record:*
The Diaries and Journals of Joseph Smith
[Salt Lake City: Signature Books in association
with Smith Research Associates, 1987], pp. 398-400)

It has gone abroad that I was no longer a prophet. I said it Ironically.
I supposed you would all understand. I[t] was not that I would
renounce the idea of being a prophet but that I would renounce the
idea of proclaiming myself such, and saying that I bear the testimony
of Jesus.

No greater love than that a man lay down his life for his friends. I
discover 100s and 1000s ready to do it for me.

In the midst of business, and find the spirit willing but the flesh is
weak subject to like passions with other men. Although I am under
the necessity of bearing the infirmities of other men, &c. On the other
hand the same characters when they discover a weakness in brother
Joseph, blast his character &c. All that law &c. [which has been
revealed] through him to the church, he [Joseph] cannot be bourne
with a moment.

Men mouth my troubles when I have trouble [but when] they
[have problems they] forget it all. I believe in a principle of reciprosip-
rocity. If we live in a devilish world &c.

I see no faults in the church. Let me be resurrected with the
Saints, whether to heaven or hell or any other good place—good
society. What do we care if the society is good? Don't care what a
character is if he's my firend. A friend, a true friend, and I will be a
friend to him. Friendship is the grand fundamental principle of Mormonism, to revolution[ize and] civilize the world, [to] pour forth
love. Friendship [is] like [the metals bonded in] Bro[ther Theodore]
Turly['s] Blacksmith shop. I do not dwell upon your faults. You shall
not upon mine. After you have covered up all the faults among you
the prettyest thing is [to] have no faults at all. Meek, quiet, &c. [If]

Presbyterians [have] any truth, embrace that. Baptist, Methodist, &c. Get all the good in the world. Come out a pure Mormon.

Last Monday Morning certain men came to me. "Bro[ther] Joseph[,] Hyrum is no prophet. He cant lead the church" You must lead the church. If you resign[, etc.] I felt curious and said here we learn in [the church about] a priesthood after the order of Melchisedeck—Prophet, Priest and King, and I will advance from Prophet to Priest and then to King not to the kingdoms of this Earth but of the most High God.

If I should would there be a great many dissappointed in M[iss]o[uri]? Law and prophets &c. Suffereth violence and the violent taketh it by force. Heaven and Earth shall pass away &c. says Christ. He was the rock &c. Gave the law &c. Ex[odus] 30:31 v[erse] and thou shalt annoint A[a]ron &c. Last chap[ter] Ex[odus], 15th [verse] and thou shalt anoint them &c. A tittle of law which must be fulfilled, forever hereditary, fixed on the law of A[a]ron down to Zachariah the father of John. Zachariah had no child. Had not God gave him a son? Sent his angel to declare a son name[d] John with the keys. John [was a] King and lawgiver.

The kingdom of Heaven suffereth violence &c. The kingdom of heaven continueth in authority until John. The authority taketh it by absolute power. John having the power, take[s] the kingdom by authority.

How do you know all this knowledge? By the gift of the H[oly] G[host. Jesus] arrested the kingdom from the Jews[, saying] of these stony Gentiles[,] these dogs[, he was] to raise up children unto Abraham.

John [said] I must be baptized by you. [Jesus said you must baptize me.] Why, to answer my decrees. John refuses. Jesus had no legal administrator before John. No Salvation between the two lids of the Bible without a legal administrator.

Tis contrary to a Governor's oath to send a man to M[iss]o[uri] where he is prescribed in his religious opinions.

Jesus was then the legal administrator and ordained his apostles.

I will resume the subject at some future time.

{43}

"He Was Not Like Other Men,"
A Sermon Delivered on 13 August 1843

(from Scott H. Faulring, ed., *An American Prophet's Record:
The Diaries and Journals of Joseph Smith
[Salt Lake City: Signature Books in association with
Smith Research Associates, 1987], pp. 403-405)

[S]aid he was not like other men. His mind was continually occupied with the business of the day, and he had to depend entirely upon the Living God for everything he said on such occasions.

The great thing for us to know is to comprehend what God did institute before the foundation of the world. Who knows it?

It is the constitutional disposition of mankind to set up stakes and set bounds to the works and ways of the Almighty.

We are called thus [to] mourn this morning the death of a good man, a great man and a mighty man. It is a solemn idea that man has no hope of seeing a friend after he has lost him, but I will give you a more painful thought. The thought is simple and I never design to communicate no ideas but what are simple, for to this end I am sent. Suppose we have an idea of a resurrection &c. &c. and yet know nothing at all of the gospel and could not comprehend one principle of the orders of Heaven, but found yourselves disappointed. Yes, at last find yourselfs disappointed in every hope or anticipation when decisions goes forth from the lips of the almighty at last. Would not this be a greater disappointment. A more painful thought than annihilation.

Had I inspiration, Revelation, and lungs to communicate what my soul has contemplated in times past there is not a soul in this congregation but would go to their homes and shut their mouths in everlasting silence on religion till they had learned something.

Why be so certain that you comprehend the things of God when all things with you are so uncertain. You are welcome to all the knowledge.

I do not grudge the world of all the religion the[y] have got. They are welcome to all the knowledge they possess.

The sound saluted my ears. We are come unto Mt. Zion &c. What could profit us to come unto the spirits of just men but to learn and come to the knowledge of spirits of the Just.

Where has Judge [Elias] Higby gone? Who is there that would not give all his goods to feed the poor and pour out his gold and silver to the four winds to come where Judge Higby has gone.

That which hath been hid from before the foundation of the world is revealed to babes and sucklings in the last days.

The world is reserved unto burning in the last days. He shall send Elijah the prophet and he shall reveal the covenants of the fathers in relation to the children and the covenants of the children in relation to the fathers.

Four destroying angels holding power over the 4 quarters of the earth until the servants of God are sealed in their foreheads. What is that seal? Shall I tell you? No.

Doctrine [of] Election [and] Sealing of the servants of God on the top of their heads tis not the cross as the Catholics would have it. Doctrine of Election to Abraham was in relation to the Lord. A man wishes to be embraced in the covenant of Abraham. A man [like] Judge Higby in world of spirits, is sealed unto the throne, and [the] doctrine of Election [is] sealing the father and children together.

To the mourner, do as the husband and the father would instruct you. [Then] You shall be reunited.

I have been acquainted with Judge Higby a long time. I never knew a more tender hearted man.

{44}

"An Appeal to the Freemen of the State of Vermont, the 'Brave Green Mountain Boys,' and Honest Men,"

(in *The Voice of Truth . . .*
[Nauvoo, Illinois: Printed by John Taylor, 1844],
pp. 15-20; with William W. Phelps)

I was born in Sharon, Vermont, in 1805,—where the first quarter of my life, grew with the growth, and strengthened with the strength of that "first born" State of the "United Thirteen." From the old "French War" to the final consummation of American Independence, my fathers, heart to heart, and shoulder to shoulder, with the noble fathers of our liberty, fought and bled; and, with the most of that venerable band of patriots, they have gone to rest,—bequeathing a glorious country with all her inherent rights to millions of posterity. Like other honest citizens, I not only, (when manhood came,) sought my own peace, prosperity, and happiness, but also the peace, prosperity, and happiness of my friends; and, with all the rights and realm before me, and the revelations of Jesus Christ, to guide me into all truth, I had good reason to enter into the blessings and privileges of an American citizen;—the rights of a Green Mountain Boy, unmolested, and enjoy life and religion according to the most virtuous and enlightened, customs, rules and etiquette of the nineteenth century. But to the disgrace of the United States, it is not so. These rights and privileges, together with a large amount of property, have been wrested from me and thousands of my friends, by lawless mobs in Missouri, supported by executive authority; and the crime of plundering our property; and the unconstitutional and barbarous act of our expulsion; and even the inhumanity of murdering men, women, and children, have received the *pass-word* of *"justifiable"* by legislative enactments, and the horrid deeds, doleful and disgraceful as they are, have been paid for by government.

In vain have we sought for redress of grievances and a restoration to our rights in the courts and legislature of Missouri. In vain have we sought for our rights and the remuneration for our property in the

halls of Congress, and at the hands of the President. The only consolation yet experienced from these highest tribunals, and *mercy seats* of
our bleeding country, is, *that, "our cause is just, but the government has no
power to redress us."*

Our arms were forcibly taken from us by those Missouri maraud-
ers;—and in spite of every effort to have them returned, the State of
Missouri still retains them; and the United States' militia law, with this
fact before the government, still compels us to do military duty, and
for a lack of said arms the *law* forces *us to pay our fines.* As Shakespeare
would say; *"thereby hangs a tale."*

Several hundred thousand dollars worth of land in Missouri, was
purchased at the United States' Land Offices in that district of country;
and the money[,] without doubt, has been appropriated to strengthen
the army and navy, or increase the power and glory of the nation in
some other way: and notwithstanding Missouri has robbed and
mobbed me and twelve or fifteen thousand innocent inhabitants,
murdered hundreds, and expelled the residue, at the point of the
bayonet, without law, contrary to the express language of the Constitution of the United States, and every State in the Union; and contrary
to the custom and usage of civilized nations; and[,] especially, one
holding up the motto: *"The asylum of the oppressed;"* yet the comfort
we receive, to raise our wounded bodies, and invigorate our troubled
spirits, on account of such immense sacrifices of life, property, patience, and right; and as an equivalent for the enormous taxes we are
compelled to pay to support these functionaries in a dignified manner,
after we have petitioned, and plead with tears, and been showed like a
caravan of foreign animals, for the peculiar gratification, of connois-
seurs in humanity, that flare along in public life, like lamps upon lamp
posts, because they are better calculated for the schemes of the night
than for the scenes of the day, is, as President [Martin] Van Buren said,
your cause is just, but government has no power to redress you!

No wonder, after the Pharisee's prayer, the Publican smote his
breast and said, *Lord be merciful to me a sinner!* What must the manacled
nations think of freemen's rights in the land of liberty?

Were I a Chaldean I would exclaim: Keed'nauh ta-meroon le-
hoam elauhayauh dey-shemayauh veh aur'kau lau gnaubadoo,
yabadoo ma-ar'gnau oomeen tehoat shemayauh allah. (Thus shall ye
say unto them: The gods that have not made the heavens and the
earth, they shall perish from the earth, and from under these heavens.)

An Egyptian, Su-e-eh-ni; (What other persons are those?) A Grecian, Diabolos bassileuei; (The Devil reigns.) A Frenchman, Messieurs sans Dieu; (Gentlemen without God.) A Turk, Ain shems; (The fountain of light.) A German, sie sind unferstandig; (What consummate ignorance!) A Syrian, Zaubok; (Sacrifice!) A Spaniard, Il sabio muda conscio, il nescio no. (A wise man reflects, a fool does not.) A Samaritan: Saunau! (O stranger!) An Italian: Oh tempa! oh diffidanza! (O the times! O the difference!) A Hebrew: Ahtauh ail rauey. (Thou God seest me.) A Dane: Hvad tidende! (What tidings!) A Saxon. Hwæt riht; (What right!) A Swede: Hvad skilia: (What skill!) A Polander: Nav-yen-shoo bah pon na Jesu Christus; (Blessed be the name of Jesus Christ.) A western Indian: She-mo-kah she-mo-keh teh ough-ne-gah. (The white man, O the white man, he very uncertain.) A Roman: Procul, O procul este profani! (Be off, be off ye profane!) But as I am I will only add; when the wicked rule the people mourn.

Now, therefore, having failed in every attempt to obtain satisfaction at the tribunals where all men seek for it, according to the rules of right: I am compelled to appeal to the honor and patriotism of my native State; to the clemency and valor of "Green Mountain Boys;" for throughout the various periods of the world, whenever a nation, kingdom, state, family or individual has received an insult, or an injury, from a superior force, (unless satisfaction was made) it has been the custom to call in the aid of friends to assist in obtaining redress. For proof we have only to refer to the recovery of Lot and his effects, by Abraham, in the days of Sodom and Gomorrah; or, to turn to the relief afforded by France and Holland, for the achievement of the Independence of these United States: without bringing up the great bulk of historical facts, rules, laws, decrees, and treaties, and bible records, by which nations have been governed, to show that mutual alliance, for the general benefit of mankind to retaliate and repel foreign aggressions; to punish and prevent home wrongs, when the conservators of justice and the laws have failed to afford a remedy, are not only common and in the highest sense justifiable and wise, but, they are also, proper expedients to promote the enjoyment of equal rights, the pursuit of happiness, the preservation of life, and the benefit of posterity.

With all these facts before me, and a pure desire to ameliorate the condition of the poor and unfortunate among men, and if possible to entice all men from evil to good; and with a firm reliance that God will reward the just, I have been stimulated to call upon my native State, for a "union of all honest men;" and to appeal to the valor of the "Green Mountain Boys" by all honorable methods and means to assist me in obtaining justice from Missouri: not only for the property she has stolen and confiscated, the murders she has committed among my friends, and for our expulsion from the State, but also to humble and chastise, or abase her for the disgrace she has brought upon constitutional liberty, until she atones for her sins.

I appeal also, to the fraternity of brethren, who are bound by kindred ties, to assist a brother in distress, in all cases where it can be done according to the rules of the order, to extend the boon of benevolence and protection, in avenging the Lord of his enemies, as if a Solomon, a Hiram, a St. John, or a Washington raised his hands before a wondering world, and exclaimed:—*"My life for his!"* Light, liberty, and virtue forever!

I bring this appeal before my native State for the solemn reason that an injury has been done, and crimes have been committed, which a sovereign State, of the Federal compact, one of the great family of *"E pluribus unum,"* refuses to compensate, by consent of parties, rules of law, customs of nations, or in any other way: I bring it also, because the national Government has fallen short of affording the necessary relief as before stated *for want of power,* leaving a large body of her own free citizens, whose wealth went freely into her treasury for lands, and whose gold and silver for taxes, still fills the pockets of her dignitaries, "in ermine and lace," defrauded, robbed, mobbed, plundered, ravished, driven, exiled and banished from the "independent republic of Missouri!"

And in this appeal let me say: raise your towers; pile your monuments to the skies, build your steam frigates; spread yourselves far and wide, and open the iron eyes of your bulwarks by sea and land; and let the towering church steeples, marshal the country like the "dreadful splendor" of an army with bayonets: but remember the flood of Noah; remember the fate of Sodom and Gomorrah; remember the dispersion and confusion at the tower of Babel; remember the destruction of Pharaoh and his hosts; remember the hand writing upon the wall, *mene, mene, tekel, upharsin;* remember the angel's visit to Sennacherib and the one hundred and eighty-five thousand Assyrians; remember the end of the Jews and Jerusalem; and remember the Lord Almighty will avenge the blood of his Saints that now crimsons the skirts of Missouri! Shall wisdom cry aloud and not her speech be heard?

Has the majesty of American liberty sunk into such vile servitude and oppression, that justice has fled? Has the glory and influence of a Washington, an Adams, a Jefferson, a Lafayette, and a host of others forever departed;—and the wrath of a Cain, a Judas, and a Nero whirled forth in the heraldry of hell, to sprinkle our garments with blood; and lighten the darkness of midnight, with the blaze of our dwellings?—Where is the patriotism of '76? Where is the virtue of our forefathers? and where is the sacred honor of freemen?

Must we, because we believe in the fulness of the gospel of Jesus Christ; the administration of angels, and the communion of the Holy Ghost, like the prophets and apostles of old,—must we be mobbed with impunity—be exiled from our habitations and property without remedy; murdered without mercy—and government find the weapons, and pay the vagabonds for doing the jobs, and give them the plunder into the bargain? Must we, because we believe in enjoying the constitutional privilege and right of worshipping Almighty God according to the dictates of our own consciences; and because we believe in repentance, and baptism for the remission of sins; the gift of the Holy Ghost by the laying on of the hands; the resurrection of the dead; the millennium; the day of judgment; and the Book of Mormon as the history of the aborigines of this continent,—must we be expelled from the institutions of our country; the rights of citizenship, and the graves of our friends and brethren, and the government lock the gate of humanity, and shut the door of redress against us?—If so, farewell freedom; adieu to personal safety,—and let the red hot wrath of an offended God purify the nation of such sinks of corruption! For that realm is hurrying to ruin where vice has the power to expel virtue.

My father, who stood, several times in the battles of the American Revolution, till his companions, in arms, had been shot dead, at his feet, was forced from his home in Far West, Missouri, by those civilized, or satanized savages, in the dreary season of winter, to seek a shelter in another State; and the vicissitudes and sufferings consequent to his flight, brought his honored grey head to the grave, a few months after.—And my youngest brother, also, in the vigor and bloom of youth, from his great exposure and fatigue in endeavoring to assist his parents on their journey, (I and my brother Hyrum being in chains, in

dungeons—*where they tried to feed us upon human flesh*—in Missouri,)
was likewise so debilitated that he found a premature grave shortly
after my father, And my mother, too, though she yet lingers among
us, from her extreme exposure in that dreadful tragedy, was filled with
rheumatic affections and other diseases, which leaves her no enjoyment of health. She is sinking in grief and pain, broken hearted, from
Missouri persecution.

O death! wilt thou not give to every honest man, *a heated dart to
sting* those wretches while they pollute the land? and O grave! wilt
thou not open the *trap door to the pit* of ungodly men, that they may
stumble in?

I appeal to the "Green Mountain Boys" of my native State, to rise
in the majesty of virtuous freemen, and by all honorable means help
bring Missouri to the bar of justice. If there is one whisper from the
spirit of an Ethen Allen; or a gleam from the shade of a Gen. Stark,
let it mingle with our sense of honor, and fire our bosoms for the cause
of suffering innocence,—for the reputation of our disgraced country,
and for the glory of God: and may all the earth bear me witness, if
Missouri, blood-stained Missouri;—escapes the due demerit of her
crimes, the vengeance she so justly deserves, that Vermont is a hypocrite—*a coward*—and this nation the hot bed of political demagogues!

I make this appeal to the sons of liberty of my native State for
help, to frustrate the wicked designs of sinful men; I make it to hush
the violence of mobs; I make it to cope with the unhallowed influence
of wicked men in high places; I make it to resent the insult and injury
made to an innocent, unoffending people, by a lawless ruffian State; I
make it to obtain justice where law is put at defiance; I make it to
wipe off the stain of blood from our nation's escutchion; I make it to
show presidents, governors, and rulers, prudence; I make it to fill
honorable men with discretion; I make it to teach senators wisdom; I
make it to learn judges justice: I make it to point clergymen to the
path of virtue; and I make it to turn the hearts of this nation to the
truth and realities of pure and undefiled religion, that they may escape
the perdition of ungodly men; and Jesus Christ, the son of God, is my
Great Counsellor.

Wherefore let the rich and the learned, the wise and the noble,
the poor and the needy, the bond and the free, both black and white,
take heed to their ways, and cleave to the knowledge of God; and
execute justice and judgment upon the earth in righteousness; and

prepare to meet the judge of the quick and the dead, for the hour of his coming is nigh.

> And I must go on as the herald of grace,
>> Till the wide-spreading conflict is over,
> And burst through the curtains of tyrannic night.
>> Yea, I must go on to gather our race,
> Till the high blazing flame of Jehovah,
>> Illumines the globe as a triumph of right.

As a friend of equal rights to all men, and a messenger of the everlasting gospel of Jesus Christ,
I have the honor to be,
Your devoted servant,

{45}

"When I Consider the Surrounding Circumstances," A Sermon Delivered on 21 January 1844

(from Scott G. Kenney, ed., *Wilford Woodruff's Journal,* 9 vols. [Midvale, Utah: Signature Books, 1983-85], 2:341-43)

When I consider the surrounding circumstances in which I am placed in this day, standing in the open air with week lungs & sumwhat out of health, I feel that I must have prayers & faith of my brethren that God may strengthen me & pour out his special blessings upon me if you get much from me this day.

Their are many people assembled here to day & throughout this city, & from various parts of the world who say that they have recieved to a certainty a portion of knowledge from God by revelation in the way that he has ordained & pointed out. I shall take the broad ground then that if we have or can receive a portion of knowledge from God by immediate revelation by the same source we can receive all knowledge.

What shall I talk about today? I know what Br [Reynolds] Cahoon wants me to speak about, he wants me to speak about the comeing of Elijah in the last days. I can see it in his eye. I will speak upon that Subject then. The Bible says "I will send you Elijah before the great & dredful day of the Lord Come that he shall turn the hearts of the fathers to the Children & the hearts of the children to their fathers lest I come & smite the whole earth with a Curse." Now the word turn here should be translated (bind or seal).

But what is the object of this important mission or how is it to be fulfilled? The keys are to be deliverd[,] the spirit of Elijah is to come, The gospel to be esstablished[,] the Saints of God gatherd, Zion built up, & the Saints to come up as Saviors on mount Zion. But how are they to become Saviors on Mount Zion? By building their temples erecting their Baptismal fonts & going forth & receiving all the ordinances, Baptisms, confirmations, washings anointings ordinations, & sealing powers upon our heads in behalf of all our Progenitors who are dead & redeem them that they may come forth in the first resurrection & be exhalted to thrones of glory with us, & herein is the

Chain that binds the hearts of the fathers to the Children & the Children to the Fathers which fulfills the mission of Elijah & I would to God that this temple was now done that we might go into it & go to work & improve our time & make use of the seals while they are on earth.

And the Saints have none to[o] much time to save & redeem their dead, & gather together their living relatives that they may be saved also, before the earth will be smitten & the consumption decreed falls upon the world & I would advise all the Saints to go to with their might & gather together all their living relatives to this place that they may be sealed & saved that they may be prepared against the day that the destroying angel goes forth & if the whole Church should go to with all their might to save their dead seal their posterity & gather their living friends & spend none of their time in behalf of the world they would hardly get through before night would come when no man Could work.

And my ownly trouble at the present time is concerning ourselves that the Saints will be divided & broken up & scattered before we get our salvation secure. For their is so many fools in the world for the devil to operate upon it gives him the advantage often times.

The question is frequently asked can we not be saved without going through with all thes ordinances &c. I would answer No not the fulness of Salvation. Jesus Said their was many mansions in his fathers house & he would go & prepare a place for them. House here named should have been translated (Kingdom) & any person who is exhalted to the highest mansion has to abide a celestial law & the whole law to[o].

But their has been a great difficulty in getting anything into the heads of this generation. It has been like splitting hemlock knots with a corndoger for a wedge & a pumpkin for a beetle; even the Saints are slow to understand. I have tried for a number of years to get the minds of the saints prepared to recieve the things of God, but we freequently see some of them after suffering all they have for the work of God will fly to peaces like glass as soon as any thing Comes that is Contrary to their traditions. They cannot stand the fire at all. How many will be able to abide a Celestial law & go through & recieve their exhaltation I am unable to say but many are called & few are Chosen.

{46}

"Views of the Powers
and Policy of the Government of the U.S."

(in *The Voice of Truth* . . .
[Nauvoo, Illinois: Printed by John Taylor, 1844],
pp. 26-38; with William W. Phelps)

Born in a land of liberty, and breathing an air uncorrupted with the sirocco of barbarous climes, I ever feel a double anxiety for the happiness of all men, both in time and eternity. My cogitations like Daniel's have for a long time troubled me, when I viewed the condition of men throughout the world, and more especially in this boasted realm, where the Declaration of Independence "holds these truths to be self-evident; that all men are created equal: that they are endowed by their Creator, with certain unalienable rights; that among these are life, liberty, and the pursuit of happiness," but at the same time, some two or three millions of people are held as slaves for life, because the spirit in them is covered with a darker skin than ours: and hundreds of our own kindred for an infraction, or supposed infraction of some over-wise statute, have to be incarcerated in dungeon glooms, or suffer the more moral penitentiary gravitation of mercy in a nut-shell, while the duellist, the debauchee, and the defaulter for millions, and other criminals, take the uppermost rooms at feasts, or, like the bird of passage, find a more congenial clime by flight.

The wisdom, which ought to characterize the freest, wisest, and most noble nation of the nineteenth century, should, like the sun in his meridian splendor, warm every object beneath its rays: and the main efforts of her officers, who are nothing more or less than the servants of the people, ought to be directed to ameliorate the condition of all: black or white, bond or free; for the best of books says, "God hath made of one blood all nations of men, for to dwell on all the face of the earth."

Our common country presents to all men the same advantages; the same facilities; the same prospects; the same honors; and the same rewards: and without hypocrisy, the Constitution when it says, "We, the people of the United States, in order to form a more perfect union, establish justice, ensure tranquility, provide for the common defence, promote the general welfare, and secure the blessings of liberty to ourselves and our posterity, do ordain and establish this Constitution for the United States of America," meant just what it said, without reference to color or condition: *ad infinitum.* The aspirations and expectations of a virtuous people, environed with so wise, so liberal, so deep, so broad, and so high a charter of *equal rights,* as appears in said Constitution, ought to be treated, by those to whom the administration of the laws are intrusted, with as much sanctity, as the prayers of the saints are treated in heaven, that love, confidence and union, like the sun, moon and stars should bear witness,

> "Forever singing as they shine,
> *The hand that made us is divine.*"

Unity is power, and when I reflect on the importance of it to the stability of all governments, I am astounded at the silly moves of persons and parties, to foment discord in order to ride into power on the current of popular excitement; nor am I less surprised at the stretches of power, or restrictions of right, which too often appear as acts of legislators, to pave the way to some favorite political schemes, as destitute of intrinsic merit as a wolf's heart is of the milk of human kindness: a Frenchman would say, "prosqué tout aimer richesses êt pouvoir:" (almost all men like wealth and power.)

I must dwell on this subject longer than others, for nearly one hundred years ago that golden patriot, Benjamin Franklin, drew up a plan of union for the then colonies of Great Britain that *now* are such an independent nation, which among many wise provisions for obedient children under their father's more rugged hand, had this:—"they have power to make laws, and lay and levy such general duties, imports, or taxes, as to them shall appear most equal and just, (considering the ability and other circumstances of the inhabitants in the several colonies,) and such as may be collected with the least inconvenience to the people; rather discouraging luxury, than loading industry with unnecessary burthens." Great Britain surely lacked the laudable humanity and fostering clemency to grant such a just plan of union—but the sentiment remains like the land that honored its birth, as a pattern for wise men *to study the convenience of the people more than the comfort of the cabinet.*

And one of the most noble fathers of our freedom and country's glory: great in war, great in peace, great in the estimation of the world, and great in the hearts of his countrymen, the illustrious Washington, said in his first inaugural address to Congress: "I behold the surest pledges that as, on one side, no local prejudices or attachments, no separate views or party animosities, will misdirect the comprehensive and equal eye which ought to watch over this great assemblage of communities and interests, so, on another, that the foundations of our national policy will be laid in the pure and immutable principles of private morality; and the pre-eminence of free government be exemplified by all the attributes which can win the affections of its citizens, and command the respect of the world." Verily, here shines the virtue and wisdom of a statesman in such lucid rays that had every succeeding Congress followed the rich instruction, in all their deliberations and enactments, for the benefit and convenience of the whole community and the communities of which it is composed, no sound of a rebellion in South Carolina; no rupture in Rhode Island; no mob in Missouri expelling her citizens by executive authority; corruption in the ballot boxes; a border warfare between Ohio and Michigan; hard times and distress; outbreak upon outbreak in the principal cities; murder, robbery, and defalcation, scarcity of money and a thousand other difficulties, would have torn asunder the bonds of the union; destroyed the confidence of man with man; and left the great body of the people to mourn over misfortunes in poverty, brought on by corrupt legislation in an hour of proud vanity, for self aggrandizement. The great Washington soon after the foregoing faithful admonition for the common welfare of his nation, further advised Congress that "among the many interesting objects which will engage your attention, that of providing for the common defence will merit particular regard. To be prepared for war is one of the most effectual means of preserving peace." As the Italian would say: *Buona aviso*, (good advice.)

The elder Adams in his inaugural address, gives national pride such a grand turn of justification, that every honest citizen must look back upon the infancy of the United States with an approving smile and rejoice, that patriotism in their rulers, virtue in the people, and prosperity in the union, once crowned the expectations of hope; unveiled the sophistry of the hypocrite and silenced the folly of foes: Mr. Adams said, "If national pride is ever justifiable, or excusable, it is when it springs, not from *power* or riches, grandeur or glory, but from conviction of national innocence, information and benevolence." There is no doubt such was actually the case with our young realm at the close of the last century; peace, prosperity, and union, filled the country with religious toleration, temporal enjoyment and virtuous enterprize; and grandly, too, when the deadly winter of the "Stamp Act," the "Tea Act," and other *close communion* acts of royalty had choked the growth of freedom of speech, liberty of the press, and liberty of conscience, did light, liberty and loyalty flourish like the cedars of God.

The respected and venerable Thomas Jefferson, in his inaugural address, made more than forty years ago, shews what a beautiful prospect an innocent, virtuous nation presents to the sage's eye, where there is space for enterprize; hands for industry; heads for heroes, and hearts for moral greatness. He said, "A rising nation, spread over a wide and fruitful land, traversing all the seas with the rich productions of their industry, engaged in commerce with nations who feel power and forget right, advancing rapidly to destinies beyond the reach of mortal eye; when I contemplate these transcendant objects, and see the honor, the happiness, and the hopes of this beloved country committed to the issue and the auspices of this day, I shrink from the contemplation and humble myself before the magnitude of the undertaking." Such a prospect was truly soul stirring to a good man, but "since the Fathers have fallen asleep," wicked and designing men, have unrobed the government of its glory,—and the people, if not in dust and ashes, or in sack cloth, have to lament in poverty, her departed greatness: while demagogues build fires in the north and south, east and west, to keep up their spirits *till it is better times*: but year after year has left the people to *hope* till the very name of *Congress*, or *State Legislature*, is as horrible to the sensitive friend of his country, as the house of "Blue Beard" is to children; or "Crockford's" hell of London, to meek men. When the people are secure and their rights properly respected, then the four main pillars of prosperity, viz: agriculture, manufactures, navigation, and commerce, need the fostering care of government and in so goodly a country as ours, where the soil, the climate, the rivers, the lakes, and the sea coast; the productions, the timber, the minerals; and the inhabitants are so diversified, that a pleasing variety accommodates all tastes, trades, and calculations, it certainly is the highest point of supervision to protect the whole northern and southern, eastern and western, centre and circumference of the realm, by a judicious tariff. It is an old saying and a true one, "if you wish to be *respected*, respect yourselves."

I will adopt, in part, the language of Mr. Madison's, inaugural address, "To cherish peace and friendly intercourse with all nations, having correspondent dispositions; to maintain sincere neutrality towards belligerent nations; to prefer in all cases amicable discussion and reasonable accommodation of differences to a decision of them by an appeal to arms; to exclude foreign intrigues and foreign partialities, so degrading to all countries, and so baneful to free ones; to foster a spirit of independence too just to invade the rights of others, too proud to surrender our own, too liberal to indulge unworthy prejudicies ourselves, and too elevated not to look down upon them in others; to hold the union of the states as the basis of their peace and happiness; to support the constitution, which is the cement of the union, as well as in its authorities; to respect the rights and authorities reserved to the states and to the people, as equally incorporated with, and essential to the success, of the general system; to avoid the slightest interference with the rights of conscience, or the functions of religion, so wisely exempted from civil jurisdiction; to preserve in their full energy, the other salutary provisions in behalf of private and personal rights, and of the freedom of the press;" as far as intention aids in the fulfillment of duty, are consummations too big with benefits not to captivate the energies of all honest men to achieve them, when they can be brought to pass by reciprocation, friendly alliances, wise legislation, and honorable treaties.

The government has once flourished under the guidance of trusty servants; and the Hon. Mr. Monroe in his day, while speaking of the constitution: says, "Our commerce has been wisely regulated with foreign nations, and between the states; new states have been admitted into our union; our territory has been enlarged by fair and honorable treaty, and with great advantage to the original states; the states respectively protected by the national government, under a mild paternal system against foreign dangers, and enjoying within their separate spheres, by a wise partition of power, a just proportion of the sovereignty, have improved their police, extended their settlements, and attained a strength and maturity which are the best proofs of wholesome law well administered. And if we look to the condition of individuals, what a proud spectacle does it exhibit? who has been deprived of any right of person or property? who [is] restrained from offering his vows in the mode in which he prefers, to the Divine Author of his being. It is well known that all these blessings have been enjoyed in their fullest extent; and I add, with peculiar satisfaction, that there has been no example of a capital punishment being inflicted on any one for the crime of high treason." What a delightful picture, of power, policy, and prosperity! Truly the wise man's proverb is just: "Sedàukauh teromain goy, veh-ka-sade le-u-méem khahmáut." Righteousness exalteth a nation, but sin is a reproach to any people.

But this is not all. The same honorable statesman, after having had about forty years experience in the government, under the full tide of successful experiment, gives the following commendatory assurance of the efficiency of the *magna charta* to answer its great end and aim: *to protect the people in their rights.* "Such, then, is the happy government under which we live; a government adequate to every purpose for which the social compact is formed; a government elective in all its branches, under which every citizen may, by his merit, obtain the highest trust recognized by the constitution; which contains within it no cause of discord; none to put at variance one portion of the community with another; a government which protects every citizen in the full enjoyment of his rights, and is able to protect the nation against injustice from foreign powers."

Again, the younger Adams in the silver age of our country's advancement to fame, in his inaugural address, (1825) thus candidly declares the majesty of the youthful Republic, in its increasing greatness: "The year of jubilee since the first formation of our union has just elapsed; that of the declaration of Independence is at hand. The consummation of both was effected by this constitution. Since that period, a population of four millions has multiplied to twelve. A territory, bounded by the Mississippi, has been extended from sea to sea. New states have been admitted to the union, in numbers nearly equal to those of the first confederation. Treaties of peace, amity and commerce, have been concluded with the principal dominions of the earth. The people of other nations, the inhabitants of regions acquired, not by conquest, but by compact, have been united with us in the participation of our rights and duties, of our burdens and blessings. The forest has fallen by the axe of our woodsmen; the soil has been made to teem by the tillage of our farmers; our commerce has whitened every ocean. The dominion of man over physical nature has been extended by the invention of our artists. Liberty and law have walked hand in hand. All the purposes of human association have been accomplished as effectively as under any other government on the globe, and at a cost little exceeding, in a whole generation, the expenditures of other nations in a single year."

In continuation of such noble sentiments, Gen. Jackson, upon his accession to the great chair of the chief magistracy: said, "As long as our government is administered for the good of the people, and is regulated by their will; as long as it secures to us the rights of person and property, liberty of conscience, and of the press, it will be worth defending; and so long as it is worth defending, a patriotic militia will cover it with an impenetrable ægis."

General Jackson's administration may be denominated the *acme* of American glory, liberty and prosperity, for the national debt, which in 1815, on account of the late war, was $125,000,000, and lessened gradually, was paid up in his golden day; and preparations were made to distribute the surplus revenue among the several states: and that august patriot, to use his own words in his farewell address, retired leaving "A great people prosperous and happy, in the full enjoyment of liberty and peace, honored and respected by every nation of the world."

At the age, then, of sixty years our blooming republic began to decline under the withering touch of Martin Van Buren! Disappointed ambition; thirst for power, pride, corruption, party spirit, faction, patronage; perquisites, fame, tangling alliances; priest-craft and spiritual wickedness in *high places*, struck hands, and revelled in midnight splendor.—Trouble, vexation, perplexity and contention mingled with hope, fear and murmuring, rumbled through the union and agitated the whole nation as would an earthquake at the centre of the earth, the world, heaving the sea beyond its bounds, and shaking the everlasting hills: so, in hopes of better times, while jealousy, hypocritical pretensions, and pompous ambition, were luxuriating on the ill-gotten spoils of the people, they rose in their majesty like a tornado, and swept through the land, till Gen. Harrison appeared, as a star among the storm clouds, for better weather.

The calm came; and the language of that venerable patriot, in his inaugural address, while descanting upon the merits of the constitution and its framers, thus expressed himself: "There were in it, features which appeared not to be in harmony with their ideas of a simple representative democracy or republic. And knowing the tendency of power to increase itself, particularly when executed by a single individual, predictions were made that, at no very remote period, the government would terminate in virtual monarchy. It would not become me to say that the fears of these patriots have been already realized.—But as I sincerely believe that the tendency of measures and of men's opinions, for some years past, has been in that direction, it is, I conceive, strictly proper that I should take this occasion to repeat the assurances I have heretofore given, of my determination to arrest the progress of that tendency if it really exists, and restore the government to its pristine health and vigor." This good man died before he had the opportunity of applying one balm to ease the pain of our groaning country, and I am willing the nation should be the judge, whether General Harrison, in his exalted station, upon the eve of his entrance into the world of spirits, *told the truth or not*: with acting president Tyler's three years of perplexity and pseudo whig democratic reign, to heal the breaches, or show the wounds, *secundum artum*, (according to art.—) Subsequent events, all things considered, Van Buren's downfall, Harrison's exit, and Tyler's self-sufficient turn to the whole, go to show, as a Chaldean might exclaim: Beràm etài elàuh beshmayàuh gauháh rauzèen: (*Certainly there is a God in heaven to reveal secrets.*)

No honest man can doubt for a moment, but the glory of American liberty is on the wane; and, that calamity and confusion will sooner or later, destroy the peace of the people. Speculators will urge a national bank as a savior of credit and comfort. A hireling pseudo priesthood will plausibly push abolition doctrines and doings, and "human rights," into Congress and into every other place, where conquest smells of fame, or opposition swells to popularity. Democracy, Whiggery and Cliquery, will attract their elements and foment divisions among the people, to accomplish fancied schemes and accumulate power, while poverty driven to despair, like hunger forcing its way through a wall, will break through the statutes of men, to save life, and mend the breach in prison glooms.

A still higher grade, of what the "nobility of nations" call, "great men," will dally with all rights in order to smuggle a fortune at "one fell swoop," mortgage Texas, possess Oregon, and claim all the unsettled regions of the world for hunting and trapping: and should a humble honest man, red, black, or white, exhibit a better title, these gentry have only to clothe the judge with richer ermine, and spangle the lawyer's fingers with finer rings, to have the judgment of his peers, and the honor of his lords, as a pattern of honesty, virtue and humanity, while the motto hangs on his nation's escutcheon: *"Every man has his price!"*

Now, oh! people! people! turn unto the Lord and live; and reform this nation. Frustrate the designs of wicked men. Reduce Congress at least one half. Two senators from a state and two members to a million of population, will do more business than the army that now occupy the halls of the national legislature. Pay them two dollars and their board per diem; (except Sundays,) that is more than the farmer gets, and he lives honestly. Curtail the offices of government in pay, number, and power, for the Philistine lords have shorn our nation of its goodly locks in the lap of Delilah.

Petition your state legislatures to pardon every convict in their several penitentiaries: blessing them as they go, and saying to them in the name of the Lord, *go thy way and sin no more.* Advise your legislators when they make laws for larceny, burglary or any felony, to make the penalty applicable to work upon roads, public works, or any place where the culprit can be taught more wisdom and more virtue; and become more enlightened. Rigor and seclusion will never do as much to reform the propensities of man, as reason and friendship. Murder only can claim confinement or death. Let the penitentiaries be turned into seminaries of learning, where intelligence, like the angels of heaven, would banish such fragments of barbarism: imprisonment for debt is a meaner practice than the savage tolerates with all his ferocity. "Amor vincit omnia." Love conquers all.

Petition also, ye goodly inhabitants of the slave states, your legislators to abolish slavery by the year 1850, or now; and save the abolitionist from reproach and ruin, infamy and shame. Pray Congress to pay every man a reasonable price for his slaves out of the surplus revenue arising from the sale of public lands, and from the deduction of pay from the members of Congress. Break off the shackles from the poor black man; and hire him to labor like other human beings; for "an hour of virtuous liberty on earth, is worth a whole eternity of bondage!" Abolish the practice in the army and navy of trying men by court martial for desertion; if a soldier or marine runs away, send him his wages, with this instruction, that *his country will never trust him again; he has forfeited his honor.* Make HONOR the standard with all men: be sure that good is rendered for evil in all cases: and the whole nation, like a kingdom of kings and priests, will rise up in righteousness: and be respected as wise and worthy on earth; and as just and holy for heaven, by Jehovah the author of perfection. More economy in the national and state governments, would make less taxes among the people; more equality through the cities, towns and country, would make less distinction among the people; and more honesty and familiarity in societies, would make less hypocrisy and flattery in all branches of the community; and open, frank, candid, decorum to all men, in this boasted land of liberty, would beget esteem, confidence, union and love; and the neighbor from any state, or from any country, of whatever color, clime or tongue, could rejoice when he puts his foot on the sacred soil of freedom, and exclaim: the very name of "*American*," is fraught with *friendship*! Oh! then, create confidence! restore freedom! break down slavery! banish imprisonment for debt, and be in love, fellowship and peace with all the world! Remember that honesty is not subject to law: the law was made for transgressors: wherefore a Dutchman might exclaim: *Ein erlicher namo ist besser als Reichthum,* (a good name is better than riches.)

For the accommodation of the people in every state and territory, let Congress show their wisdom by granting a national bank, with branches in each state and territory, where the capital stock shall be held by the nation for the mother bank: and by the states and territories, for the branches: and whose officers and directors shall be elected yearly by the people with wages at the rate of two dollars per day for services: which several banks shall never issue any more bills than the amount of capital stock in her vaults and the interest. The net gain of the mother bank shall be applied to the national revenue, and that of the branches to the states and territories' revenues. And the bills shall be par throughout the nation, which will mercifully cure that fatal disorder known in cities, as *brokerage*; and leave the people's money in their own pockets.

Give every man his constitutional freedom, and the president full power to send an army to suppress mobs; and the states authority to repeal and impugn that relic of folly, which makes it necessary for the governor of a state to make the demand of the president for troops, in cases of invasion or rebellion. The governor himself may be a mobber and, instead of being punished, as he should be for murder and treason, he may destroy the very lives, rights, and property he should protect. Like the good Samaritan, send every lawyer as soon as he repents and obeys the ordinances of heaven, to preach the gospel to the destitute, without purse or scrip, pouring in the oil and the wine: a learned priesthood is certainly more honorable than *"an hireling clergy."*

As to the contiguous territories to the United States, wisdom would direct no tangling alliance: Oregon belongs to this government honorably, and when we have the red man's consent, let the union spread from the east to the west sea; and if Texas petitions Congress to be adopted among the sons of liberty, give her the right hand of fellowship; and refuse not the same friendly grip to Canada and Mexico: and when the right arm of freemen is stretched out in the character of a navy, for the protection of rights, commerce and honor, let the iron eyes of power, watch from Maine to Mexico, and from California to Columbia; thus may union be strengthened, and foreign speculation prevented from opposing broadside to broadside.

Seventy years have done much for this goodly land; they have burst the chains of oppression and monarchy; and multiplied its inhabitants from two to twenty millions; with a proportionate share of knowledge; keen enough to circumnavigate the globe; draw the lightning from the clouds; and cope with all the crowned heads of the world.

Then why? Oh! why! will a once flourishing people not arise, phoenix like, over the cinders of Martin Van Buren's power; and over the sinking fragments and smoking ruins of other catamount politicians; and over the wind-falls of Benton, Calhoun, Clay, Wright, and a caravan of other equally unfortunate law doctors, and cheerfully help to spread a plaster and bind up the *burnt, bleeding wounds* of a sore but blessed country? The southern people are hospitable and noble; they will help to rid so *free* a country of every vestige of slavery, when ever they are assured of an equivalent for their property. The country will be full of money and confidence, when a national bank of twenty millions, and a state bank in every state, with a million or more, gives a tone to monetary matters, and make a circulating medium as valuable in the purses of a whole community, as in the coffers of a speculating banker or broker.

The people may have faults but they should never be trifled with. I think Mr. Pitt's quotation in the British Parliament of Mr. Prior's couplet for the husband and wife, to apply to the course which the king and ministry of England should pursue to the then colonies, of the *now* United States, might be a genuine rule of action for some of the *breath made* men in high places, to use towards the posterity of that noble daring people:

> "Be to her faults a little blind;
> Be to her virtues very kind."

We have had democratic presidents: whig presidents; a pseudo democratic whig president; and now it is time to have *a president of the United States*; and let the people of the whole union; like the inflexible Romans, whenever they find a *promise* made by a candidate, that is not practised as an officer, hurl the miserable sycophant from his exaltation, as God did Nebuchadnezzar, to crop the grass of the field, with a beast's heart among the cattle.

Mr. Van Buren said in his inaugural address, that he went "into the presidential chair the inflexible and uncompromising opponent of every attempt, on the part of Congress, to abolish slavery in the District of Columbia, against the wishes of the slave holding states; and also with a determination equally decided to resist the slightest interference with it in the states where it exists." Poor little Matty made this rhapsodical sweep with the fact before his eyes, that the State of New York, his native state, had abolished slavery, without a struggle or a groan. Great God, how independent! From henceforth slavery is tolerated where it exists; constitution or no constitution; people or no people; right or wrong; vox Matti, vox Diaboli; "the voice of Matty," "the voice of the devil;" and peradventure, his great "Sub-Treasury" scheme was a piece of the same mind: but the man and his measures have such a stricking resemblance to the anecdote of the Welchman and his cart tongue, that, when the constitution was so long that it allowed slavery at the capitol of a free people, it could not be cut off; but when it was so short that it needed a *Sub-Treasury*, to save the funds of the nation, it *could be spliced*! Oh, granny, granny, what a long tail our puss has got! As a Greek might say, *hysteron proteron*: the cart before the horse; but his mighty whisk through the great national fire, for the presidential chestnuts, *burnt the locks of his glory with the blaze of his folly*!

In the United States the people are the government; and their united voice is the only sovereign that should rule; the only power that should be obeyed; and the only gentlemen that should be honored; at home and abroad; on the land and on the sea: wherefore, were I the president of the United States, by the voice of a virtuous people, I would honor the old paths of the venerated fathers of freedom: I would walk in the tracks of the illustrious patriots, who carried the ark of the government upon their shoulders with an eye single to the glory of the people: and when that people petitioned to abolish slavery in the slave states, I would use all honorable means to have their prayers granted: and give liberty to the captive; by paying the southern gentleman a reasonable equivalent for his property, that the whole nation might be free indeed! When the people petitioned for a national bank, I would use my best endeavors to have their prayers answered, and establish one on national principles to save taxes, and make them the controllers of its way and means; and when the people petitioned to possess the territory of Oregon, or any other contiguous territory; I would lend the influence of a chief magistrate to grant so reasonable a request, that they might extend the mighty efforts and enterprise of a free people from the east to the west sea; and make the wilderness blossom as the rose; and when a neighboring realm petitioned to join the union of the sons of liberty, my voice would be, *come*: yea come Texas; come Mexico; come Canada; and come all the world—let us be brethren; let us be one great family; and let there be universal peace. Abolish the cruel custom of prisons, (except certain cases,) penitentiaries, and court-martials for desertion; and let reason and friendship reign over the ruins of ignorance and barbarity; yea, I would, as the universal friend of man, open the prisons; open the eyes; open the ears and open the hearts of all people, to behold and enjoy freedom, unadulterated freedom; and God, who once cleansed the violence of the earth with a flood; whose Son laid down his life for the salvation of all his father gave him out of the world; and who has promised that he will come and purify the world again with fire in the last days, should be supplicated by me for the good of all people.

With the highest esteem, I am a friend of virtue, and of the people,

{47}

"Their Is a Differance Between the Spirit & Office of Elias & Eligah," A Sermon Delivered on 10 March 1844

(from Scott G. Kenney, ed., *Wilford Woodruff's Journal*, 9 vols. [Midvale, Utah: Signature Books, 1983-85], 2:359-66)

Their is a differance between the spirit & office of Elias & Eligah. It is the spirit of Elias I wish first to speak of. And in order to Come at the subject I will bring some of the testimony from the scripture & give my own. In the first place suffice it to say I went into the woods to inquire of the Lord by prayer his will concerning me, & I saw an angel & he laid his hands upon my head & ordained me to be a priest after the order of Aaron & to hold the keys of this priesthood which office was to preach repentance & Baptism for the remission of sins & also to baptise. But [I] was informed that this office did not extend to the laying on of hands for the giving of the Holy Ghost that that office was a greater work & was to be given afterwards. But that my ordination was a preparetory work or a going before which was the spirit of Elias for the spirit of Elias was a going before to prepare the way for the greater, which was the case with John the Baptist.

He came bawling through the wilderness prepare ye the way of the Lord & make his paths strait & they were informed if they could receive it it was the spirit of Elias & John was vary particular to tell the people He was not that light but was sent to bear witness of that light. He told the people that his mission was to preach repentance & baptize with water, but it was he that Should Come after him that should baptise with fire & the Holy Ghost. If he had been an imposture he might have gone to work beyound his bounds & undertook to have performed ordinances that did not belong to that office & calling under the spirit of Elias.

The spirit of Elias is to prepare the way for a greater revelation of God which is the priesthood of Elias or the Priesthood that Aaron was ordained unto. And when God sends a man into the world to prepare for a greater work [he] holds the keys of the power of Elias. It was called the doctrin of

Elias even from the early ages of the world. John's mission was limited to preaching & Baptizing but what he done was legal & when Jesus Christ Came to any of John's deciples He baptized them with fire & the Holy Ghost.

We find the Apostles endowed with greater power than John. Their office was more under the spirit & power of Elijah than Elias. In the Case of Philip when he went down to Samaria [he] was under the spirit of Elias. He baptised both men & women. When Peter & John herd of it they went down & lade hands on them & they received the Holy Ghost. This shows the distinction between the two powers. When Paul came to certain deciples He asked if they had received the Holy Ghost. They said no. Who baptized you then? We were Baptized unto Johns Baptism. No John did not baptized you for he did his work right, & so Paul went & baptized them for He knew what the true doctrin was & he knew that John Had not Baptised them & these [are] principles and [it] is strange to me that men who have red the scriptures of the New Testament are so far from it.

What I want to impress upon your minds is the difference of power in the different parts of the Priesthood, so that when any man comes among you saying I have the spirit of Elias you can know whether he be true or fals. For any man that comes having the spirit & power of Elias he will not transend his bounds. John did not transend his bound but faithfully performed that part belonging to his office, and evry portion of the great building should be prepared right & assigned to its proper place, & it is necessary to know who holds the keys of power & who dont or we may be likely to be decieved. That person who holds the keys of Elias hath a preparitory work.

But if I spend much more time in conversing about the spirit of Elias I shall not have time to do justice to the spirit & power of Elijah. This is the Elias spoken of in the last days & here is the rock upon which many split thinking the time was past in the days of John & Christ & no more to be. But the spirit of Elias was revealed to me & I know it is true. Therefore I speak with boldness for I know varily my doctrin is true. Now for Elijah, the spirit power & Calling of Elijah is that ye have power to hold the keys of the revelations ordinances, oricles powers & endowments of the fulness of the Melchezedek Priesthood & of the kingdom of God on the Earth & to recieve, obtain & perform all the ordinances belonging to the kingdom of God even unto the sealing of the hearts of the fathers unto the Children &

the hearts of the Children unto the fathers even those who are in heaven. Malachi says I will send Elijah befor the great and dredful day of the Lord come & He shall turn the hearts of the Fathers to the Children and the hearts of the Children to the Fathers lest I come & smite the earth with a curse.

Now what I am after is the knowledge of God & I take my own Course to obtain it. What are we to understand by this in the last days? In the days of Noah God destroyed the world by a flood & has promised to destroy it by fire in the last days. But before it took place Elijah should first Come & turn the hearts of the Fathers to the Children &c.

Now comes the point. What is this office & work of Elijah? It is one of the greatest & most important subjects that God has revealed. He should send Elijah to seal the Children to the fathers & fathers to the Children. Now was this merely confined to the living to settle difficulties with families on earth? By no means. It was a far greater work. Elijah what would you do if you was here? Would you confine your work to the living alone? No. I would refer you to the scriptures whare the subject is manifest. Ie without us they could not be made perfect nor we without them, the fathers without the Children nor the Children without the fathers. I wish you to understand this subject for it is important & if you will recieve it this is the spirit of Elijah that we redeem our dead & connect ourselves with our fathers which are in heaven & seal up our dead to come forth in the first resurrection & here we want the power of Elijah to seal those who dwell on earth to those which dwell in heaven. This is the power of Elijah & the keys of the kingdom of Jehovah.

Let us suppose a case. Suppose the great God who dwells in heaven should reveal himself to Father Cutler here by the opening heavens and tell him I offer up a decree that whatsoever you seal on earth with your decree I will seal it in heaven. You have power then. Can it be taken of[f]? No. Then what you seal on earth by the keys of Elijah is sealed in heaven & this is the power of Elijah, & this is the difference between the spirit & power of Elias and Elijah. For while the spirit of Elias is a fore runner the power of Elijah is sufficient to make our Calling & Election sure & the same doctrin whare we are exhorted to go on to perfection not laying again the foundation of repentance from dead works but of laying on of hands resurrection of the dead &c. We cannot be perfect without the fathers, &c.

We must have revelations then & we can see that the doctrin of revelation as far transcends the doctrin of no revelation as knowledge is above ignorance. For one truth revealed from heaven is worth all the sectarian notions in exhistance.

This spirit of Elijah was manifest in the days of the Apostles in delivering certain ones to the buffitings of Satan that they may be saved in the day of the Lord Jesus. They were sealed by the spirit of Elijah unto the damnation of Hell untill the day of the Lord or revelation of Jesus Christ.

Here is the doctrin of Election that the world have quarreled so much about but they do not know any thing about it. The doctrin that the Prysbeterians & Methodist[s] have quarreled so much about once in grace always in grace, or falling away from Grace I will say a word about. They are both wrong. Truth takes a road between them both. For while the Presbyterian Says once in grace you cannot fall the Methodist says you can have grace to day, fall from it to morrow, next day have grace again & so follow it. But the doctrin of the scriptures & the spirit of Elijah would show them both fals & take a road between them both. For according to the scriptures if a man has receive the good word of God & tasted of the powers of the world to come if they shall fall away it is impossible to renew them again seeing they have Crucified the son of God afresh & put him to an open shame. So their is a possibility of falling away. Y[ou] could not be renewed again, & the power of Elijah Cannot seal against this sin for this is a reserve made in the seals & power of the priesthood.

I will make evry doctrin plain that I present & it shall stand upon a firm bases. And I am at the defiance of the world for I will take shelter under the broad cover of the wings of the work in which I am ingaged. It matters not to me if all hell boils over. I regard it ownly as I would the Crackling of thorns under a pot.

A murderer, for instance one that sheds innocent Blood cannot have forgiveness. David sought repentance at the hand of God Carefully with tears but he could ownly get it through Hell. He got a promise that his soul should not be left in Hell. Although David was a king he never did obtain the spirit & power of Elijah & the fulness of the Priesthood, and the priesthood that he received & the throne & kingdom of David is to be taken from him & given to another by the name of David in the last days raised up out of his linage.

Peter refered to the same subject on the day of pentecost, but the multitude did not get the endowment that Peter had. But several days after the people asked what shall we do? Peter says I would ye had done it ignorantly speaking of crucifying the Lord &c. He did not say to them repent & be baptized for the remission of your sins but he said repent therefore & be converted that your sins may be blotted out when the times of refreshing shall come from the presence of the Lord. Acts III 19. This is the case with murderers. They could not be baptized for the remission of sins for they had shed innocent Blood.

Again the doctrin or sealing power of Elijah is as follows: If you have power to seal on earth & in heaven then we should be crafty. The first thing you do go & seal on earth your sons & daughters unto yourself & yourself unto your fathers in eternal glory & go ahead and not go back but use a little Craftiness & seal all you can & when you get to heaven tell your father that what you seal on earth should be sealed in heaven. I will walk through the gate of heaven and Claim what I seal & those that follow me & my Council.

The Lord once told me that what I asked for I should have. I have been afraid to ask God to kill my enemies lest some of them should peradventure repent. I asked a short time since for the Lord to deliver me out of the hands of the govornor of Missouri & if it must needs be to accomplish it to take him away & the next news that came pouring down from their was Govornor Reynolds had shot himself. And I would now say beware O earth how you fight against the saints of God & shed innocent Blood, for in the days of Elijah his enemies came upon him & fire was called down from heaven & destroyed them.

The spirit of Elias is first, Elijah second, & Mesiah last. Elias is a fore runner to prepare the way, & the spirit & power of Elijah is to come after holding the keys of power building the Temple to the cap stone placing the seals of the Melchezedeck priesthood up on the house of Israel & making all things ready. Then Mesiah comes to his Temple which is last of all. Mesiah is above the spirit & power of Elijah for he made the world & was that spiritual rock unto Moses in the wilderness. Elijah was to come & prepare the way & build up the kingdom before the coming of the great day of the Lord.

Although the spirit of Elias might begin it, I have asked of the Lord concerning his Coming & while asking, the Lord gave me a sign & said in the days of Noah I set a bow in the heavens as a sign & token that in any year that the bow should be seen the Lord would not come, but their should be seed time—harvest during that year. But whenever you see the bow withdraw it shall be a token that their shall be famin pestilence & great distress among the nations.

But I take the responsibility upon myself to prophesy in the name of the Lord, that Christ will not come this year as Miller has prophecyed, for we have seen the bow. And I also Prophecy in the name of the Lord that Christ will not Come in *forty years* & if God ever spake by my mouth he will not come in that length of time, & Jesus Christ never did reveal to any man the precise time that he would Come. Go & read the scriptures & you cannot find any thing that specifies the exact [time] he would come & all that say so are fals teachers.

Their are some important things concerning the office of the Mesiah in the organization of the world which I will speak of hereafter. May God Almighty bless you & pour out his spirit upon you is the prayer of your unworthy servant Amen.

{48}

"I Now Call the Attention of this Congregation," A Sermon Delivered on 7 April 1844

(see Stan Larson, ed.,
"The King Follett Discourse: A Newly Amalgamated Text,"
Brigham Young University Studies 18 [Winter 1978]: 193-208)

I now call the attention of this congregation while I address you on the subject which was contemplated in the fore-part of the conference. As the wind blows very hard it will be hardly possible for me to make you all hear unless there is profound attention. It is a subject of the greatest importance and the most solemn of any that could occupy our attention, and that is the subject of the dead. I have been requested to speak on the subject on the decease of our beloved brother, Elder King Follett, who was crushed to death in a well, by the falling of a rub of rock on him. I have been requested to speak by his friends and relatives but inasmuch as there are a great many others here in this congregation, who live in this city as well as elsewhere, who have lost friends, their case will be had in mind this afternoon, and I feel disposed to speak on the subject in general and offer you my ideas as far as I have ability and as far as I will be inspired by the Holy Spirit to treat and dwell upon this subject. I want your prayers, faith, the inspiration of Almighty God, and the gift of the Holy Ghost that I may set forth things that are true and that can easily be comprehended and which shall carry the testimony to your hearts. I pray that the Lord may strengthen my lungs, stay the winds, and let the prayer of the Saints to heaven appear that it may enter into the ear of the Lord of Sabaoth, for the fervent effectual prayer of a righteous man availeth much. There is strength here and I verily believe that your prayers will be heard. I will speak in order to hold out.

Before I enter fully into the investigation of the subject that is lying before us, I wish to pave the way, make a few preliminaries, and bring up the subject from the beginning in order that you may understand the subject when I come to it. I do not calculate to please your ears with superfluity of words, with oratory, or with much learning, but I calculate to edify you with the simple truths of heaven.

In the first place I wish to go back to the beginning of creation. There is the starting point in order to know and be fully acquainted with the mind, purposes, decrees, and ordinations of the great Elohim that sits in the heavens. For us to take up beginning at the creation it is necessary for us to understand something of God Himself in the beginning. If we start right, it is very easy for us to go right all the time; but if we start wrong, we may go wrong, and it is a hard matter to get right.

There are but very few beings in the world who understand rightly the character of God. If men do not comprehend the character of God, they do not comprehend their own character. They cannot comprehend anything that is past or that which is to come; they do not know—they do not understand their own relationship to God. The world knows and comprehends but little more than the brute beast. If a man knows nothing more than to eat, drink, sleep, arise, and not any more, and does not comprehend what any of the designs of Jehovah are, what better is he than the beast, for it comprehends the same things—it eats, drinks, sleeps, comprehends the present and knows nothing more about God or His existence. This is as much as we know unless we are able to comprehend by the inspiration of Almighty God. And how are we to do it by any other way?

I want to go back, then, to the beginning that you may under-stand and so get you to lift your minds into a more lofty sphere and exalted standing than what the human mind generally understands. I want to ask this congregation—every man, woman, and child—to answer this question in their own heart: What kind of a being is God? Ask yourselves! I again repeat the question: What kind of a being is God? Does any man or woman know? Turn your thoughts in your hearts, and say, Have any of you seen Him? Or heard Him? Or communed with Him? Here is a question that will, peradventure, from this time henceforth occupy your attention while you live.

The Apostle says that this is eternal life to know the only wise God and Jesus Christ whom He has sent—that is eternal life. If any man inquire, What kind of a being is God?—if he will cast his mind to know and search diligently his own heart—if the declaration of the Apostle be true, he will realize that unless he knows God he has not eternal life for there can be eternal life on no other principle.

233

My first object is to go back and find out the character of the only wise and true God and what kind of a being He is. If I should be the man so fortunate as to comprehend God and explain to your hearts what kind of a being God is, so that the Spirit seals it, then let every man and woman henceforth put his hand on his mouth, sit in silence, and never say anything or lift his voice against the servants of God again. But if I fail to do it, I have no right to revelation and inspiration and it becomes my duty to renounce all of my pretensions to inspiration or to being a prophet, etc. If I should do so, should I not be as bad as all the rest of the false teachers of the world? They will all be as badly off as I am. They will all say I ought to be damned. There is not a man or a woman who would not breathe out an anathema on my head if they knew I was a false prophet. Some would feel authorized to take away my life, but you might just as well take the lives of other false teachers as mine, if I were false. If any man is authorized to take away my life who says I am a false teacher, then, upon the same principle, I should have the same right to take the life of all false teachers and who would not be the sufferer and where would be the end of the blood?

But meddle not with any man for his religion, for no man is authorized to take away life in consequence of religion. All laws and government ought to tolerate and permit every man to enjoy his religion, whether right or wrong. There is no law in the heart of God that would allow anyone to interfere with the rights of man. Every man has a right to be a false prophet, as well as a true prophet. If I show verily that I have the truth of God, show the world is wrong by showing what God is, and show that ninety-nine out of a hundred are false prophets and teachers while they pretend to hold the keys of God, and go to killing them, would it not deluge the whole world with blood?

I am going to inquire after God because I want you all to know God and to be familiar with Him. If I can get you to know Him, I can bring you to Him. And if so, all persecution against me will cease. This will let you know that I am His servant, for I speak as one having authority and not as a scribe.

What kind of a being was God in the beginning, before the world was? I will go back to the beginning to show you. I will tell you, so open your ears and eyes, all ye ends of the earth, and hear, for I am going to prove it to you with the Bible. I am going to tell you the designs of God for the human race, the relation the human family sustains with God, and why He interferes with the affairs of man. First,

God Himself who sits enthroned in yonder heavens is a Man like unto one of yourselves—that is the great secret! If the veil were rent today and the great God that holds this world in its sphere and the planets in their orbit and who upholds all things by His power—if you were to see Him today, you would see Him in all the person, image, fashion, and very form of a man, like yourselves. For Adam was a man formed in His likeness and created in the very fashion and image of God. Adam received instruction, walked, talked, and conversed with Him as one man talks and communicates with another.

In order to understand the subject of the dead and to speak for the consolation of those who mourn for the loss of their friends, it is necessary to understand the character and being of God. For I am going to tell you how God came to be God and what sort of a being He is. For we have imagined that God was God from the beginning of all eternity. I will refute that idea and take away the veil so you may see. Truth is the touchstone. These things are incomprehensible to some, but they are simple. The first principle of truth and of the Gospel is to know for a certainty the character of God, and that we may converse with Him the same as one man with another, and that He once was a man like one of us and that God Himself, the Father of us all, once dwelled on an earth the same as Jesus Christ himself did in the flesh and like us.

I will show it from the Bible. I wish I were in a suitable place to tell it. I wish I had the trump of an archangel. If I had the privilege, I could tell the story in such a manner that persecution would cease forever. The scriptures inform us (Mark it, Brother [Sidney] Rigdon) that Jesus Christ said:—What did Jesus say?—As the Father has power in Himself, even so has the Son power in himself. To do what? Why, what the Father did. That answer is obvious; even in a manner to lay down His body and take it up again. Jesus, what are you going to do? "To lay down my life as my Father laid down His body that I might take it up again." Do you believe it? If you don't believe it, you don't believe the Bible. The Scriptures say it and I defy all hell—all the learned wisdom and records and all the combined powers of earth and hell together to refute it!

Here then is eternal life—to know the only wise and true God. You have got to learn how to make yourselves Gods in order to save yourselves and be kings and priests to God, the same as all Gods have done—by going from a small capacity to a great capacity, from a small degree to another, from grace to grace, until the resurrection of the dead from exaltation to exaltation—till you are able to sit in everlasting burnings and everlasting power and glory as those who have gone before, sit enthroned. I want you to know that God in the last days, while certain individuals are proclaiming His name, is not trifling with you nor me.

I want you to know the first principles of consolation. How consoling to the mourners when they are called to part with a husband, father, wife, mother, child, dear relative, or friend, to know, though they lay down this body and all earthly tabernacles shall be dissolved, that their very being shall rise in immortal glory to dwell in everlasting burnings and to sorrow, die, and suffer no more. And not only that, but to contemplate the saying that they will be heirs of God and joint-heirs with Jesus Christ. What is it? To inherit and enjoy the same glory, powers, and exaltation until you ascend a throne of eternal power and arrive at the station of a God the same as those who have gone before. What did Jesus Christ do? "Why I do the same things that I saw my Father do when worlds came rolling into existence." Saw the Father do what? "I saw the Father work out His kingdom with fear and trembling and I am doing the same, too. When I get my kingdom, I will give it to the Father and it will add to and exalt His glory. He will take a higher exaltation and I will take His place and am also exalted, so that He obtains kingdom rolling upon kingdom." So that Jesus treads in His tracks as He had gone before and then inherits what God did before. God is glorified in the salvation and exaltation of His creatures.

It is plain beyond comprehension and you thus learn that these are some of the first principles of the Gospel, about which so much has been said. When you climb a ladder, you must begin at the bottom rung. You have got to find the beginning of the history and go on until you have learned the last principle of the Gospel. It will be a great while after the grave before you learn to understand the last, for it is a great thing to learn salvation beyond the grave and it is not all to be comprehended in this world.

I suppose I am not allowed to go into an investigation of anything that is not contained in the Bible. If I should, you would cry treason, and I think there are so many learned and wise men here who would put me to death for treason. I will, then, go to the old Bible and turn commentator today. I will go to the very first Hebrew word—BER-

ESHITH—in the Bible and make a comment on the first sentence of the history of creation: "In the beginning . . . . " I want to analyze the word BERESHITH. BE-in, by, through, and everything else; next, ROSH-the head; ITH. Where did it come from? When the inspired man wrote it, he did not put the first part—the BE—there; but a man—an old Jew without any authority—put it there. He thought it too bad to begin to talk about the head of any man. It read in the first: "The Head One of the Gods brought forth the Gods." This is the true meaning of the words. ROSHITH signifies to bring forth the Elohim. If you do not believe it, you do not believe the learned man of God. No learned man can tell you any more than what I have told you. Thus, the Head God brought forth the Head Gods in the grand, head council. I want to simplify it in the English language.

O, ye lawyers, ye learned doctors, who have persecuted me, I want to let you know and learn that the Holy Ghost knows something as well as you do. The Head One of the Gods called together the Gods and the grand councillors sat in grand council at the head in yonder heavens to bring forth the world and contemplated the creation of the worlds that were created at that time. When I say doctors and lawyers, I mean the doctors and lawyers of the Scriptures. I have done so hitherto, to let the lawyers flutter and let everybody laugh at them. Some learned doctor might take a notion to say that the Scriptures say thus and so and we must believe the Scriptures, for they are not to be altered. But I am going to show you an example of an error.

I have an old book (New Testament) in the four languages: Latin, Greek, Hebrew, and German. I have been reading the German. I find it to be the most correct that I have found and find it corresponds the nearest to the revelations that I have received and given the last fourteen years. What does this text say? It tells about JAKOBUS, the son of Zebedee, which means Jacob. In the English New Testament it says James, the son of Zebedee, but this says Jacob, the son of Zebedee. Now, if Jacob had the keys, you might talk about James through all eternity and never get the keys. Matthew 4:21 gives the testimony that it is the word of Jacob, instead of James. The doctors (I mean doctors of law, not of physic) say, "If you say anything not according to the Bible, we will cry treason." How can we escape the damnation of hell, unless God be with us and reveal it to us. Men bind us with chains. The Latin says IACOBUS, which means Jacob; the Hebrew says YA'AQOB, which means Jacob; the Greek says IAKOBOS—Jacob; and the German says Jacob. I thank God

I have got the oldest book in the world and the Holy Ghost. I thank Him for the old book, but more for having the oldest book in my heart—the gift of the Holy Ghost. Here I have all four testimonies: Greek, Hebrew, German, and Latin.

Come here, ye learned men, and read, if you can. I should not have introduced this testimony, only to show that I am right and to back up the word ROSH—the Head Father of the Gods. In the beginning the Head of the Gods called a council of the Gods. The Gods came together and concocted a scheme to create this world and the inhabitants. When we begin to learn in this way we begin to learn the only true God. We find out God and what kind of a being we have got to worship. Having a knowledge of God, we know how to approach Him and ask so that He will answer. When we begin to know how to come to Him, He begins to come to us. When we are ready to come to Him, He is ready to receive us. As soon as we begin to understand the character of God, He begins to unfold the heavens to us and tell us all about it before our prayers get to His ears.

Now, I ask all the learned men who hear me, why the learned doctors who are preaching salvation say that God created the heavens and the earth out of nothing. They account it blasphemy to contradict the idea. If you tell them that God made the world out of something, they will call you a fool. The reason is that they are unlearned but I am learned and know more than all the world put together—the Holy Ghost does, anyhow. If the Holy Ghost in me comprehends more than all the world, I will associate myself with it.

You ask them why, and they say, "Doesn't the Bible say He created the world?" And they infer that it must be out of nothing. The word create came from the word BARA, but it doesn't mean so. What does BARA mean? It means to organize; the same as a man would organize and use things to build a ship. Hence, we infer that God Himself had materials to organize the world out of chaos—chaotic matter—which is element and in which dwells all the glory. Element had an existence from the time He had. The pure principles of element are principles that never can be destroyed. They may be organized and reorganized, but not destroyed. Nothing can be destroyed. They never can have a beginning or an ending; they exist eternally. It is associated with the subject in question, the resurrection of the dead.

I have another subject to dwell on which is calculated to exalt man, but it isn't possible for me to say much but to touch upon it.

238

Time will not permit me to say all. So I must come to what I wish to speak of—the resurrection of the dead—the soul—the immortal spirit—the mind of man. Where did it come from? All doctors of divinity say that God created it in the beginning, but it is not so. The very idea lessens the character of man, in my estimation. I don't believe the doctrine. Hear it, all ye ends of the earth: I know better for God has told me so. I will make a man appear a fool before he gets through. If he doesn't believe it it won't make the truth without effect. I am going to tell of things more noble.

We say that God Himself is a self-existent God. Who told you so? It's correct enough, but how did it get into your heads? Who told you that man did not exist in like manner upon the same principle? How does it read in the Hebrew? It doesn't say so in the old Hebrew. God made the tabernacle of man out of the earth and put into him Adam's spirit (which was created before), and then it became a living body or human soul. Man existed in spirit; the mind of man—the intelligent part—is as immortal as, and is coequal with, God Himself. I know that my testimony is true.

Hence when I talk to these mourners, what have they lost? You who mourn the loss of friends are only separated for a small moment from their spirits, and their spirits are only separated from their bodies for a short season. But their spirits existed coequal with God and they now exist in a place where they hold converse together one with another the same as we do on the earth. Does not this give you satisfaction?

I want to reason more on the spirit of man for I am dwelling on the immutability of the spirit and on the body of man—on the subject of the dead. Is it logical to say that a spirit is immortal and yet have a beginning? Because if a spirit of man had a beginning, it will have an end, but it does not have a beginning or end. This is good logic and is illustrated by my ring. I take my ring from my finger and liken it unto the mind of man—the immortal spirit—because it has no beginning or end. Suppose you cut it in two—as the Lord lives there would be a beginning and an end. So it is with man. All the fools and learned and wise men from the beginning of creation who come and say that, man had a beginning, prove that he must have an end. If that doctrine be true, then the doctrine of annihilation would be true. But if I am right, then I might with boldness proclaim from the housetop that God never had the power to create the spirit of man at all. God Himself could not create Himself.

239

Intelligence is eternal and exists upon a self-existent principle. It is a spirit from age to age and there is no creation about it. The first principles of man are self-existent with God. All the minds and spirits that God ever sent into the world are susceptible of enlargement and improvement. The relationship we have with God places us in a situation to advance in knowledge. God Himself found Himself in the midst of spirits and glory. Because He was greater He saw proper to institute laws whereby the rest who were less in intelligence, could have a privilege to advance like Himself and be exalted with Him, so that they might have one glory upon another in all that knowledge, power, and glory. So He took in hand to save the world of spirits.

This is good doctrine. It tastes good. You say honey is sweet and so do I. I can also taste the spirit and principles of eternal life, and so can you. I know it is good and that when I tell you of these words of eternal life that are given to me by the inspiration of the Holy Spirit and the revelations of Jesus Christ, you are bound to receive them as sweet. You taste them and I know you believe them. I rejoice more and more.

I want to talk more of man's relation to God. I will open your eyes in relation to your dead. All things whatsoever God in His infinite reason has seen fit and proper to reveal to us while we are dwelling in our mortal state, in regard to our mortal bodies, are revealed to us in the abstract and independent of affinity of this mortal tabernacle. His commandments are revealed to our spirits precisely the same as though we had no bodies at all and those revelations which must of necessity save our spirits will save our bodies. God reveals them to us in the view of no eternal dissolution of our bodily tabernacles. Hence, the responsibility, the awful responsibility, that rests upon us in relation to our dead; for all the spirits who have not obeyed the Gospel in the flesh must either obey the Gospel and be baptized, or be damned. Solemn thought! Dreadful thought!

Is there no preparation for—no salvation for—nothing to be done for—our fathers and friends who have gone before us and not obeyed the decrees of the Son of Man? I would to God that I had forty days and nights to talk, and to tell you all, to let you know that I am not a fallen prophet. What promises are made? What can be said if in the grave? What kind of characters are those who can be saved, although their bodies are moldering and decaying in the grave? We are looked upon by God, who dwells in eternity, as though we were in eternity, and when His commandments touch us it is in view of eternity. He does not view things as we to. The greatest responsibility that God has laid upon us in this world is to seek after our dead.

The Apostle says, "They without us cannot be made perfect." Now I am talking of them. I say to you, Paul, "You can't be made perfect without us." I will meet Paul half way. It is necessary that those who have gone before and those who come after us must be made perfect and have salvation in common with us. For it is necessary that the seats be in our hands, to seat our children and our dead for the dispensation of the fulness of times—a dispensation to meet the promises made by Jesus Christ before the foundation of the world for the salvation of man. God has made it obligatory to man and thus has He laid it upon the eaves of the world. Hence, the saying of Elijah: God said He shall send Elijah, etc.

I have a declaration to make in relation to the provisions which God made for every creature from before the foundation of the world to suit the conditions of man. What has Jesus said? All sins and all blasphemies—every transgression that man may be guilty of—shall be forgiven in this world or the world to come, except one—the sin against the Holy Ghost. There is a provision for salvation for him, either in this world or in the world of spirits which is to come. Hence, God has made a provision that the spirits of our friends and every spirit in that eternal world can be ferreted out and saved, unless he has committed that unpardonable sin which can't be remitted to him, whether in this world or in the world of spirits. God has wrought out salvation for all men, unless they have committed a certain sin. Every man who has got a friend in the eternal world can save him, unless he has committed the unpardonable sin. You can save any man who has not committed the unpardonable sin. So you can see how far you can be a savior.

A man cannot commit the unpardonable sin after the dissolution of the body. He cannot be damned through all eternity; there is a way possible for his escape in a little time, so he is not particularly damned. If a man has knowledge he can be saved, for knowledge saves a man. There are those that are without wisdom until they get exalted to wisdom, and in the world of spirits there is no way for a man to come to understanding and be exalted but by knowledge. If he has been guilty of great sins, he is punished for them. So long as a man will not give consent and heed to the commandments, he must abide without salvation. When he consents to obey the Gospel, whether alive or dead, he is saved.

A sinner has his own mind and his own mind damns him. He is damned by mortification and is his own condemner and tormenter. Hence the saying: They shall go into the lake that burns with fire and brimstone. I have no fear of hell fire, that doesn't exist, but the torment and disappointment of the mind of man is as exquisite as a lake burning with fire and brimstone—so is the torment of man.

I know the Scriptures; I understand them. I said that no man can commit the unpardonable sin after the dissolution of the body. Why? Because they must commit the unpardonable sin in this world after they receive the Holy Ghost. All will suffer in the eternal world until they obey Christ himself and are exalted. Hence, the salvation of the Savior Jesus Christ was wrought out for all men to triumph over the works of the devil; if the plan did not catch them in one place, it would in another. The devil came to save the world and stood up as a savior. The contention in heaven was that Jesus contended that there would be certain souls that would be condemned and not saved, but the devil said. "I am a savior," and that he could save them all. As the grand council gave in for Jesus Christ, the lot fell on him. So the devil rose up, rebelled against God, fell, and was thrust down, with all who put up their heads for him.

All sin shall be forgiven, except the sin against the Holy Ghost, for Jesus Christ will save all except the sons of perdition. What must a man do to commit the unpardonable sin? He has got to deny the plan of salvation; he has got to say that the sun does not shine while he sees it with his eyes open; he has got to receive the Holy Ghost, deny Jesus Christ when the heavens are open to him, know God, and then sin against Him. After a man has sinned the sin against the Holy Ghost, there is no repentance for him.

Hence, from that time they begin to be enemies, like many of the apostates of Christ—of The Church of Jesus Christ of Latter-day Saints. They go too far, and the Spirit leaves them. Hence, when a man begins to be an enemy, he hunts me, he seeks to kill me, he thirsts for my blood, he never ceases to try to hurt me. For he has got the same spirit of the devil that they had who crucified Jesus, the Lord of Life—the same spirit that sins against the Holy Ghost. You can't renew them to repentance—you cannot save them; awful is the consequence, for they make open war like the devil.

I advise all to be careful what you do. Stay, all that hear. Do not give way. Don't make any hasty moves. You may be saved, or you may by and by find out that someone has laid a snare for you and you have been deceived. Be cautious: await. If a spirit of bitterness is in you, don't be in haste. When you find a spirit that wants bloodshed—murder—the same is not of God, but is of the devil. Say you, "That man is a sinner;" well, if he repents, he shall be forgiven. Out of the abundance of the heart, man speaks. The man that tells you words of life is the man that can save you. The best men bring forth the best works. I warn you against all evil characters who sin against the Holy Ghost; for there is no redemption for them in this world nor in the world to come.

I could go back and trace every subject of interest concerning the relationship of man to God, if I had time. I can enter into the mysteries; I can enter largely into the eternal worlds; for Jesus said, "In my Father's kingdom there are many mansions," etc. There is one glory of the moon, sun, and stars, etc. What have we to console us in relation to our dead? We have reason to have the greatest hope and consolation for our dead of any people on earth. For we have aided them in the first principles. For we have seen them walk worthily on earth in our midst, and sink asleep in the arms of Jesus; and those who have died in the faith are now in the celestial kingdom of God. Hence, is the glory of the sun.

You mourners have occasion to rejoice, for your friend has gone to wait until the perfection of the reunion and the resurrection of the dead. At the resurrection of your friend in felicity, he will go to the celestial glory, while there are many who die in the world who must wait many myriads of years before they can receive the like blessings. Your expectation and hope is far above what man can conceive. For why has God revealed it to us?

I am authorized to say to you my friends, by the authority of the Holy Ghost and in the name of the Lord, that you have no occasion to fear; for he is gone to the home of the just. Don't mourn; don't weep. I know it by the testimony of the Holy Ghost that is within me. You may wait for your friends to come forth to meet you in eternity in the morn of the celestial world. Rejoice, O Israel! Your friends who have been murdered in the persecutions shall triumph gloriously in the celestial world, while their murderers shall welter and dwell in torment for years, until they pay the uttermost farthing. I say this for the benefit of strangers. I leave the subject.

I have a father, brothers, children, and friends who are gone to eternity to a world of spirits soon to meet me. I bless those who have lost friends. They are only absent for a few moments and the time will soon be gone. They are in the spirit. The trump will soon be blown, and then shall we hail our mothers, fathers, friends, and all. There will be no fear of mobs, etc., but all will have an eternity of felicity.

A question about parents receiving their children. Will mothers have their children in eternity? Yes! Yes! Mothers, you will have your children. For they will have it without price; for their debt of redemption is paid. There is no damnation awaiting them for they are in the spirit. But as the child dies, so will it rise from the dead and be living in the burning of God and possessing all the intelligence of a God. It will never grow, it will be the child in its precise form as it was before it died out of your arms. Children dwell and exercise power throne upon throne, dominion upon dominion, in the same form just as you laid them down. Eternity is full of thrones upon which dwell thousands of children, reigning on thrones of glory, with not one cubit added to their stature.

I will leave this subject here, and make a few remarks upon baptism. The baptism of water with the baptism of fire and the Holy Ghost attending it is necessary and inseparably connected. He must be born of water and the Spirit in order to get into the kingdom of God. Found in the German Bible is a text that bears me out the same as the revelations which I have given and taught for fourteen years about baptism. I have the testimony to put in their teeth that my testimony has been true all the time. You will find it in the declaration of John the Baptist. I will read a text in German upon baptism. John says, "I baptize you with water, but when Jesus Christ comes, who has the power and keys, He will administer the baptism of fire and the Holy Ghost." Great God! Now where is all the sectarian world? If this testimony is true, they are all damned as clearly as any anathema ever was. I know the text is true. I call upon all to say, Aye. Alexander Campbell, how are you going to save them with water? For John said his baptism was good for nothing without the baptism of Jesus Christ. Many talk of any baptism not being essential to salvation, but this would lay the foundation of their damnation. Leaving the principles of the doctrine of baptism, etc. There is one God, one Father, one Jesus, one hope of our calling, one baptism; that is, all three baptisms make one.

I have the truth and I am at the defiance of the world to contradict it. I have preached Latin, Hebrew, Greek, and German, and I have fulfilled all. I am not so big a fool as many have taken me for. The Germans know that I read the German correctly.

Hear it, all ye ends of the earth: I call upon all men—priests, sinners, and all. Repent! Repent! Turn to God and obey the gospel. For your religion won't save you, and if you do not, you will be damned, but I do not say how long. There have also been remarks made concerning all men being redeemed from hell, but those who sin against the Holy Ghost cannot be forgiven in this world or in the world to come. But I say that those who commit the unpardonable sin are doomed to GNOLAUM and must dwell in hell, worlds without end; they shall die the second death. As they concoct scenes of bloodshed in this world, so they shall rise to that resurrection which is as the lake of fire and brimstone. Some shall rise to the everlasting burning of God, for God dwells in everlasting burnings; and some shall rise to the damnation of their own filthiness, which is the same as the lake of fire and brimstone.

I have intended my remarks to all—to all the rich and poor, bond and free, great and small. I have no enmity against any man. I love all men—I love you all, but hate your deeds. I am their best friend, and if persons miss their mark it is their own fault. If I reprove a man, and he hate me, he is a fool; for I love all men, especially these my brethren and sisters. I rejoice in hearing the testimony of my aged friend.

You don't know me—you never will. You never knew my heart. No man knows my history. I cannot do it. I shall never undertake it. I don't blame you for not believing my history. If I had not experienced what I have, I could not have believed it myself. I never did harm any man since I have been born in the world. My voice is always for peace. I cannot lie down until my work is finished. I never think evil nor think anything to the harm of my fellowman. When I am called at the trump and weighed in the balance, you will know me then. I add no more. God bless you. Amen.

{49}

"The Savior Has the Words of Eternal Life," A Sermon Delivered on 12 May 1844

(from a manuscript by Thomas Bullock, original in archives, Historical Department, Church of Jesus Christ of Latter-day Saints, Salt Lake City, Utah)

The Savior has the words of Eternal life— nothing else can profit us— there is no salvation in believing an evil report against our neighbor— I advise all to go on to perfection and search deeper and deeper into the mysteries of Godliness— a man can do nothing for himself unless God direct him in the right way, and the Priesthood is reserved for that purpose— the last time I spoke on this stand, it was on the resurrection of the dead; when I promised to continue my remarks upon that subject. I still feel a desire to say something on this subject— let us this very day begin anew, and now say with all our hearts, we will forsake our sins and be righteous— I shall read the 24th. ch[apter] of Matthew and give it a litteral rendering and reading, and when it is rightly understood it will be edifying (he then read & translated it from the German) I thought the very oddity of its rendering would be edifying any how— "And it will preached be; the Gospel of the Kingdom in the whole world, to a witness over all people, and then will the end come." I will now read it in German— (which he did, and many Germans who were present said he translated it correct) the Savior said, when those tribulations should take place, it should be committed to a man, who should be a witness over the whole world. The keys of knowledge power, and revelations, should be revealed to a witness who hold the testimony to the world; it has always been my soul province to dig up hidden mysteries, new things, for my hearers— just at the time when some men think that I have no right to the keys of the Priesthood just at that time, I have the greatest right— the Germans are an exalted people. The old German translators are the most correct; most honest of any of the translators, and therefore I get testimony to bear me out in the revelations that I have preached for the last 14 year[s]— the old German, Latin, Greek and Hebrew translations all say it is true, they cannot be impeached, and therefore I am in good company— all the testimony is, that the Lord in the last days would commit the keys of the Priesthood to a witness over all people— has the Gospel of the Kingdom commenced in the last days? and will God take it from the man, until he takes him, himself? I have read it precisely as the words flowed from the lips of Jesus Christ— John the Revelator saw an angel flying thro' the midst of heaven, having the everlasting Gospel to preach unto them that dwell on the earth, &c. The Scripture is ready to be fulfilled when great wars, famines, pestilence, great distress, judgements, &c are ready to be poured out on the Inhabitants of the Earth— John saw the angel having the holy Priesthood who should preach the everlasting gospel to all nations,— God had an angel, a special messenger, ordained, & prepared for that purpose in the last days— Woe! Woe! be to that man, or set of men, who lift up their hands against God and his Witness in these last days.— For they shall deceive almost the very chosen ones— my enemies say that I have been a true prophet— & I had rather be a fallen true prophet, than a false prophet; when a man goes about prophesying and commands men to obey his teachings, he must be either a true or false prophet; false prophets always arise to oppose the true prophets, and they will prophesy so very near the truth that they will deceive almost the very chosen ones— the doctrine of eternal judgments belong to the 1st. principles of the Gospel in the last days— in relation to the Kingdom of God—the devil always sets up his Kingdom at the very same time in opposition to God,— every man who has a calling to mininster to the Inhabitants of the world, was ordained to that very purpose in the grand Council of Heaven before this world was— I suppose that I was ordained to this very office in that grand Council— It is the testimony that I want, that I am God's servant, and this people his people— The Ancient Prophets declared in the last days the God of Heaven shall set up a Kingdom which should never be destroyed, nor, left to other people; & the very time that was calculated on; this people was struggling to bring it out— he that arms himself with Gun, sword, or Pistol except in the defense of truth, will some time be sorry for it— I never carry any weapon with me bigger than my Pen Knife— When I was dragged before the Cannon and muskets in Missouri, I was unarmed. God will always protect me until my mission is fulfilled. I calculate to be one of the Instruments of setting up the Kingdom of

247

Daniel, by the word of the Lord, and I intend to lay a foundation that will revolutionize the whole world— I once offered my life to the Missouri Mob as a sacrifice for my people—and here I am— it will not be by Sword or Gun that this Kingdom will roll on— the power of truth is such that—all nations will be under the necessity of obeying the Gospel[.] the prediction is that army will be against army—it may be that the Saints will have to beat their Ploughes into Swords. It will not do for men to sit down and see their women & children destroyed patientl[y],— my text is on the resurrection of the dead, which you will find in the 14 ch[apter]. of John. In my Fathers house are many mansions &c it should be In my Father's Kingdom are many Kingdoms—in order that ye may be heirs of God and joint heirs with me— I do not believe the methodist doctrine of sending honest men, and noble minded men to hell, along with the murderer and adulterer— they may hurl all their hell and fiery billows upon me, for they will roll off me as fast as they come on— but I have an order of things to save the poor fellows at any rate, and get them saved for I will send men to preach to them in prison and save them if I can. There are many mansions for those who obey a celestial law—& there are other mansions for those who come short of that law—every man in his own order[.] there is baptism &c for those to exercise who are alive, and baptism for the dead, who died without the knowledge of the gospel[.] I am going on in my progress for eternal life— it is not only necessary that you should be baptized for your dead, but you will have to go thro' all the ordinances for them, same as you have gone through, to save yourselves; there will be 144,000 Saviors on Mount Zion, and with them an innumerable host, that no man can number— Oh! I beseech you to forward, go forward and make your calling and your election sure— and if any man preach any other gospel with that which I have preached, he shall be cursed, and some of you who now hear me, shall see it & know that I testify the truth concerning them; in regard to the law of the Priesthood—there should be a place where all nations shall come up from time to time to receive their endowments, and the Lord has said, this shall be the place for the baptism for the dead— every man that has been baptized and belongs to the Kingdom, has a right to be baptized for those who are gone before, and, as soon as the Law of the Gospel is obeyed here by their friends, who act as proxy for them, the Lord has administrators there to set them free— a man may act as proxy for his own relatives— the ordinances of the

248

Gospel which was laid out before the foundation of the world has been thus fulfilled, by them, and we may be baptized for those who we have much friendship for, but it must be first revealed to the man of God, lest we should run too far— as in Adam all die, so in Christ shall all be made alive, all shall be raised from the dead— the Lamb of God hath brought to pass the resurrection so that all shall rise from the dead— God Almighty himself dwells in Eternal fire, flesh and blood cannot go there for all corruption is devoured by the fire— our God is a consuming fire— when our flesh is quickened by the Spirit, there will be no blood in the tabernacles,— some dwell in higher glory than others—those who have done wrong, always have that wrong knawing them— Immortality dwells in everlasting burnings— I will from time to time reveal to you the subjects that are revealed by the Holy Ghost to me— all the lies that are now hatched up against me are of the devil & all the influence of the devil & his servants will be used against the kingdom of God— the Servants of God teach nothing but the principles of eternal life— by their works ye shall know them— a good man will speak good things, & holy principles and an evil man, evil things;— I feel in the name of the Lord, to rebuke all such bad principles, liars &c and I warn all of you to look out who you are going after— I exhort you to give heed to all the virtue and the teachings which I have given you; all men who are immortal, dwell in everlasting burnings; you cannot go any where, but where God can find you out; all men are born to die & all must rise, all must enter eternity— in order for you to receive your children to yourself, you must have a promise, some ordinance some blessing in order to assend above principalities or else it may be an angel— they must rise just as they died— we can there hail our lovely infants with the same glory, the same loveliness in the celestial glory where they all enjoy alike— they differ in stature, in size— the same glorious spirit gives them the likeness of glory and bloom— the old man with his silvery hairs will glory in bloom & beauty— no man can describe it to you— no man can write it— when did I ever teach any thing wrong from this stand? when was I ever confounded? I want to triumph in Israel before I depart hence and am no more seen— I never told you I was perfect—but there is no error in the revelations which I have taught— must I then be thrown away as a thing of nought?— I enjoin for your consideration, add to your faith, virtue, love &C. I say in the name of the Lord, if these things are in you, you shall be fruitful. I testify that no man has power to reveal it, but myself, things in heaven, in earth and hell— and all shut your mouths for the future— I commend you all to God, that you may inherit all things— & may God add his blessings. Amen.

{50}

"K[ings] & P[riests] unto God & His Fa[the]r," A Sermon Delivered on 16 June 1844

(from a manuscript by Thomas Bullock, original in archives, Historical Department, Church of Jesus Christ of Latter-day Saints, Salt Lake City, Utah)

The Prophet [Joseph Smith] read the 3rd Rev text 6th. v. & made us K[ings] & P[riests] unto God & his Fa[the]r. to him be glory & dom[inion] for evermore—

It is altog[ethe]r correct in the translat[io]n.— now you know that of late some have sprung up & apostat[ized]. & they declare that [the] Pro[phet] bel[ieves] in a plurality of Gods—&c. & behold a very great secret[,] they cry it has been my intent[io]n to take up this subj[ec]t & show what my Faith is in the matter— I have contemplated the saying of Je[sus] as it was in the days of Noah so shall it be at his 2nd. coming & if it rains I'll preach—the plurality of Gods— I have selected this text[.] I wish to declare I have allways—& in all congregat[ion]s when I have preached it has been the plurality of Gods[.] it has been preached 15 years— I have always decl[are]d God to be a distinct personage—J[esus] C[hrist] a sep[erate] & distinct pers[onage] from God the Fa[the]r. the H[oly] G[host] was a distinct personage & or Sp[irit] & these 3 constit[ute] 3 distinct personages & 3 Gods— if this is in accordance with the New Test[ament]— lo & behold we have 3 Gods any how & they are plural any how—our text says

the apostl[es] have disc[overe]d that there were Gods above— God was the Fa[the]r of our L[or]d J[esus] C[hrist].— my object was to preach the Scrip[tures]—& preach the doctrine there being a God above the Fa[the]r of our L[or]d J[esus] C[hrist].— I am bold to declare I have tau[gh]t all the strong doctrines publicly—& always stronger than what I preach in private— John was one of the men & the apos[tles] declare they were made K[ings] & P[riests] unto God the Fat[he]r of our L[or]d J[esus] C[hrist]. it reads just so[,] hence the doctrine of a plurality of Gods is as prominent in the Bible as any doctrine— it is all over the face of the Bible, it stands beyond the

251

power of controversy— a wayfaring man tho a fool need not fail— Paul says there are gods many & Lords many— I want to set it in a plain simple manner— but to us there is but one God pertaining to us, in all thro all,— but if J[oseph] Smith says there is Gods many & L[or]ds many they cry away with him crucify him[.] mankind verily say that the Scrip[ture] [i]s with them— Search the Script[ures] & & they testify of things that apostates wo[ul]d blaspheme— Paul[,] if Jo Smith is a blasphemer you are— I say there are Gods many & L[or]ds many but to us only one & we are to be in subject to that one & no man can limit the bounds, or the eternal existence of eternal time— hath he beheld the et[ernal] world & is he auth[orize]d to say that there is only God he makes himself a fool—& there is an end of his career in knowledge[.] he cannot obt[ai]n all knowledge for he has sealed up the gate to [it.]

some say I do not interpret same as you— they say it means the heathen God. Paul says there are Gods many &c it makes a plurality of Gods any how— with[ou]t a rev[elatio]n I am not going to give the God of Heaven to them any how— you know & I testify that Paul had no allusions to it— I have it from God & get over it if you can— I have a witness of the H[oly] G[host] & a test[imony]. that Paul had no allusion to the Heathen G[od] in the text— Twice I will shew from the Heb[rew] Bible & the 1st. word shews a plurality of Gods— & I want the apostate & learned men to come here—& prove to the contrary[.] an unlearned boy must give you a little Hebrew—Berosheit &c In the begin[ing]. rosheit—the head—it sho[ul]d read the heads of—to organ- ize the Gods—Eloiheam[.] Eloi. God in sing[ular] heam, reanders Gods[.] I want a little learning as well as other fools

[Alexander] Popes quot[ation]: Drink deep

all the confusion is for want of drinking and draught[.] the head God—organized the heavens & the Earth— I defy all the learning in the world to refute me.

In the begin[ning] the heads of the Gods organized the heaven & the Earth— now the learned Priest— [and] the people rage—& the heathen imagine a vain thing— if we pursue the Heb[rew] further—it reads

The Head one of the Gods said let us make man in our image[.] I once asked a learned Jew once—if the Heb. language compels us to render all words ending in heam in the plural—why not render the first plural— he replied it would ruin the Bible— he acknowledged I was right. I came here to investigate these things precisely as I believe it— hear & judge for yourself—& if you go away satisfied—well & good— in the very beginning there is a plurality of Gods beyond the power of refutation— it is a great subject I am dwelling on— the word Eloiheam ought to be in the plural all the way thro—Gods— the heads of the Gods appointed one God for us—& when you take a view of the subject it sets one free to see all the beauty holiness & perfection of the God— all I want is to get the simple truth—naked & the whole truth— Men say there is one God—the Fa[the]r Son & the H[oly] G[host] are only 1 God— it is a strange God any how 3 in 1. & 1 in 3. it is a curious thing any how— Fa[the]r. I pray not for the world but I pray for those that thou givest me &c &c all are to be crammed into 1 God— it wo[ul]d make the biggest God in all the world— he is a wonderful big God— he would be a Giant[.] I want to read the text to you myself— I am agreed with the Fa[the]r & the Fa[the]r is agreed with me & we are agreed as one— the Greek shews that is sho[ul]d be agreed— Fa[the]r. I pray for them that thou hast given me out of the world &c &c that they may be agreed & all come to dwell in unity & in all the Glory & Everlasting burn[in]gs of God & then we shall see as we are seen & be as God— & he as the God of his Fa[the]r.— I want to reason— I learned it by translating the papyrus now in my house—I learned a test[imony] concerning Abraham & he reasoned concern[in]g the God of Heaven— in order to do that s[ai]d he—suppose we have two facts that supposes that anot[he]r fact may exist[;] two men on the earth—one wiser than the other— wo[ul]d shew that an[o]t[he]r who is wiser than the wisest may exist— intelligences exist one above anot[he]r that there is no end to it— if Abra[ham] reasoned thus— if J[esus] C[hrist] was the Son of God & John disc[overe]d that god the Fa[the]r of J[esus] C[hrist] had a fa[the]r you may suppose that he had a Fa[the]r also— where was ther[e] ever a Son with[ou]t a Fa[the]r— where ever did tree or any thing spring into existence with[ou]t. a progenitor— & every thing comes in this way— Paul says that which is Earthly is in likeness of that which is Heavenly— hence if J[esus] had a Fa[the]r can we not believe that he had a Fa[the]r also— I despise the idea of being scared to death— I want you all to pay partic[ula]r attent[ion]. J[esus] s[ai]d as the Fa[the]r wrought precisely in the same way as his Fa[the]r had done bef[ore]— as the Fa[the]r had done bef[ore]— he laid down his life & took it up same as his Fa[the]r had done bef[ore]— he did as he was sent to lay down his life & take it up again & was then committed unto him the keys &c[.] I know it is good reasoning— I have reason to think that the Church is being purged— I saw Satan fall from heaven— & the way they ran was a caution. all these are wonders & marvellous in our eyes in these last days— so long as men are under the law of God they have no fears, they do not scarce themselves— I want to stick to my text—to shew that when men open their lips—they do not injure me—but injure themselves— To the law & to the testimony— they are poured all over the Scrip[tures.]

when things that are great are passed over with[ou]t even a tho[ugh]t I want to see all in all its bearings & hug it to my bosom— I bel[ieve] all that God ever rev[eale]d. & I never hear of a man being d[amne]d for bel[ievin]g too much but they are d[amne]d for un-bel[ief].

they found fault with J[esus] C[hrist] bec[ause] he s[ai]d he was the Son of God & made himself equal with God— they say like the apost[ates] of old [that] I must be put down— what [did] Je[sus] say[s]— it is written in your law[:] I said Ye are Gods— it was thro' him that they drink of the rock— of course he wo[ul]d take the honor to himself— J[esus] if they were called Gods unto whom the word of God [was given] why sh[ou]ld it be tho[ugh]t incredible that I sho[oul]d say I am the Son of God. Oh Apostates did ye never think of this bef[ore]. these are the quotations that the apostates take to the Scrip[tures.] they swear that they bel[ieve] the Bible & the Book of Mormon &c & then you will get filth & slander & bogus makers plenty— & one of the Church members prophesied that Jo[seph] Smith sh[ou]ld never preach any more—& yet I am now pr[e]ach[in]g.— go & read the vision— there is glory & glory—Sun, moon & Stars—& so do they differ in glory & every man who reigns is a God— & the text of the Do[ctrine] & Cov[evan]t[s] damns themselves— Paul[,] what do you say— they impeached Paul & all went & left him— Paul had 7 churches & they drove him off from among them— & yet they cannot do it by me— I rej[oice] in that— my test[imony] is good— Paul—says there is one Glory of the Sun the moon & the Stars— & as the Star differs &— They are exalted far above princ[ipalities] thrones dom[inions] & angels—& are expressly decl[are]d to be heirs of God & j[oin]t heirs with J[esus] C[hrist] all hav[in]g et[erna]l power— the Scrip[tures] are a very strange doct[rine].— I have an[othe]r Scrip[ture]— now says God when [he] visited Moses in the Bush— moses was a stuttlerling sort of a boy like me— God said thou shalt be a God unto the children of Israel— God said thou shalt be a God unto Aaron & he shall be thy spokes[man]. I bel[ieve] in these Gods that God reveals as Gods—to be Sons of God & all can cry Abba Father—Sons of God who exalt themselves to be Gods even from bef[ore] the foundat[io]n of the world & are all the only Gods I have a reverence for—

John s[ai]d he was a K[ing].— J[esus] C[hrist] who hath by his own blood made us K[ings] & P[riests] to God. Oh thou God Who are K[ing] of K[ing]'s & L[or]d of L[or]ds— We cannot bel[ieve] thee— [the] old Catholic Church is worth more than all— here is a princ[iple] of logic—that men have no more sense— I will illustrate an old apple tree—here jumps off a branch & says I am the true tree & you are corrupt— if the whole tree is corrupt how can any true thing come out of it— the char[acte]r of the old ones have always been sland[ere]d by all apos[tates] since the world began— I testify again as God never will acknowledge any apost[ate]: any man who will betray the Catholics will betray you— & if he will betray one anoth[e]r he will betray you— all men are liars who say that they are of the true— God always sent a new dispensat[io]n into the world— when men come out & build upon o[the]r men's foundat[io]n.— did I build on anot[he]r mans found[a]t[io]n but my own— I have got all the truth & an indepen[den]t rev[elatio]n in the bargain— God will bear me off triumphant— I will drop this subj[ec]t. I wish I co[ul]d speak for 3 or 4 hours[;] it is not exped[ien]t on acc[oun]t of the rain— I will still go on & shew you proof on proof. all the Bible is as equal one part as another.

Index

A

Aaron, 198; and John the Baptist, 201; Moses a God to, 254

Aaron, order or priesthood of: also called priesthood of Elias, 226-27; to continue with his seed, 169; Joseph receives from an angel, 226

Abel, 65; became an angel, 144; first martyr, 51-52; his sacrifice, 143-44; holds keys of his dispensation, appeared to Paul, 144

abolitionists, 85-90, 221-22

Abraham, 37, 38, 39, 104, 128, 177, 197, 198, 206, 253; and adoption or election, 149-50, 201, 203; effect of Holy Ghost on his literal seed, 120; giving father's blessing, 125; Joseph Smith one of literal seed, 195; patriarchs from his lineage, 121; and plural marriage, 192, 195-96, 199; and sacrifice of Isaac, 195, 197; and slavery, 87-88

Adam, 9, 128, 142, 177, 180, 239, 249; at Ah-dam-ondi-Ahman, gave patriarchal blessings to children, to assemble those with keys of all dispensations in last days, 125-26; as Ancient of Days, 124, 127, 142; begins chain of authority and power to present, 151; directs ministering angels and reveals gospel, 143; experience with God, 143-44, 235; founds Kingdom of God, 168; holds keys of first presidency and priesthood, 124, 144; holds keys to Dispensation of Fulness of Times, 143; and law of sacrifice, 146; as Michael, 124, 142, 143; relation to Jesus Christ, 125, 143, 144

Adams, Charles Francis, xvi, xxi

Adams, John, 208, 215-16

Adams, John Quincy, 218

adoption, 201; effect of Holy Ghost on Gentiles, 120; or election, and seed of Abraham, 149-50

adultery, 12-13, 15, 21; defends against reports of, 96-97; what constitutes, 196, 198

Ah-dam-ondi-Ahman, place where Adam gave patriarchal blessings to children, to assemble those with keys of all dispensations in last days, 125-26

Allen, Ethen, 209

Ancient of Days, as Adam, 124, 127, 142

angel(s), 2, 3, 4, 17, 18, 19, 65, 106, 126, 162, 208; Abel became one, 144; Adam can send to reveal gospel, 143; administer to telestial worlds, 20; appear to John the Revelator, 151; appear to Joseph Smith, 2, 226; appear to Zechariah, 169; compared to gods on basis of plural marriage, 193, 194, 196; compared to spirits, 151; destroying, 203; dwell with God on planet like crystal, 173; nature of bodies of, 151; never has wings, 128; as sentinels, 194. *See also* ministering of angels

anointing, of King David to reign over Israel, 166; one leader on earth with power and keys of priesthood, 192-94. *See also* washings and anointings

Anthon Transcript, account of, 29

Apollos, 20, 63

apostasy, 34-35, 251

apostates, 98, 103-4, 242, 252, 254, 255. *See also* enemies

apostles, 8, 28, 39, 53-54, 62, 70-74, 82, 83, 120, 170, 171, 201; becoming kings and priests, 251-52; ordination of Jesus Christ: and endowment, 227-28; ordination of Joseph Smith and Oliver Cowdery, 2; and spirit of Elijah, 229; those who have fallen, 122

aspiring men, 11, 12, 105, 160, 161

Atchison, General, 102

Atonement, 19

autobiography (Joseph Smith), 204; earliest, 26-30; no man knows my history, 245

Avard, Sampson, 97, 113

B

Baldwin, Caleb, 99, 108

banking, 222, 223

baptism, 4, 5, 61-64, 75, 119, 156, 169, 244; and children of Israel, 126; essential for salvation, 240, 244; and little children, 154-55; sectarian, 152

baptism for dead, 151-53, 183-84, 211, 240, 248. *See also* dead, ordinances for; temple

basses, 175

beasts, of Revelation, 175-79

belief, man never damned for believing too much, 254

Benton, Thomas Hart, xxii

Bible, 12, 251-52, 255; Joseph Smith's translation of, 32, 78; limitations of, 177, 179, 236-38, 251

bishops, 15; and consecration, 13, 41-42

blacks, 25, 87, 208, 213, 221-22. *See also* abolitionists; slavery

blood, shedding, 19, 194, 195, 209, 213, 228, 230, 234, 242, 243, 245, 255; of innocent, 123, 141, 149, 194; of Joseph Smith, 187; and King David, 149, 196, 229; of Saints, 208; spilling own, 188, 191; and thunder, 187, 190. *See also* enemies; Holy Ghost, sin against; sin, unpardonable

Bogart, Captain, 137

Boggs, Governor, 99, 134, 138

bogus makers, 254

Book of Abraham, 83, 253

Book of Mormon, xi, xii, 2, 9-10, 11, 12, 46, 67, 74, 75, 78, 85, 107, 115, 208, 254; background of, 2, 29-30, 35-36, 46; copyright, 1; lost 116 pages of, 29-30

Book of Moses, 65

bread, and the sacrament, 5-6

brothers, 80-82

Brown, Pelatiah, 176

Brown, Sam, xx, xxiii

Bullock, Thomas, 246, 251

Burnett, Peter H., xvii, xix, xx, xxii

C

Cahoon, Reynolds, 107, 211

Cain, his curse, 144, 208

California, 223

calling and election, making sure, 120, 181, 182, 203, 228, 248. *See also* election; temple, ordinances

Campbell, Alexander, 76, 244

Canada, 223, 225

Carpenter, Benjamin, 46

Carter, Joana, 117

Carthage, Illinois, 189

celestial kingdom, 18-19, 35, 57, 157, 194, 212, 243, 248, 254; crystal, new name, key word for inhabitant, 173

children, 22, 67-70, 91, 92, 132-33, 135; advice to, 111, 117; baptism of, 154-55; and resurrection, nothing added to stature, 156-57, 244

cholera, 24, 25

Church of Christ, xii, 2, 4, 5, 6, 46; laws for, 12-15

church of the first born, 19, 21, 121

Church of Jesus Christ of Latter Day Saints, 108

Church of Latter Day Saints, 58, 74, 78, 99, 108, 131, 137

Clark, General, 136, 137

Clark, John B., 91

Clay, Henry, xxii

Clayton, William 172, 175

Colesville, New York, 7-11

Columbia, South America, 9, 223

concubines, 192, 195-96

conferences, of the church, 5, 6,

consecration, 13, 15, 41-42, 97

Cornelius, 156

Corrill, John, 91, 94-95

Council of Fifty, xiii

council in heaven. *See* pre-existence

Cowdery, Oliver, 1; blessing of, 43; ordained an apostle and elder, 2; sees plates in a vision, 30

Crary, Christopher, xix, xx

creation, 124, 125, 231, 233, 237, 238-39, 252-53

Crosby, Jonathan, xvii

crucifixion, 184, 229

crystal, for those in celestial kingdom, 173

D

Daniel, vision of, 174, 213, 248

David, King, 81, 83, 166; and murder, 149, 196, 229; and plural marriage, 192, 196

Day of Pentecost, 120, 184, 199; and endowment, 229-30; and Kingdom of God, 169-70

deacons, 4, 5

dead, ordinances for, 241, 248-49. *See also* baptism for dead; temple

debating school, Kirtland, 79-80

Declaration of Independence, 213

deism, xi

dispensation of fulness of times, 43, 106, 107, 125, 144, 153

divorce, 196

doctrine, against censuring, 176

E

elders, 2, 4, 5, 6, 11, 13, 15, 45, 46, 56, 58, 68

election, 10, 119, 149-50, 229. *See also* calling and election

Elias, 20, 125; contrast with Elijah, Jesus Christ, 226-31

Elijah, 39, 126, 146-47, 153, 203, 211-12, 229, 230, 241; background for, 67-70; and Elias, 226-31; and ordinances, work for dead, 227-28

Elohim, 190, 233, 252, 253; the Head God, 237

end of world, 8, 9, 23-24, 35-36, 46-47, 77, 101, 139, 212. *See also* last days; second coming

endowment, 198; and Elijah, 227-28; and gathering, 183; key words and signs, 155, 156; and Kirtland, 46, 56-57; and mission work, 17; and Pentecost, 170, 227-30. *See also* temple, ordinances; sealing

enemies, 19, 21, 43, 46, 54, 55, 65, 67, 68, 75-76, 81, 91, 95-96, 98, 103-4, 107, 110, 122, 129, 171, 181, 188, 189, 205, 207-9, 243, 247-48; crucify Christ afresh, 242; Joseph will defend self, 190; and Missouri, 109, 129-41; and *Mormonism Unvailed*, 74;

vengeance, 141, 188, 207-9; will be punished, 7-8, 10, 94, 230. *See also* blood, shedding; mobs

Enoch, 9, 19, 21, 39, 65, 125, 144, 177; appears to Jude and Paul, 144-45

Esaias, 21, 71

eternal matter, 124

Ether, 67

ethics, situational, 158

eunuch, 62

evangelist, a patriarch, 121

exaltation, 194, 196

excommunication, xiii, 6

Ezekiel, 121

F

families, 60, 67-68, 228, 230

Far West, Missouri, 111, 129-41

Fayette, New York, 9

figural interpretation, 176-78

first estate, 181

first presidency, 97, 124, 127, 144

first principles, 35, 60-61, 148-49, 151, 208, 247

first vision, Joseph Smith's first account, 26-28

Follett, King, funeral speech, 232-45

for time and eternity, 192, 193

Franklin, Benjamin, 214

freemasonry, 10, 207

friendship, 103, 123, 166, 188, 222, 225, 243, 245; and baptism for dead, 249; God and, 22, 24, 94, 171; grand fundamental principle of Mormonism, 200-1; weakened by oaths and secrecy, 113

G

Gabriel, 56, 124

Galland, Isaac, 108

gathering, 8, 13, 34, 46-47, 59-60, 66-68, 70-74, 77-78, 111, 183, 211; temple ordinances the purpose of, 183, 185

Gauss, Jesse, 32

Gentiles, 2, 10, 13, 34, 67, 120, 169, 201

German, and Bible, 237-38, 244-47

gift of discerning spirits, 128

gift of tongues, 128, 164

God, 3, 39-40, 50, 107, 155, 168, 171, 178, 181, 233-35, 240, 246; and Adam, 143-44; bound by sealing power, 196-97; and creation, 125, 234-35, 252; the Father, 5, 16-17, 48-49, 172, 193, 194, 251, 253-54; his planet, 173; and intelligence(s), 239, 240; Joseph Smith's vision of, 28; once a man, 235; one pertaining to us, 252; whatever he requires is right, 158; and women, 162-63. *See also* Godhead

Godhead, 3, 5, 16, 19, 35, 60-64, 75, 144, 156, 172, 184, 193, 194, 236, 240, 243, 244, 253-54; distinct personages, have always taught, 251; not three in one, 253-54; office of Messiah, 231; two members in, 48-52. *See also* God; Holy Ghost; Jesus Christ

gods, and angels, 194; and creation, 237, 253; each has father, 253-54; humans as, xiii, 19, 235; and marriage, 193, 194, 196; Moses a god to Aaron, 254-55; plurality of, 106, 172, 193, 251, 252

Gold Book, 1

gold plates, 28, 30

Goliath, 81

government, 137, 140-41, 168-69, 186, 209, 234. *See also* United States

grace, 3, 7, 98

Granger, Carlos, 166

Great Britain, 223

Greek, and Bible, 237-38, 245, 247

Green Mountain Boys, 204, 206, 207, 209

Guilliam, Cornelius, 137

H

habeas corpus, 101, 102, 186, 189, 190, 191

Hades, or Hell, 184

Hagar, and plural marriage, 195, 199

Hale, Isaac, xvi, xix, xxi

Haman, 93

Hamilton, Alexander, xv

Harmony, Pennsylvania, xii, 29

Harris, Martin, xix, 1, 11, 22, 29-30

Harrison, President Benjamin, 219-20

Haun's Mill, 102, 109

healing the sick, 14, 156; women and, 164

Hebrew, 237-38, 239, 245, 247, 252

Hendrix, Daniel, xvi, xix, xx

Higbee, Judge, 203

high council, 45-46

Hill, Marvin S., xv

Hinkle, George M., 94, 95, 132, 133, 134

Hiram, 207

history, keeping records, 53-54

Holy Ghost, 3, 4, 5, 60-61, 74, 75, 106, 110, 123, 148, 156, 199, 201, 208, 232, 237, 238, 240, 249, 252; baptism of fire and, 226-27, 244; effect on gentiles, 120; first comforter, 12, 120; gift of, compared to personage of, 156, 173; mind of God, in *Lectures on Faith*, 48-49; a personage, 173, 251; sin against, 195, 241, 242, 243, 245. *See also* blood, shedding; Godhead; Perdition, sons of

Holy Spirit of Promise, 19, 109, 119, 192, 194-95

House of Israel, 9, 10, 13

House of the Lord. *See* temple, House of the Lord

Howe, Eber, 74, 75-76

Humphry, Solomon, 31-32

Hurlburt, Doctor Philastus, xxi, 75-76

Hyde, Orson, 162, 172

I

Indians, American, 66

innocent blood. *See* blood, of innocent; enemies; Holy Ghost, sin against; Perdition, sons of

intelligence(s), 173; eternal, self-existent, 239, 240; learn about while translating Book of Abraham, 253

interpretation, of scripture, 175-79

Isaac, 38, 39; and plural marriage, 192, 196; and sacrifice, 195, 197

Isaiah, 21, 121

J

Jackson, President Andrew, xxii, 219

Jacob, 38, 39; and plural marriage, 192, 196

Jefferson, Thomas, xv, 208, 216

Jehovah, 139, 146, 160, 162, 210, 222, 228, 233

Jessee, Dean, xiii

Jesus Christ, xii, xxiv, 1, 2, 3, 5, 9, 16-17, 20, 27-28, 34-35, 39, 50, 55, 58, 60-61, 65-66, 76-77, 78, 93, 95, 111, 140, 143, 144, 148, 149, 177, 180, 183, 184, 194, 201, 204, 209, 210, 229, 240, 241, 246, 249, 254; and Adam, 124, 125-26, 143; an angel, 151; a distinct personage, 251; and Elias, 230; and Elijah, 229, 230; and endowment, 183, 227-28; and gathering, 70-74; and God the Father, 193, 235-36, 243, 253-54; and John the Baptist, 170, 201, 226-27, 244; and Kirtland temple, 57; in *Lectures on Faith*, 48-49; makes humans kings and priests, 255; a man, 172; a ministering spirit, 19, 151; and office of Savior or Messiah, 231, 242; and priesthood, 146, 170; the Second Comforter, 120-21; and washing of feet, 56. *See also* Godhead; Messiah; Second Comforter

Jethro, and high priesthood, 165

Jews, 2, 34, 77, 169, 183, 184, 201

John the Baptist, 20, 74, 168, 169-70, 201; and baptism, 170, 244; and Elias, 226-27; and Jesus Christ, 201, 226-27; a king, 201, 251-52, 255; and Kingdom of God, 169-70; and priesthood of Aaron, 169, 170, 201

John the Revelator, 56, 121, 174, 177, 247

Johnson, Benjamin F., xx, xxi, xxiv

Johnson, Luke, xvii

Johnson, Lyman, 32

Judas, 122, 208

Jude, Enoch appeared to, 144

justification, 3

K

key words (and signs), 156; need for interpretation, 179; the new name in celestial kingdom, 173

keys, 124, 182; and Adam, 124, 125, 143; and Elijah, 146, 228, 230; and Jehovah, 146; and Jesus Christ, 254; and Joseph Smith, 192-94, 196, 246; and Kingdom of God, 26, 98, 142, 162; and Lamech, 145-46; and mysteries, 105; and plural marriage, 196; and priesthood, 124, 146, 194, 198, 247;

and Relief Society, 162, 164; and sacrifice, 146; and violence, 188

King, Judge, 129-30

king, Joseph Smith progresses from prophet to priest to king, 201

Kingdom of God, xiii, 82, 168, 247; and Adam, 168; and John the Baptist, 169-70; and priesthood, 168, 171; and Satan, 249; and violence, 248

kings and priests, 19, 221, 235, 251-52, 255

Kirtland, Ohio, xvii-xviii, xx, xxii, 11, 40, 45-47, 53-54, 59, 79-84, 111, 127

Kirtland Bank, xii, xx, xxiii

Knight, Joseph, xix

Knight, Newel, xvii, 7

knowledge, 175-76, 241-42

L

Lamb's Book of Life, 194

Lamech, 145-46

languages, learning, 84, 205-6

last days, 34, 35-36, 127, 246-47. *See also* end of world; second coming

Latin, and Bible, 237-38, 245, 247

law, God's, 155, 173, 193, 201, 212; whatever God requires is right, 158

Law of Moses, 6, 146, 147

lawyers, xxii, 101, 102, 136, 186, 187, 188, 190, 191, 222

laying on of hands, 4; by women, 161, 164

Lectures on Faith, 48-52

Levi, sons of, 146

liars, 249, 255

Liberty Jail, xii, 91, 102-3, 136-37, 138; advice from, 93-115, 117; arrest, 186-90

license, or certificate, for priest, teacher, elder, 5

Lincoln, Abraham, xv

lineage, 61, 120, 201; and Joseph Smith, 78, 121, 165, 195; and priesthood, 103-4, 121, 147, 165

Lucas, General, 108, 135, 137

Lucifer. *See* Satan

Lyman, Amasa, 135

M

Mace, Wandle, xix-xx

Madison, President James, 217

magic, 74

Maine, 223

Malachi, 228

man, relationship to God, 235, 239, 243

Manchester, New York, xi, 10, 28

marriage. *See* new and everlasting covenant; plural marriage; women

McDaniel, John, xvii

McIntyre, Alexander, 10

McLellen, William, 23, 32, 80

McRae, Alexander, 99, 108

Melchizedek priesthood. *See* priesthood, order of Melchizedek

membership records, 6

Messiah, office of, 231. *See also* savior

Methodism, xi, 229

Mexico, 223, 225

Michael, as Adam, 124, 142, 143

Michigan, 215

Millennial Harbinger, 74

millennium, xii, 9, 172

Miller, Emeline, 23

Miller, William, 231

ministering of angels, 26, 45, 78, 115, 127, 145; and Adam, 143; and Enoch, 144; and marriage, 193. *See also* angel(s)

ministering spirits, compared to ministering angels, 151

miracles, 14; and the endowment, 57

missionary work, 14, 85; and the endowment, 57

Mississippi, 218

Missouri, xvii, 60, 91, 96, 100, 131-32, 189, 201, 204-5, 207-8, 209, 215, 230, 247; Caldwell County, 130, 132, 133; Carroll County, 130; Chariton County, 136; Clay County, 117, 132; Daviess County, 96, 116, 129, 132, 133, 134; and enemies, 100, 101, 102, 117, 134; and Illinois 186, 187; Jackson County, xii, 16, 36, 41, 55-56, 58, 59, 91, 135; Ray County, 96. *See also* enemies

mobs, 94, 100, 101. *See also* enemies; Missouri

Monroe, President James, 217

Mordecai, 93

more sure word of prophecy, 180

Mormonism, 59, 91, 102; God is the author of it, 107

Mormonism Unvailed, 74, 75-76

Moroni, 28-29, 35-36

Morse, Michael, xvii

Moses, 20, 125, 126; and gathering, 66; as a god to Aaron and House of Israel, 254-55; and Joseph Smith, 191; and plural marriage, 192, 196; and priesthood, 125, 170

Mount of Transfiguration, 125

murder. *See* blood, shedding

mysteries, 16, 21, 143, 183, 243

mysticism, xi

N

Nathan, 196

Nauvoo, Illinois, xiii, xviii, xxii, xxiii, 186-89, 190

Nauvoo City Council, 190

Nauvoo Expositor, xiii

Nauvoo Legion, xviii-ix, 173

Nauvoo Relief Society, 160-64

new and everlasting covenant, 6, 64, 70, 98, 192, 194, 195, 196. *See also* plural marriage

New Hampshire, xi

New Jerusalem, xii, 13, 14, 36, 65, 67, 70

new name, in celestial kingdom, 173

New York, xii, 224; Seneca County, 58

New York City, New York, Joseph Smith visits, 23-25

Ninevah, 24

no man knows my history, 245

Noah, 37, 128, 207, 228, 230-31; is Gabriel, 124; and priesthood, 145-46

O

oaths, 113, 192

obedience, and plural marriage, 197-98

Ohio, xii, 215; Geauga County, 58

Old Major, Joseph Smith's horse, 117

144,000, anointed priests, 174; Saviors on

Mount Zion performing ordinances for dead, 248

ordinances, 125; and Adam, 142; and Elijah, 227-28; and salvation, 142, 155, 212; and temple, 183. *See also* baptism for dead; endowment; rituals; sealing; temple

ordination, 5, 12, 35, 143

Oregon, 220, 223, 225

Osborne, David, xx

P

Packard, Noah, 31-32

Page, John, 162

Paine, Thomas, xv

Palmyra, New York, xi, xv-xvi, xx, 30

papyrus, Egyptian, 253

parables, Jesus and secrets, 71-78

paradise, world of spirits, 184

Partridge, Edward, 41-42, 99, 102, 108

passions, 200

patriarch, oldest descendant of Abraham, 121

Patten, David W., 109, 133

Paul, 20, 38-39, 63, 74, 81, 83, 119, 121, 125, 126, 143, 145, 149; Abel appears to, 144; Enoch appears to, 144-45; and plurality of gods, 252; and salvation of dead, 241; and slavery, 88-89; and three heavens, 184

Peck, Reed, 95

Perdition, sons of, 17-18, 151, 242. *See also* blood, of innocent; Holy Ghost, sin against; Satan; sin, unpardonable

persecution, xix, 1, 140. *See also* enemies; mobs

Peter, 60, 81, 149, 156; and endowment, 229-30

Peter, James, and John, 125

Pharoah, of Egypt, 150, 207

Phelps, W. W., 95

Philip, 62, 227

plan of salvation, 152, 242

plural marriage, xii, xiii, 192-99; and Abraham, 195-96; charges of "a community of wives," 97; distinguishes gods from angels, 193; and Holy Spirit of Promise, 193; Joseph Smith hiding from Emma Smith, 166; and Nancy Rigdon, 158; prophets have keys, 196; and Sarah Ann Whitney,

165-67. *See also* new and everlasting covenant; women

plural worlds, xiii, 17

plurality of gods, 252, 253. *See also* God; Godhead; gods

polygamy. *See* new and everlasting covenant; plural marriage; women

Potter, Elisah, xx

Pratt, Orson, 8, 32, 161-62

Pratt, Parley P., xvi, xx, xxi, xxiii, xxiv, 135, 161

prayer, xviii, 7

pre-existence, xiii, 106, 142, 198, 237, 242, 249, 255

predestination. *See* calling and election; election

Presbyterian, 229

Price, Colonel, 136, 137

pride, 105

priesthood, 124, 142-47, 152, 198, 246, 248; and Adam, 124, 151; and angels, 26; and apostates, 103-4; and Cain, 144; and doctrine of translation, 145; and Elias, 226-27; and Elijah, 146-47; high, 26, 45, 165; holy, 26, 98, 123, 195-96; and John the Baptist, 170; keys of, 145-46, 196, 246, 247; and Kingdom of God, 168; and lineage, 147, 165; and Noah, 146; order of Aaron, 46, 142, 170, 226-27; order of Enoch, 19; order of Melchizedek, 19, 142, 147, 170, 201; order of Son of God, 19, 26, 142; restoration of, 26; and restoration of sacrifice, 146-47; rights of, 109-11

priests, 4, 5, 6, 14, 19

primitivism, xi

prophets, 3, 13, 21, 65, 109, 126, 168, 177, 180, 247; false, 200, 234, 247; holy, 8, 28, 39, 146, 147; progress to priests and then kings, 201

Q

Quincy, Illinois, 99, 137

R

rape, 100

Relief Society, Joseph Smith delivers keys to,

192, 193, 194-95; power to bind heaven, 119, 196-97. *See also* endowment; ordinances; plural marriage; temple

Second Comforter, Jesus Christ, 120-21. *See also* Holy Ghost; Jesus Christ

second coming, 8-10, 19, 57, 77-78, 101, 126, 128, 139, 174; if Joseph Smith lives to be 84 years old will see, 172; won't be for at least forty years, 231. *See also* end of world; last days

second death, 18

secrets, 43-44, 181, 251; keep plural marriage from Emma Smith, 166; keep work on Bible translation to self, 14; knowing God's, 16; and use of parables, 76; weaken friendship, 113-14

sectarianism, xi

sentinels, angels as, 194

servants, 89. *See also* abolitionists; blacks; slavery; women

sexual disgressions, 15

Shakespeare, 205

Sharon, Vermont, xi, 26, 204

shedding of blood. *See* blood, shedding; enemies

Shoal Creek, 129, 137

signs, and ordinances, required for salvation, 155

Silas, 63

Simon, 62

sin, unpardonable, 151, 241, 242. *See also* blood, shedding; enemies; Holy Ghost, sin against; Perdition, sons of

slavery, 67-70, 213, 221-22, 223, 224; and the Bible, 87; defense of, 85-90. *See also* abolitionists, blacks

Smith, Alexander, 117

Smith, Alvin, 83, 152

Smith, Bathsheba, xvi, xxi

Smith, Catherine, 31, 83

Smith, Don Carlos, 83, 102

Smith, Emma, xvii, xviii, xxii, 22-25, 91-92, 102, 116-18, 135; marriage of, 29; and plural marriage, 166, 197-98, 198-99; as scribe, 30

Smith, Frederick, 117

Smith, Hyrum, xiii, 10, 11, 22, 23, 80, 83, 99, 108, 135, 166, 208; blessing by Joseph Smith, 43-44; whether can lead the church, Joseph Smith's resignation, 201

Smith, Jerusha, 23

Smith, Job, xx

Smith, John, 108

Smith, Joseph, III, xviii, 117

Smith, Joseph, Jr., his autobiography, 26-30, 31, 204, 245; his calling, 161, 192, 196, 201

Smith, Joseph, Sr., xi, xix, xxi, 1, 10, 11, 23, 26, 28, 80-82, 83, 208; blessing by Joseph Smith, 43

Smith, Julia, 23, 24, 113

Smith, Lucy Mack, xi, xxi, 1, 23, 83, 208; blessing by Joseph Smith, 43

Smith, Samuel Harrison, 10, 30, 83; blessing by Joseph Smith, 44

Smith, Silas, 37-40

Smith, Sophronia, 23, 31, 83

Smith, William, xvi-xviii; blessing by Joseph Smith, 44; whether he will lose his apostleship, 79-84

Sodom and Gomorrah, 168, 206, 207

solemn assembly, at Kirtland, 56, 57

Solomon, 158, 207; and plural marriage, 192, 196

Son of God, office of, 254, 255. *See also* Messiah; savior

sons of Perdition. *See* Holy Ghost, sin against; Perdition, sons of

South Carolina, 215

spirit(s), 19, 124, 127-28, 181, 183-84, 239, 248

spiritual wifery, xiii

spiritualizing interpretations, Joseph Smith against, 178-79

Stout, Allen, xxii

Stowell, Josiah, 1

swearing, 180

symbol. *See* figural interpretation

T

Taylor, John, 125, 204, 213

teachers, 4, 5, 14

telestial kingdom, 20, 254

temple, and gathering, 183; House of the Lord (in Kirtland), xviii, 56-57; ordinances, 153, 183, 184, 211-12; organization of church requires, 161; restoration of sacrifice, 147

tenors, 175

terrestrial kingdom, 19-20, 254; and Enoch, 144; and translated bodies, 144, 145

Texas, 220, 223

theocracy, xiii

Thompson, Robert B., 142

time, reckoned according to planet on which reside, 172-73

tower of Babel, 207

Towles, Nancy, xvii

transfiguration, 181

translation, doctrine of, xviii, 144, 145, 151

tribes of Israel, 66

Tucker, Pomeroy, xvi

Turnham, Judge, 136

Tyler, Daniel, xvii-xviii, 220

type. *See* figural interpretation; spiritualizing interpretations

U

Unitarianism, xi

United States, 36, 204, 224; constitution of, 114-15, 135, 141, 188, 189, 190, 191, 204, 205, 213-14, 222; government of, 140-41, 204, 213-25, 221

Universalism, xx

unpardonable sin. *See* blood, shedding; Holy Ghost, sin against; Perdition, sons of; sin, unpardonable

Uriah, 196

Urim and Thummim, God's planet a, 173

V

Van Allen, Isaac, 108

Van Buren, Martin, 205, 219-20, 223, 224

vanity, 148

vengeance. *See* blood, shedding; enemies

Vermont, xi

vigilantes, xii, xiii

Vision, the, 16-21, 127

W

Walker, Cyrus, 191

washings and anointings, 56, 183, 211

Washington, George, xv, 207, 215

Wayne Sentinel, xvi

West, William, xviii

West Indies, and signs of the times, 9

Whitmer, David, xx, 95

Whitney, Elizabeth Ann, 22, 165-67

Whitney, Newel K., 11, 22, 23, 24, 25, 79, 165-67

Whitney, Sarah Ann, 165-67

Wight, Lyman, 99, 108, 133, 134, 135

Williams, Frederick G., 23, 31

Wilson, General, 134-35, 137

Wilson, Moses G., 91

wine, and the sacrament, 5-6

witnesses, and Book of Mormon, 2

women, 132-33, 135, 161, 162, 163, 203, 244; compared to slaves, 67-70; and gift of tongues, 164; how should behave, 162-64; and law of Sarah, 199; and laying on of hands, 160-61, 164; to Nancy Rigdon, whatever God requires is right, 160; and plural marriage, 197-99; sphere of, 160; submit to husbands, 69-70

Woodruff, Wilford, 122, 154, 168, 183, 186, 211, 226

works, 6

Y

Young, Brigham, xxiii-xxiv

Z

Zecheriah, 169

Zion, xii, 46, 65; and Missouri, 36, 41, 58